Junges Nachhaltigkeitsrecht

Felix Aiwanger | Maximilian Richard Götze
Biset Sena Güneș | Vincent Hoppmann
Hans Flemming Maltzahn | Antonia Sommerfeld [eds.]

Sustainability Law: Comparative, Interdisciplinary, and Intradisciplinary Perspectives

JUNGES NACHHALTIGKEITS RECHT

Nomos

Open-Access-Förderung durch die Max-Planck-Gesellschaft.

The Deutsche Nationalbibliothek lists this publication in the Deutsche Nationalbibliografie; detailed bibliographic data are available on the Internet at http://dnb.d-nb.de

1st Edition 2026

Published by
Nomos Verlagsgesellschaft mbH & Co. KG
Waldseestraße 3–5 | 76530 Baden-Baden
www.nomos.de

Production of the printed version:
Nomos Verlagsgesellschaft mbH & Co. KG
Waldseestraße 3–5 | 76530 Baden-Baden

ISBN 978-3-7560-3566-3 (Print)
ISBN 978-3-7489-6626-5 (ePDF)

DOI https://doi.org/10.5771/9783748966265

Onlineversion
Inlibra

Editors' Preface

The present volume constitutes a collection of papers from the 4th Young Sustainability Law Conference – Junges Nachhaltigkeitsrecht (JNR) 2025, which was held from 19 to 21 June 2025 in Hamburg, Germany. This interdisciplinary conference united international early-career researchers, established scholars, and practitioners to engage in dynamic and forward-looking discussions on the legal dimensions of sustainability.

The JNR 2025 Conference was organized by an interdisciplinary team of scholars from three academic institutions in Hamburg: the Max Planck Institute for Comparative and International Private Law, the Bucerius Law School, and the University of Hamburg (Institute of Law and Economics). Building on the success of previous JNR conferences in Munich, Halle, and Vienna, we set out to provide a platform for exploring sustainability within legal discourse, through an integrated approach that combines comparative, interdisciplinary, and intradisciplinary perspectives.

The call for abstracts for this conference received an overwhelming response, with 421 submissions from across the globe. The level of scholarly rigour, creativity, and intellectual commitment reflected in these proposals was exceptional. Following a thorough and careful review process, we are proud to present this volume, which brings together the outstanding and thought-provoking contributions delivered at the conference. Each paper exemplifies cutting-edge research and a deep commitment to advancing sustainability through law. We hope that the ideas assembled here will stimulate further debate, encourage innovative research, and promote reflection beyond established boundaries within legal scholarship.

The Conference Programme

The JNR 2025 Conference featured a diverse and intellectually stimulating programme structured around seven thematic sessions, bringing together over 30 speakers from 15 different jurisdictions. The contributions covered a broad spectrum of topics, ranging from global supply chains and private and company law, to law and economics approaches, sustainable governance and public (international) law, as well as natural disaster insurance law, investment law, and environmental criminal law.

A particular highlight of the conference was the panel discussion on the role of private actors in sustainable development. The panel brought together distinguished discussants from academia and practice: Prof. Dr. Frank Adloff (University of Hamburg); Larisa Alwin (Appellate Judge at the Amsterdam Court of Appeal); Prof. Dr. Hajer Gueldich (Legal Counsel of the African Union/Carthage University); Prof. Dr. Remo Klinger (Partner at Geulen & Klinger/Eberswalde University); and Benjamin Köhler (Head of Sustainability Management at OTTO GmbH & Co. KG). The discussion, moderated by Dr. Antonia Sommerfeld and Dr. Felix Aiwanger (both MPI Hamburg), offered a robust and multifaceted exploration of how private actors – including courts, legal practitioners, corporations, and international organisations – shape the evolving legal framework and contemporary developments in sustainability.

The programme was framed by three keynote lectures, which provided in-depth academic reflections on the complexity and current challenges of sustainability law. Dr. Marta Santos Silva (University of Minho) opened with a keynote on intradisciplinary perspectives, followed by Prof. Dr. Damilola S. Olawuyi (Afe Babalola University/Hamad Bin Khalifa University), who offered insights on comparative perspectives. The conference concluded with a keynote on interdisciplinary perspectives by Prof. Dr. André Nollkaemper (University of Amsterdam), which synthesized many of the conference's central themes and provided an overarching conceptual framework. We are therefore particularly honoured to include this final keynote as the opening contribution and intellectual basis of this volume.

Acknowledgements

The success of JNR 2025 was the result of a collective effort. We would like to extend our sincere gratitude to everyone who contributed to the success of the conference: the speakers, whose expertise and dedication provided invaluable insights; the participants, whose engagement enriched the discussions; and the extended organising team, whose commitment and professionalism ensured a seamless and rewarding experience for all. We are especially grateful to Anja Hell-Mynarik and Ava Héloïse Hoffmann as well as the participating student assistants – Carolin Rüsseler, Yasemine Uyan, and Johannes Lenz – for their exceptional commitment and support before, during, and after the conference. This volume reflects the collaborative efforts of everyone who came together to explore, debate, and shape the future of sustainability law.

We would also like to express our special thanks to the Max Planck Institute for Comparative and International Private Law, Max Planck Law, Bucerius Law School, Nomos Verlagsgesellschaft, Mohr Siebeck, and Duncker & Humblot for their generous support.

We hope that this volume will continue to encourage discussion and cooperation across boundaries, thereby furthering the development of sustainability law and helping to create legal frameworks that support a more sustainable future.

Hamburg, February 2026

Antonia Sommerfeld, Biset Sena Güneş, Felix Aiwanger, Hans Flemming Maltzahn, Maximilian Götze, Vincent Hoppmann

Table of Contents

System error in international law: exposing and addressing cumulative harm

*André Nollkaemper**

In this short contribution, I propose an angle for engaging with the scholarly work on sustainability law contained in this volume. I suggest that the lens of *cumulative harm* offers a productive way to read these diverse contributions together. By focusing on how dispersed, individually minor actions and decisions interact to generate large-scale environmental degradation, the frame of cumulative harm helps reveal both common challenges and systemic blind spots in law's capacity to respond. With occasional reference to papers in this volume, the chapter identifies recurring themes in how legal rules and institutions struggle with, reproduce, or begin to address such harms.

A. *Death by a thousand cuts: understanding cumulative environmental harm*

The phrase 'Death by a thousand cuts' originates from a historical method of execution in imperial China. The condemned was slowly killed through many small, non-fatal incisions. Over time, these cuts accumulated into a fatal outcome.[1]

---

* SEVEN – University of Amsterdam.
1 Timothy Brook/Jérôme Bourgon/Gregory Blue, Death by a thousand cuts (2008).

Today, the phrase has come to describe how large-scale damage to our planet can result from numerous small, seemingly insignificant actions.[2]

It is a fitting metaphor for cumulative environmental harm: not caused by a single act of destruction, but by countless lawful and often invisible actions whose effects compound over time. Each act may appear negligible, yet together they drive systemic and sometimes irreversible environmental degradation.

The examples are well known. Plastic pollution, stemming from everyday practices around the world like buying bottled drinks and carelessly disposing of the bottle, using single-use straws, or washing synthetic clothing—that each release only small amounts of plastic, but collectively result in vast accumulations in oceans, rivers, our own bodies.[3] Greenhouse gas accumulation results from billions of daily decisions to drive, fly or eat meat.[4] And biodiversity loss results from countless decisions to consume fruits grown by pesticides, by building houses with timber from tropical forests, or by consuming beef produced with soy grown on deforested land —all acts that individually seem insignificant but together erode ecosystems and drive species extinction.[5]

These examples illustrate not only the scale of the problem but also why law, with its emphasis on discrete causation, struggles to respond. The papers prepared for this conference provide further illustrations of such

2 Jacqueline Peel, 'Issues in climate change litigation' (2011), 5(1) CCLR, p. 15, 20; Jessica T. Dales, 'Death by a thousand cuts: incorporating cumulative effects in Australia's Environment Protection and Biodiversity Conservation Act' (2011), 20(1) Wash. Int'l L. J., p. 149, 152.

3 David K. A. Barnes et al., 'Accumulation and fragmentation of plastic debris in global environments' (2009), 364(1526) Phil. Trans. R. Soc. B, p. 1985, 1987; Marja H. Lamoree et al., 'Health impacts of microplastic and nanoplastic exposure' (2025), 31 Nat. Med., p. 2873.

4 IPCC, Climate Change 2022: Impacts, Adaptation, and Vulnerability. Contribution of Working Group II to the Sixth Assessment Report of the Intergovernmental Panel on Climate Change (2022), p. 2418 (noting that 'Cascading effects can indeed lead to cumulative risks, including acceleration of ecosystem degradation, or the reaching of thresholds and irreversible states, as well as increasing the likelihood of crossing tipping points.').

5 IPBES, 'Global assessment report on biodiversity and ecosystem services. Summary for policymakers' (2019), https://files.ipbes.net/ipbes-web-prod-public-files/inline/files/ipbes_global_assessment_report_summary_for_policymakers.pdf (last accessed: 23 September 2025), p. 4 (highlighting that biodiversity loss results from the *cumulative action of many drivers*—land-use change (eg deforestation for soy or timber), pesticide use, and consumption choices that drive production).

deaths by a thousand cuts. Examples are hidden supply chains in the luxury fashion industry, that enable cumulative harm;[6] cumulation of individual consumer choices that have massive cumulative ecological consequences;[7] and how urban transport emissions, though individually minor, aggregate across cities.[8]

This phenomenon of cumulative harm presents a major challenge for international law. Because this harm is dispersed across actors, borders, and timescales, it escapes the grasp of international law, which remains focused on discrete breaches and linear causality. As such, cumulative harm reveals a systemic blind spot in international law: the inability to account for, regulate, or even clearly perceive the scale and interaction of these diffuse contributions.

Indeed, it is my contention that together, these examples expose a system error in international law: a foundational mismatch between how environmental harm accumulates and how legal obligations and legal responsibility are structured. The harms described are not outliers—they are the norm in a world of complex interdependence. What becomes visible through the lens of cumulative harm is not only the scale of environmental degradation, but also the structural limitations of existing regulatory systems in seeing and responding to it.

B. A problem of many hands: diffusion of responsibility for cumulative environmental harm

If we delve deeper into why and how cumulative environmental harm poses a challenge for international law, it is helpful to use the frame of the so-called problem of many hands, a term originating in public administration theory, notably in the original paper by Dennis Thompson.[9] The concept of 'the problem of many hands' stands for the proposition that the more widely a harm is spread across actors, the harder it becomes to assign ac-

6 Shuma Talukdar, 'From Galli to Paris Fashion Week: Law, Sustainability, and the Hidden Faces of Karegari', this volume, p. 23-41.

7 María Elisa Morales/Sara Moreno, 'Towards a Sustainable Consumer Law: A Preliminary Assessment of the French Example for Chile', this volume, p. 59-78.

8 Vincent-Carlos Barduhn, 'Sustainable Urban Mobility Plans (SUMPs): A German and Spanish comparative legal overview', this volume, p. 263-278.

9 Dennis F. Thompson, 'Moral responsibility of public officials: the problem of many hands' (1980), 74(4) Am. Polit. Sci. Rev., p. 905.

countability to any one of them. Marc Bovens has defined the phenomenon as one in which 'the responsibility for any given instance of conduct is scattered among more people, [so that] the discrete responsibility of every individual diminishes proportionately.'[10] That proportionate reduction of responsibility is true in moral, political, and practical terms. It is often also true in legal terms.

This perspective is particularly salient in the context of cumulative global environmental harm. When environmental degradation results not from one actor's conduct but from the incremental, lawful actions of thousands or millions—operating independently but cumulatively—it becomes difficult to determine who did what in causing harm, who ought to bear obligations, and who is to blame.

On the one hand, this dilution of responsibility undermines the forward-looking, preventative functions of international law. The traditional structure of international legal responsibility hinges on identifying a duty-bearer and articulating a specific obligation aimed at preventing a harmful outcome. However, in the context of cumulative harm, the contribution of any single actor often falls below the threshold required for breach.

This is especially true in the case of obligations of result, such as the duty to prevent significant transboundary environmental harm. When contributions are individually minimal, they may fall 'below the radar' of legal wrongfulness, even as they collectively produce devastating consequences. Transport-related carbon emissions illustrate this phenomenon. The cumulative effect of millions of actions—individual car trips, freight deliveries, commercial flights—is a major driver of climate change. Yet each of these actions, when viewed in isolation, typically falls below the threshold of legal significance under international law.

Despite a growing number of cases against corporations, the dominant position still is that companies that invest in fossil fuels, or build and operate transport systems, and individuals who use fossil fuels all act perfectly legal under international law. The same may be true for the financial sector, where banks and investors provide funding to acts that cause environmental harm.

These problems are particularly visible in supply chains, where the question is who bears obligations for what part of the chain. Are all actors

10 Mark Bovens, The quest for responsibility: accountability and citizenship in complex organizations (1998), p. 46.

in the chain under obligations, or only some, the most important ones? And what does that then mean for all others upstream and downstream? If the ongoing negotiations in Brussels on the due diligence directive have learned anything, it is how complex and controversial this is. Similar complexity and uncertainty arise in discussions of scope 3 emissions, as exemplified by the Shell litigation.[11]

On the other hand, the dilution of responsibility has consequences for the backward-looking function of international law. A key function of responsibility is to enable redress for victims. Where harm is real, but no actor's contribution rises to the level of individual liability—or where information about causal roles is scattered across many actors—victims may be left without remedy. In such cases, the multitude of causes makes it all the more difficult for victims to identify who harmed them, and on what legal basis they may claim redress. If neither individuals nor collectives can be held accountable, the system fails to fulfil a core function of international law of responsibility.

This inability to grasp accountability feeds back on the performance of obligations. As Bovens observed, '[i]f no one can be meaningfully called to account after the event, no one need feel responsible beforehand.'[12] The consequence is that actors may defer responsibility to others or downplay their own role, resulting in inaction or minimal compliance.

This logic parallels the free-rider problem in the provision of public goods: when individual efforts appear dispensable, motivation to contribute weakens. As Mancur Olson's work suggests, in large groups, individuals tend to underestimate both the impact and necessity of their own actions, particularly when others are perceived as more capable of addressing the issue.[13] The same is true for companies and states.

In sum, the problem of many hands reveals that the very structure of cumulative environmental harm resists conventional legal approaches to causation, obligation, and accountability.

---

11 André Nollkaemper, 'Lessons of a landmark lost: the judgment of the Hague Court of Appeal in *Shell v. Milieudefensie*' (12 November 2024), VerfBlog, https://verfassungsblog.de/shell-milieudefensie-climate-litigation (last accessed: 26 September 2025).

12 Bovens (1998), p. 49.

13 Mancur Olson, The logic of collective action: public goods and the theory of groups (1965).

C. System failure by design: when international law produces what it fails to prevent

This leads me to the main point of these reflections. The challenges posed by cumulative environmental harm are not merely evidentiary difficulties that international law struggles to address. They are, in important ways, problems that international law itself helps to create. The fragmentation of responsibility, and the invisibility of small-scale but widespread harms, are not accidental oversights. Rather, they are features embedded in the very architecture of international legal governance.

Through its narrow focus on state-to-state responsibility, its fundamental bond to bilateralism, its reliance on discrete causal chains, and its failure to account for systemic and collective dynamics, international law reproduces and legitimises the very conditions that allow cumulative harm to flourish. In this sense, the law does not simply fail to prevent environmental degradation—it contributes to its production. What appears, at first glance, to be regulatory insufficiency is, upon closer examination, a deeper systemic failure by design.

This point is supported in a variety of forms, often implicitly, by other contributions in this volume that demonstrate how cumulative harm often emerges not despite legal systems, but because of their structure. For instance, clean energy policies in the Netherlands, despite their sustainability framing, reproduce inequality and extractive patterns—suggesting that law entrenches the very vulnerabilities it seeks to address.[14] And consumer law in France and Chile treats consumers as isolated agents, ignoring the cumulative environmental impacts of their consumption.[15] Similarly, the analysis of Sustainable Urban Mobility Plans shows that, despite their sustainability rhetoric, these lead to continued emissions through weak implementation—but now legitimized by such plans.[16] And the discussion of deep seabed mining shows how the regime for the International Seabed Authority prioritises commercial over ecological interests, legitimising harm through international regulation.[17]

---

14 Kate O'Reilly, 'Law, power and the climate crisis: proposing a critical theory approach for EU sustainability law', this volume, p. 279-291.

15 Morales/Moreno, this volume, p. 59-78.

16 Barduhn, this volume, p. 263-278.

17 Sanjeet Ruhal, 'The ambivalent promise of the abyss: Deep-seabed mining, governance gap and the race for critical minerals', this volume, p. 115-135.

These examples show that cumulative harm often stems not from regulatory failure alone, but from legal design. The law frequently acts as producer of the very harms it purports to regulate.

While many of these examples arise from domestic or regional law, the problem is amplified in international law. Strong protection of state sovereignty and deference to national policy choices restrict the capacity of international law to address harmful decisions. This structural permissiveness, combined with narrow doctrines of responsibility, impedes systemic intervention.

A stark example is the role of international law in structuring the global meat industry, on which I have been working recently.[18] Far from being a neutral background condition, international law has played an enabling role in the global expansion of meat production—a major driver of cumulative environmental harm, including greenhouse gas emissions, biodiversity loss, deforestation, and water depletion.

International law has supported the intensification and globalisation of livestock through multiple legal and institutional pathways.

On the one hand, international law has anchored the liberties that allow states and companies to do what they do. It has protected the freedom of states to expand such production to infinite degrees. No international legal norms exist to prohibit or even meaningfully restrain the environmental and animal welfare harms generated by these systems.

On the other hand, international law has actively promoted harmful intensification, for instance by trade agreements that reduce tariffs and facilitate cross-border meat exports; by investment treaties that protect agribusiness ventures; and by lending practices of international financial institutions that subsidise industrial livestock infrastructure in the Global South. In short, international law has not merely tolerated industrial meat production—it has helped build the legal, financial, and institutional scaffolding that makes it possible.

If we take a step back from such specific examples, we can identify several interrelated features of international law that help explain why cumulative harm remains so difficult to regulate.

First, international law grants deep legal liberties that allow harmful conduct to remain below the threshold of legal wrongfulness—especially when that conduct is diffuse, individually minor, and widely distributed.

---

18 André Nollkaemper, 'International law and the agony of animals in industrial meat production' (2023), 34(4) Eur. J. Int'l L., p. 939.

Second, the narrow scope of legal subjects means that only states and international organisations are directly bound by international obligations, leaving private actors—despite being major contributors to environmental harm—beyond the direct reach of legal accountability. Any consequences for harm caused by corporations or individuals arise, at best, only indirectly, through the responsibilities of states to regulate them.

Third, international legal doctrine imposes high thresholds for establishing causation. The International Court of Justice, for instance, requires 'a "sufficiently direct and certain causal nexus" between an alleged wrongful action or omission and the alleged damage'.[19] This makes it difficult (though not impossible) to attribute responsibility for cumulative harm to any individual state.

Finally, legal frameworks governing trade, investment, and finance actively shape markets in ways that promote environmental degradation. Rather than curbing unsustainable practices, these frameworks often incentivise them, by creating market access, transborder flows of goods and services that we all want, but that come with a price.

Together, these elements reveal how the architecture of international law not only fails to prevent cumulative harm—it structurally reproduces it.

D. Tilting the system: incremental responses to cumulative harm in international law

The structural nature of cumulative environmental harm, and the enabling role played by international law, suggest that meaningful solutions must go beyond isolated reforms. Instead, they must aim at systemic transformation. There are no indications that anything resembling such a systemic transformation is about to happen. However, the absence of a structural overhaul need not mean that international law is entirely static or without leverage.

A range of more modest, piecemeal interventions—whether through reinterpretation, institutional practice, soft law, or treaty innovation—may begin to tilt the legal system, however slightly, in a direction more responsive to the realities of cumulative harm. While individually limited, such changes may help open normative space, shift legal expectations, or unsettle entrenched assumptions that currently inhibit systemic responsiveness.

19 International Court of Justice, Advisory Opinion on the Obligations of States in respect of Climate Change, 23 July 2025, para. 436.

This is a line that is also present in many of the contributions to this volume, containing a range of innovative legal strategies that offer pathways toward systemic responsiveness. Some of these are fundamental and challenge the system head-on. One is the plea for institutional and ideological reconfiguration, not just technical and policy adjustments.[20] Other papers are more modest in scale, yet nonetheless suggest how law can be reoriented to confront the complexities of cumulative harm. Examples are the discussions of the role of extraterritorial due diligence laws in illuminating hidden supply chain harms;[21] investment treaties that are evolving to balance investor protections with environmental safeguards;[22] sustainability obligations in the built environment that can reshape fragmented legal responsibilities;[23] and a proposal for behavioural incentives as soft governance tools to steer individual behaviour cumulatively in more sustainable patterns.[24] All of these contributions reflect a broader legal imagination increasingly attuned to the structural nature of cumulative harm.

While most of these papers focus on domestic law, they do resonate with emerging developments in international law. Also here, certain doctrines and interpretations have begun to respond to the systemic challenges posed by cumulative environmental degradation. Of course, the speed of change is slow, the changes do not run deep, and the degrees of creativity and imagination are mostly limited and bounded by political reality.

Yet, some trends can be identified. The International Tribunal for the Law of the Sea, in its 2024 advisory opinion on climate change, affirmed that states have a due diligence obligation to ensure that activities under their jurisdiction do not cause significant harm to the marine environment; and that this extends to climate change.[25] This, of course, is not new. But with the opinion, we have moved to a different level in understanding what this means for cumulative harm; how it applies to greenhouse gas emissions

20 O'Reilly, this volume, p. 279-291.

21 Talukdar, this volume, p. 23-41.

22 Anita Grigoryan, 'Sustainable investment treaties: A comparative perspective on balancing investor rights and sustainable development', this volume, p. 169-182.

23 Nora Bouzoraa/Yassine Hasnaoui, 'Which direction to take? On (in)direct obligations to climate proof buildings in Dutch public and private law', this volume, p. 247-261.

24 Sameh Mansour/Maha Balbaa, 'Neuro-legal nudging and sustainable economics: a behavioural approach to sustainability law', this volume, p. 151-167.

25 International Tribunal for the Law of the Sea, Advisory Opinion on the Request submitted by the Commission of Small Island States on Climate Change and International Law, 21 May 2024.

from private actors, and how it applies to the protection of the marine environment from such cumulative effects.

The opinion thus recognises that shift: cumulative harm from dispersed private conduct is not beyond the reach of international obligations. States must exercise regulatory oversight over private contributions.

The International Court of Justice's advisory opinion on climate change expanded on this.[26] It clarified that state due diligence encompasses fossil fuel companies, agribusiness, and even consumption patterns. The Court made explicit that states shall adopt domestic policies to mitigate such harms. The private actors are not themselves international subjects, but their conduct that produces cumulative harm becomes relevant through state obligations to control them.[27]

The ruling of the European Court of Human Rights in *KlimaSeniorinnen v. Switzerland* is very much in the same line.[28] It recognises that human rights require states to adopt forward-looking climate policies capable of addressing cumulative risks. The court linked diffuse contributions like greenhouse gas emissions to justiciable rights, and accepted that systemic failure to regulate climate risk can violate rights under the European Convention on Human Rights. Its rejection of the 'drop in the ocean' argument goes to the root of the problem of cumulative environmental harm.

However, it is clear that all of this is a far cry from amounting to a truly systemic transformation that would change the international legal drivers of the current situations in which cumulative global environmental harm still is largely lawful and even driven by particular legal arrangements. These pushes to address systemic causes come from the courts, and their impact on legal change is naturally limited. The opinions from the International Tribunal for the Law of the Sea and the International Court of Justice are not binding. *KlimaSeniorinnen* is limited to Europe.

States have not been willing nor able to deliver the kind of far-reaching legal redesign needed to confront these problems at their root. The fate of the negotiations on the global plastics treaty is illustrative. The draft contains concrete regulatory strategies highly relevant for cumulative harm. It proposes extended producer responsibility, product bans, and design stan-

---

26 International Court of Justice, Advisory Opinion on the Obligations of States in respect of Climate Change, 23 July 2025.

27 Ibid, para. 282.

28 ECtHR (Grand Chamber), 9 April 2024 – Appl. No. 53600/20 – *Verein KlimaSeniorinnen Schweiz and Others v. Switzerland.*

dards. These could anticipate and address cumulative harm by targeting upstream behaviour.[29] If adopted, the treaty could model how international law can impose systemic obligations on private actors and tackle cumulative harm. Whether that will happen is, at the time of writing, uncertain. And all the time, planetary harms continue to accumulate. What is clear is that we remain at an early and uncertain stage in international law's reckoning with the deep structural drivers of cumulative environmental harm.

E. Conclusion

Cumulative environmental harm is not an anomaly but the prevailing pattern of degradation in a world of interdependence. It poses not just a regulatory challenge, but a systemic legal failure deeply rooted in the structure of international law itself. From the structure of obligations to the exclusion of private actors, and through the hidden doctrines of state responsibility, international law often fails to perceive—let alone prevent or redress—the harms that result from countless dispersed and lawful activities. Worse, it often facilitates or entrenches the very legal and economic arrangements that give rise to such harms.

The emergence of new interpretations—such as due diligence obligations extending to private actors, nascent treaty innovations like the plastic pollution instrument, and the human rights framing of climate obligations—suggests that international law is not entirely static. These incremental developments hint at a shift in legal thinking: from a complicit framework to one more responsive to the systemic nature of global harm.

The very rich contributions to this volume are part of that same development, both in analysing the systemic drivers of cumulative harm and in identifying possible legal pathways for response. The challenge ahead is undeniably formidable. Yet it is inspiring to see so much deep critical engagement, paired with so much forward-looking creativity. Volumes such as the present one will not be able to change the political will. But what they can do is bring together innovative legal thought and imagination. By opening new conceptual and normative doors, the chapters make impor-

29 UNEP, 'Chair's Revised Text Proposal', Intergovernmental Negotiating Committee to develop an international legally binding instrument on plastic pollution, including in the marine environment (INC-5.2) (15 August 2025), https://www.unep.org/inc-plastic-pollution/session-5.2 (last accessed: 26 September 2025).

tant contributions to enhancing the understanding and opening space for systemic change that international law urgently needs.

From *Galli* to Paris Fashion Week: law, sustainability, and the hidden faces of *Karegari*

*Shuma Talukdar**

A. *Introduction*

Sustainability has become a defining issue of our time. The United Nations' Brundtland Commission defined sustainability in 1987 as 'meeting the needs of the present without compromising the ability of future generations to meet their own needs.' It is primarily divided into three core concepts: environmental (conserving natural resources and preserving ecosystems), social (promoting equity and human rights for all people and communities), and economic (managing resources and economic growth responsibly). Embracing sustainability as a principle of corporate governance has become legally binding for companies in many countries, primarily in developed nations. However, its impact can also be seen in the industries of developing nations. One such industry is the embroidery industry, a sub-sector of the textile industry.

* Shuma Talukdar is a Doctoral Researcher at the School of Law, Mahindra University, Hyderabad (India). She is also a registered Advocate with the Bar Council of India. She holds dual Master's degrees in Business Law and Public Administration. She strongly identifies as both an environmentalist and a feminist. Her research interests include sustainability law, transnational law, and governance. E-mail: ShumaTalukdar13@gmail.com

The word embroidery comes from the French word '*broderie*', meaning embellishment, and dates back as far as 30,000 BC. India is the most hand-skilled country in the world, employing approximately 34.5 million *karegar* (craftsmen) across the nation. However, the communities involved in this work are predominantly rural and remain largely un-corporatised.[1] Since the 1980s, luxury brands have outsourced embroidery to India, for its exceptional craftsmanship, diverse traditional embroidery techniques, and cost-effective yet high-quality production,[2] with the market valued at $150–$250 billion.

India is the largest exporter of hand embroidery in the world, mainly to France and Italy.[3] By 2019, India's embroidery exports had surpassed $230 million, a nearly fivefold increase since 1999[4] and are currently flourishing, with exports reaching $3.6 billion (EUR 3.3 billion) in FY23 (including both luxury and non-luxury segments).[5]

Iconic fashion items such as Alessandro Michele's Gucci collection, Dior's embellished saddle bags, and Jennifer Lopez's famous Versace jungle dress were handcrafted by skilled Indian craftsmen. However, despite the high prices these brands command, the craftsmen often face poor working conditions, inadequate wages, and little recognition.[6]

Skilled craftsmen create intricate, couture-level work, often behind the scenes of these iconic global fashion events. With crafts like *Phulkari, Kantha*, and *Chikankari*, India offers a rich variety that helps luxury brands stand out. Additionally, favourable currency exchange rates make India a cost-efficient choice. The glamour of Paris Fashion Week stands in sharp

---

1 Bandana Tiwari, 'Luxury Brands Must Credit Craftspeople' (2015), https://www.businessoffashion.com/opinions/news-analysis/op-ed-luxury-brands-must-credit-craftspeople/ (last accessed: 30 June 2025).

2 Bloomberg Originals, 'Inside Luxury's Secret India Supply Chain' (2023), https://www.youtube.com/watch?v=Qy2JWUOwTWQ (last accessed: 30 June 2025).

3 Sheetal Jain, 'Recognising Indian Artisans' Contribution to Luxury' (2023), https://www.luxurydaily.com/recognize-indian-artisans-contributions-to-luxury/ (last accessed: 30 June 2025).

4 Kai Schultz/Elizabeth Pathon/Phyllida Jay, 'Luxury's Hidden Indian Supply Chain' (2020), https://www.nytimes.com/2020/03/11/style/dior-saint-laurent-indian-labor-exploitation.html (last accessed: 30 June 2025).

5 Shilpa Dhamija, 'Is India's Savoir-Faire Getting Its Due Credits?' (2024), https://www.luxurytribune.com/en/is-indias-savoir-faire-getting-its-due-credits (last accessed: 30 June 2025).

6 Luxe Analytics, 'Time for Indian Artisans to Shine on the Global Map' (n.d.), https://luxeanalytics.in/blog/blog_detail/44 (last accessed: 30 June 2025).

contrast to the reality of dimly lit workshops in Delhi, Mumbai, or Kolkata, where artisans work long hours for meagre pay. While some brands, such as Dior, highlight their Indian supply chains, the world is increasingly recognising India's deep-rooted contribution to global luxury fashion.[7]

Although scholarship on global supply chain and sustainability law is expanding,[8] no academic work has examined the embroidery industry, a niche yet economically significant sector in India. Existing studies on EU sustainability laws focus on formal industries or Western contexts, neglecting informal[9] fragmented sectors[10] such as Indian hand embroidery. This paper marks the starting point of a larger project examining how the EU Corporate Sustainability Reporting Directive (CSRD) and Corporate Sustainability Due-Diligence Directive (CSDDD) could reshape the luxury supply chain and improve conditions for Indian craftsmen.

Initial findings suggest that these directives hold significant potential to improve transparency and accountability in EU supply chains. However, their extraterritorial reach raises important justice concerns, particularly the risk of imposing disproportionate compliance burdens on suppliers in developing countries. Large, well-resourced exporters may adapt, but small and medium suppliers, who often employ the most vulnerable workers, risk exclusion from the EU market.

Against this backdrop, this study explores the central question: Can the CSRD and CSDDD make EU luxury supply chains more transparent and accountable, while meaningfully improving the working conditions of Indian embroidery craftsmen?

---

7 Mankiran, 'The Supply Chain of Luxury Global Ateliers in India' (2024), https://mba-esg.in/luxury-hidden-indian-supply-chain/ (last accessed: 30 June 2025).

8 See, for example, Antje Wahl/Gary Q. Bull, 'Mapping Research Topics and Theories in Private Regulation for Sustainability in Global Value Chains' (2014), 124(4) Journal of Business Ethics, p. 585.
Also see, Emma Ross, 'Overdressed and Underregulated: How the Fashion Industry's Extreme Plastic Pollution Can Be Linked to a Lack of Supply Chain Regulation' (2023), 25(1) Vermont Journal of Environmental Law.

9 Workers, primarily women engaged in home-based work alongside their household responsibilities. They are inadequately represented in official statistics and remain outside the scope of protective legislation or trade union organization. Resultantly, they lack basic safeguards such as contracts, health benefits, or social security, leaving them structurally invisible and vulnerable to exploitation.

10 Groups of different size involved with this industry. Some of them are big players and others SMEs or even individual people working from home.

B. Environmental and social Issues in the Indian embroidery sector

I. Environmental issues

Although this paper focuses on the social dimension, it is important to briefly situate embroidery within the broader environmental impact of textiles. The embroidery industry is one of the most polluting industries globally.[11] In Europe, textiles are the fourth largest source of environmental pollution, responsible for about 20 per cent of global water pollution[12] and around 10 per cent of total greenhouse gas emissions more than those from international shipping and aviation combined.[13] These emissions occur across the entire supply chain, including raw material extraction, production, dyeing, processing, transportation, and distribution.[14] If current practices continue, emissions from the textile industry are expected to increase by over 50 per cent by 2030.[15] This may derail the EU's objective of achieving its own Sustainable Development Goals (SDGs), by 2030, as achieving sustainability in the supply chain is essential for meeting the SDGs.[16]

---

11 Air Collection, 'Sustainability in Embroidery: Eco-Friendly Materials and Techniques' (n.d.), https://www.aircollection.it/en/news/sustainability-in-embroidery-eco-friendly-materials-and-techniques.38 (last accessed: 30 June 2025).

12 European Parliament, 'The Impact of Textile Production and Waste on the Environment' (2020), https://www.europarl.europa.eu/topics/en/article/20201208STO93327/the-impact-of-textile-production-and-waste-on-the-environment-infographics (last accessed: 30 June 2025).

13 Max, 'The Environmental Impact of the Textile Sector' (2024), https://www.hhc.earth/knowledge-base/articles/the-environmental-impact-of-the-textile-sector (last accessed: 30 June 2025).

14 Nikita Shukla, 'Fast Fashion Pollution and Climate Change' (2022), https://earth.org/fast-fashion-pollution-and-climate-change/#:~:text=Fast%20Fashion%20and%20Climate%20Change,processing%20to%20transport%20and%20shipping (last accessed: 30 June 2025).

15 Ibid.

16 Walter Leal Filho/Laís Trevisan/Thais Dibbern/Julen Castillo Apraiz/Izabela Rampasso/Rosley Anholon/Beatrice Gornati /Manfredi Morello/Wim Lambrechts, 'Sustainable Supply Chain Management and the UN Sustainable Development Goals: Exploring Synergies Towards Sustainable Development' (2025), 37(1) TMQJ, https://doi.org/10.1108/TQM-04-2023-0114 (last accessed: 8 September 2025), *also see,* Rohit Agrawal/Abhijit Majumdar/Kirty Majumdar/Rakesh D. Raut/Balkrishna E. Narkhede, 'Attaining Sustainable Development Goals (SDGs) through Supply Chain Practices and Business Strategies: A Systematic Review with Bibliometric and Net-

In embroidery specifically, significant environmental waste is generated during production. Fabric scraps, embroidery threads, trims, and buttons often go unused, with 10–25 per cent of fabric wasted during the cutting stage. These losses can result from technical errors, such as misprints, poor embroidery techniques, and inaccurate sampling.[17] Furthermore, many embroidery threads are made from synthetic, petroleum-based materials that are non-biodegradable and persist in the environment for decades. The dyeing process often uses harmful chemicals, which pollute water sources and damage ecosystems.[18]

Due to its complex and fragmented supply chain, which involves multiple production sites, international transport, and diverse raw material sources, embroidery has a significant environmental footprint. Each stage, from fabric sourcing to dyeing and finishing, contributes to pollution and resource consumption.[19]

To address the environmental impact of the textile industry, including embroidery, regulatory efforts are emerging at both the union and national levels in Europe. For example, France's Anti-Waste for a Circular Economy Law (AGEC), in effect since 2022, prohibits the destruction of unsold goods and encourages reuse or recycling. It also mandates transparency about environmental impacts.[20] The European Union's Strategy for Sustainable and Circular Textiles (2022) promote the use of recycled fabrics, digital product passports, and stricter rules against misleading environmental claims. France's Climate and Resilience Law (2021) introduced a labelling

---

work Analyses' (2022), 31(7) Business Strategy and the Environment, https://doi.org/10.1002/bse.3057 (last accessed: 8 September 2025).

17 Osama Abd Elhameed Kawashty Hamzawy, 'Waste Management Implementation in Textile Industry & Waste Impacts on the Environment' (2023), https://mjaf.journals.ekb.eg/article_310211_eb311c8c859920feea71c8e5521b3e97.pdf (last accessed: 30 June 2025).

18 Central Embroidery, 'Eco-Friendly Embroidery: Embrace Sustainable Threads Today' (2025), https://www.centralembroidery.co.uk/eco-friendly-embroidery-sustainable-threads-and-processes/ (last accessed: 30 June 2025).

19 News and Views, 'Embroidery and the Environment: Small Changes for Big Impact'(2019), https://www.marathonthreads.co.uk/en/blog/industry/embroidery-and-the-environment-small-changes-for-big-impact/ (last accessed: 30 June 2025).

20 Carl Dalhammar/Flavie Vonderscher/Sandar Leonet/Jessika Luth Richter 'National Leadership for Legislating Longer Product Lifetimes: French Policies and their Interaction with European Union Policies' [Proceedings of the 6th Product Lifetimes and the Environment Conference (PLATE2025), 2025].

system to help consumers make environmentally informed choices.[21] These legal measures reflect a growing recognition of the need to address environmental harms in the textile and embroidery sectors through stricter regulation and more sustainable practices to achieve the SDGs.

However, as this paper focuses on the social dimension of the embroidery industry in India, the study will henceforth limit itself to social aspects and will not discuss the environmental aspect further.

II. Social issues

The embroidery sector, though culturally rich, artistically significant, and globally admired, faces several social challenges that primarily affect the craftsmen involved in the production process.

One key concern is the lack of fair labour standards in this largely 'unorganised sector'[22]. Wages in the embroidery sector are significantly low. 'Home-based workers'[23] earn far below the legal minimum and living wage standards. For example, average monthly earnings are ₹2,860 ($ 32.76),[24] while the national minimum wage in India is ₹178 ($ 2.04) per day, which amounts to approximately ₹5,340 ($ 61.51) per month. However, each state sets its own minimum wage, making some locations more preferred by workers than others with higher wage levels.

For instance, the minimum wage for an unskilled worker in Delhi is ₹17,494 ($ 200.38) per month, and for a skilled worker, it is ₹21,215 ($

21 ClimateSeed, 'Textile Industry: Environmental Impact and Regulations' (2022), https://climateseed.com/blog/secteur-du-textile-impact-environnemental-etreglementation#:~:text=The%20textile%20industry%20is%20a,million%20tons%20in%2020302 (last accessed: 30 June 2025).

22 Code on Social Security 2020, s 2(85), "Unorganised sector" means an enterprise owned by individuals or self-employed workers and engaged in the production or sale of goods or providing service of any kind whatsoever, and where the enterprise employs workers, the number of such workers is less than ten.

23 Code on Social Security 2020, s 2(36), "Home-based worker" means a person engaged in, the production of goods or services for an employer in his home or other premises of his choice other than the workplace of the employer, for remuneration, irrespective of whether or not the employer provides the equipment, materials or other inputs.

24 Sushil Kumar Bishnoi/Shikha Kapoor, 'A Case Study on Fair Compensation to Hand Embroidery Workers in India' (2020), Reasearch Journal of Textile and Apparel, pp. 97–110.

243).[25] In contrast, the minimum wage for an unskilled worker in West Bengal is ₹10,214 ($ 116.99), and for a skilled worker, it is ₹12,688 ($ 145.33).[26] As a result, many craftsmen from states such as West Bengal migrate to cities like Delhi in search of higher wages, despite often facing poor working conditions due to the high cost of real estate and living in larger cities.[27] These low wages not only affect the workers' quality of life but also threaten the continuity of the craft, as younger generations are discouraged from pursuing it as a profession.[28]

Beyond wages, poor working conditions persist. Craftsmen often work long hours in uncomfortable postures and sometimes in poorly lit rooms. This often leads to serious health issues,[29] such as poor eyesight and neurological disorders. These long working hours and strict deadlines are mostly set before the hosting of events and shows by brands. The demand for low-cost embroidery puts additional pressure on craftsmen without ensuring fair compensation or working conditions.[30]

While some social enterprises are working to improve the wages and working conditions of the workers and to preserve this traditional skill,[31] such efforts remain isolated. Without systemic change, to promote trans-

25 India-Briefing, 'Minimum Wages and Salary Structures in India' (2024), https://www.india-briefing.com/doing-business-guide/india/human-resources-and-payroll/minimum-wage#:~:text=Effective%20October%201%2C%202024%2C%20the,%2Dmatriculate%2C%20and%20graduate%20employees (last accessed: 30 June 2025).

26 Workforce Consulting, 'The West Bengal Minimum Wages Notification' (2024), https://www.workforce.org.in/Blog_Details.aspx?oId=416 (last accessed: 30 June 2025).

27 Kia Schultz/Elizabeth Paton/Phyllida Jay, 'Luxury's Hidden Indian Supply Chain' (2020) https://www.nytimes.com/2020/03/11/style/dior-saint-laurent-indian-labor-exploitation.html (last accessed: 23 August 2025).

28 Disha Poray, 'The Fading Art of Indian Embroidery and Its Impact on Luxury Fashion' (2019), https://www.researchgate.net/profile/Disha-Poray/publication/338817265_The_Fading_Art_of_Indian_Embroidery_and_its_Impact_on_Luxury_Fashion/links/5e2bc98e4585150ee780a147/The-Fading-Art-of-Indian-Embroidery-and-its-Impact-on-Luxury-Fashion.pdf?__cf_chl_tk (last accessed: 30 June 2025).

29 Somnath Gangopadhyay/Sabarni Chakrabarty/Krishnendu Sarkar/Samrat Dev/Tamal Das/Sunetra Banerjee, 'An Ergonomics Study on the Evaluation of Carpal Tunnel Syndrome Among Chikan Embroidery Workers of West Bengal, India' (2015), https://pmc.ncbi.nlm.nih.gov/articles/PMC4597008/pdf/oeh-21-199.pdf (last accessed: 30 June 2025).

30 Tiwari, 'Luxury Brands Must Credit Craftspeople' (2015).

31 Sangeetha Swaroop, 'Embroidery: A Dying Craft Revived, One Stitch at a Time' (2018), https://gulfnews.com/lifestyle/embroidery-a-dying-craft-revived-one-stitch-at-a-time-1.1459082 (last accessed: 30 June 2025).

parency and enforce fair wages and ethical labour practices throughout the supply chain, the exploitation of craftsmen will persist continue beneath the surface of luxury fashion.[32]

C. Extraterritorial impact of CSRD and CSDDD

To strengthen sustainability, the EU has introduced landmark instruments: the CSRD and CSDDD. Together, they aim to increase corporate accountability, prevent greenwashing, and embed social and environmental responsibility into the global supply chain.

The CSRD requires large EU companies and listed SMEs to ensure transparency by reporting on their sustainability practices using the European Sustainability Reporting Standards (ESRS), aiming to prevent greenwashing and social washing, and to promote accountability through double materiality and mandatory third-party assurance of reports.[33] Companies must integrate Environmental, Social, and Governance (ESG) policies into their strategies and disclose relevant environmental and social impacts.[34] The directive mandates disclosure not only about a company's own activities but also about its upstream and downstream value chain, including products, services, and business relationships. Thus, the directive also requires disclosure on Indian suppliers.[35]

CSDDD, on the other hand, goes a step further. It emphasises proactive risk management through mandatory due diligence, obliging companies to prevent and address social and environmental harms in their supply chains.[36] Aligned with Organisation for Economic Co-operation and Devel-

---

32 Jappis PI, 'Sustainable Practices in Embroidery Production' (2024), https://jappispi.chinagoods.com/news/sustainable-practices-in-embroidery-production.html (last accessed: 30 June 2025).

33 Directive (EU) 2022/2464 of the European Parliament and of the Council of 14 December 2022 amending Regulation (EU) No 537/2014, Directive 2004/109/EC, Directive 2006/43/EC and Directive 2013/34/EU, as regards corporate sustainability reporting [2022] OJ L 322, p. 36.

34 Ibid., p. 16.

35 Ibid., p. 25.

36 Nadia Perrone, 'Perspectives of Extraterritorial Jurisdiction for Environmental Damage in the Proposal of the European Directive on Corporate Sustainability Due Diligence' (2023), 3(2), Italian Review of International and Comparative Law, https://doi.org/10.1163/27725650-03020012 (last accessed: 7 September 2025), pp. 389–408.

opment (OECD) guidelines,[37] it legally compels firms not only to report, but also to act on issues such as fair labour, climate goals, and resource responsibility.[38]

However, political negotiations have narrowed the directive's scope. The Omnibus compromise text, which limits the CSDDD to Tier 1 suppliers,[39] raises concerns about its ability to reach the most vulnerable workers upstream. For Indian industries, such as embroidery, which largely rely on subcontracting and home-based production, this creates a significant blind spot. It risks excluding the most vulnerable home-based workers (often women from minority communities) working in the supply chain.

Despite these limitations, the directives together offer a powerful framework to transform embroidery supply chains from opaque and exploitative to transparent and accountable.[40] The CSRD enforces detailed sustainability reporting, making it mandatory for companies to disclose environmental and social risks throughout their value chains, thereby shedding light on previously hidden subcontracting practices, where, manufacturer exporters and merchant exporters were the profit makers in the supply chain.[41] Meanwhile, the CSDDD mandates concrete action, requiring brands to

37 The OECD Guidelines established comprehensive standards for the responsible business conduct of multinational companies. It covers an array of issues, such as, human rights, employment, environment, consumer protection, and many others. It extends to company's entire business relationship and also to supply chain, not just its direct employment.

38 Rebekah Mays/Tian Daphne, 'CSRD and CSDDD: What are the key differences?' (2024), https://www.circularise.com/blogs/csrd-and-csddd-what-are-the-key-differences#:~:text=The%20CSRD%20mandates%20reporting%20and,company's%20activities%20and%20preventing%20greenwashing (last accessed: 30 June 2025).

39 Directive of the European Parliament and of the Council amending Directives 2006/43/EC, 2013/34/EU, (EU) 2022/2464 and (EU) 2024/1760 as regards certain corporate sustainability reporting and due diligence requirements [2025] https://commission.europa.eu/document/download/1d14a487-f042-476f-997f-adf7c3e14950_en?filename=CSDDD%20Omnibus%20proposal.pdf (last accessed: 7 September 2025) p. 26, para 21.

40 ESG Voices, 'What is Supply Chain Transparency in ESG?' (2024), https://www.esgvoices.com/post/the-crucial-role-of-supply-chain-transparency-in-esg (last accessed: 30 June 2025).

41 Sujata Madhok, 'Report on Bonded Labour in Delhi Analysing the Effectiveness of the Programmes for the Eradication of the Bonded Labour System' (2007), New Delhi: Centre for Education and Communication.

actively identify and mitigate risks, such as labour exploitation.[42] These directives, if implemented as proposed, could mark a new phase in corporate responsibility, where companies must track and disclose not only their profits but also the environmental and social impacts of their activities. These new directives are changing how businesses work, making transparency and thorough checks on their supply chains, obligatory.[43]

However, if not implemented with adequate support and flexibility, the CSDDD could potentially violate international trade principles and norms of fairness by placing disproportionate burdens on exporters in developing countries, such as India.[44] The imposition of strict compliance requirements without technical or financial assistance amounts to indirect discrimination, as it favours well-resourced companies while excluding small firms from global markets.[45] This undermines the principle of substantive justice, as it fails to account for the unequal capacities of stakeholders across the Global South.[46] In effect, such one-size-fits-all regulations risk breaching the spirit of international law, which calls for equitable treatment and inclusive participation in global trade systems.

In short, the directives have the potential to reshape global supply chains, but without careful attention to local contexts, they may unintentionally entrench a two-tier system: formal suppliers integrated into EU markets, while informal workers remain invisible and unprotected.

---

42 Martina Puigròs, 'CSRD: Transparency and Accountability in Corporate Sustainability Reporting' (2024), https://www.finboot.com/post/csrd-transparency-and-accountability-in-corporate-sustainability-reporting (last accessed: 30 June 2025).

43 Dayrise, 'Mandatory Due Diligence and Transparency Regulations on the Rise' (2025), https://dayrize.io/mandatory-due-diligence-and-transparency-regulations-on-the-rise/ (last accessed: 30 June 2025).

44 United Nations, 'The Future of Sustainable Trade' (2025), https://unctad.org/system/files/official-document/ditctab2024d5_en.pdf (last accessed: 05 September 2025), p. 29.

45 National Board of Trade Sweden, 'Potential Impacts of EU Due Diligence Obligations on Companies' Suppliers in Developing Countries' (2023), https://www.kommerskollegium.se/globalassets/publikationer/rapporter/2023/potential-impacts-of-eu-due-diligence-obligations-on-companies-suppliers.pdf (last accessed: 05 September 2025), p. 24.

46 Maartje Smit, 'A Global South Perspective on the Corporate Sustainability Due Diligence Directive' (2024), https://blogs.lse.ac.uk/internationaldevelopment/2024/10/10/a-global-south-perspective-on-the-corporate-sustainability-due-diligence-directive/ (last accessed: 05 September 2025).

D. Lessons from France´s Duty of Vigilance Act and India's Utthan Pact

Indian embroidery is increasingly gaining global visibility, with luxury brands highlighting Indian craftsmen in response to consumer demand for transparency and sustainability.[47] This shift is driven by NGO advocacy, social media activism, and purpose-driven marketing, positioning supply chain visibility as both an ethical imperative and a competitive advantage. High-profile campaigns, such as Dior's 2023 India showcase,[48] have inspired other brands like Hermès and Balmain to credit craftsmen and disclose supply chain practices.[49]

Changes are occurring within the Indian supply chain, though it remains unclear whether these are in anticipation of the EU's directives (yet to be fully implemented) or in response to France's Duty of Vigilance (DV) Law, in effect since 2017. As the first binding due diligence law in the world, DV Law undoubtedly pioneered the model, however, its narrow scope and patchwork application across the EU created momentum for an EU-wide measure. The Act, under Article 1, states that large companies with at least 5,000 employees in France or 10,000 worldwide must adopt a vigilance plan to identify risks and prevent serious human rights, health, and environmental harms across their operations and subsidiaries.[50] This scope is too narrow and applies to only around 250 companies. Further, studies suggest that the DV Law has led to enhanced due diligence and corporate accountability, although companies retain discretion in compliance.[51] Despite its pioneering role, the law faces challenges regarding scope, enforcement, and the genuine integration of environmental and social stan-

47 DFU Publications, 'Luxury Brands Tap into India's Traditional Craftsmanship' (2023), https://www.dfupublications.com/categories/article/luxury-brands-tap-into-india-s-traditional-craftsmanship (last accessed: 30 June 2025).

48 Loïc Prigent, 'Dior Goes To India!' (2023), https://www.youtube.com/watch?v=aTUdtZWy6MY (last accessed: 30 June 2025).

49 Mankiran, 'The Supply Chain of Luxury Global Ateliers in India' (2024).

50 Business and Human Rights Resource Centre, 'French Duty of Vigilance Law – English Translation' (2016), https://www.business-humanrights.org/en/latest-news/french-duty-of-vigilance-law-english-translation/ (last accessed: 23 August 2025).

51 Almut Schilling-Vacaflor/Maria-Therese Gustafsson, 'Towards More Sustainable Global Supply Chains? Company Compliance with New Human Rights and Environmental Due Diligence Laws' (2023), 33(3), Environmental Politics, p. 422, 443, https://doi.org/10.1080/09644016.2023.2221983.

dards.[52] This is because companies have filed generic vigilance plans and the law does not mention a dedicated supervisory authority. Additionally, enforcement under the law depends on civil litigation, which is slow and resource-intensive.

Several other obstacles make civil litigation under the DV Law difficult. The first is the identification of companies with scope. The second is determining the competent court, whether civil or commercial. There is also uncertainty about who has standing before the court. The law lacks a precise standard for the vigilance plan. Victims must rely heavily on NGOs for litigation and face a heavy burden of proof. Finally, there is no clarity on how to handle cases where the harm occurred outside France.[53]

While developed countries, particularly in Europe, are increasingly adopting supply chain regulations to address the environmental and social externalities of global trade, these laws often focus narrowly on a single domain. The French DV Law attempts to integrate both, but early evidence shows that legal inclusion alone is insufficient for effective policy coherence.[54] To date, sixteen cases (as available in the public domain)[55] have been brought under the DV Law, with only five decided. The decided cases are discussed below and the pending cases are listed in the footnote.[56]

---

52 Elsa Savourey/Stéphane Brabant, 'The French Law on the Duty of Vigilance: Theoretical and Practical Challenges Since its Adoption' (2021), 6(1), Business and Human Rights Journal, p. 141–152, https://doi:10.1017/bhj.2020.30, *also see*, Maria Lancri, 'Lessons from the French Duty of Care Law on the Way to a European Text' (2021), 22, ERA Forum, p. 453–464, https://doi.org/10.1007/s12027-021-00686-2.

53 Ibid.

54 Almut Schilling-Vacaflor, 'Integrating Human Rights and the Environment in Supply Chain Regulations' (2021), 13(17), Sustainability, https://doi.org/10.3390/su13179666 (last accessed: 30 June 2025), p. 9666.

55 Simmons and Simmons, 'French Duty of Vigilance: Litigation Tracker' (2025), https://www.simmons-simmons.com/en/publications/clomu1rfn01pmu6x4dz5enms5/french-duty-of-vigilance-litigation-tracker (last accessed: 30 June 2025).

56 *Bloom and Foodwatch v. Carrefour* (2025); *Jurdi v. BNP Paribas* (2025), both are still pending. CGT and CFDT v. SNCF (2024), is decided and discussed in the main body of this paper. *Les Amis de la Terre France and others v. TotalEnergies* (2023); *Comissao Pastoral da Terra and Notre Affaire à Tous v. BNP Paribas* (2023); *Mena Rights Group v. TotalEnergies* (2023); *Zero Waste France and Others v. Danone* (2023); *Oxfam France & Others v. BNP Paribas* (2023), all the cases from 2023 are still pending before the court. *Sherpa and Others v. Yves Rocher* (2022); *Data Rights and Others v. Idemia* (2022), Data Rights is decided and discussed above. *Observatorio Ciudadano and Others v. Suez* (2021); *Sud PTT v. LaPoste* (2021); *Sherpa and Others v. Casino* (2021), out of the three cases filed in 2021, two are decided and discussed above in the main body of this paper. *Notre Affaire à Tous and Others v. Total Energies* (2020);

The decided cases show that procedural defects and strict legal formalities discourage public-interest litigants.[57] The DV Law has prompted corporate engagement and even plan modifications, often without a full trial or ruling.[58] Civil society groups face further challenges such as heavy evidentiary burdens, judicial conservatism, and rigid procedures.[59] These factors limit their ability to bring actions before the court. In one instance, however, the court directed a company to adopt proper monitoring and vigilance measures.[60] Similar obstacles may arise under the CSRD and CSDDD unless addressed with clearer procedural rules and stronger enforcement mechanisms.

In the Indian context, an earlier attempt, although a voluntary industry-led initiative, was made to improve the condition of craftsmen. The Uttan Pact, a legally non-binding pact, was signed in 2016 by major luxury fashion groups, including Kering (owner of Gucci and Saint Laurent), LVMH (owner of Dior and Fendi), Burberry, and Mulberry, along with Indian export houses such as Amal Beading & Embroideries Pvt. Ltd. and Marsil Exports.[61] The pact aimed to improve working conditions and legal compliance in Mumbai's embroidery sector. However, it was not publicly promoted, and some participants were required to sign non-disclosure agreements, reflecting its largely confidential and voluntary nature.

The pact sought to transform the sector by improving working conditions and ensuring transparency across the supply chain. It aimed to benefit workers by enforcing compliance with Indian labour laws, ensuring minimum wages, Provident Fund (PF), Employees' State Insurance (ESI), regulated working hours under the Factories Act, and strict health and safety standards.[62] It also requires craftsmen to be skill-certified and links their pay to legally recognised wage levels, moving away from the informal

---

ProDesc and ECCHR v. EDF (2020), both are pending, and *Friends of the Earth and Others v. Total Energies* (2019), decided and discussed in this paper.

57 *Observatorio Ciudadano & Others v. Suez* (2021).

58 *Data Rights & Others v. Idemia* (2022).

59 *Friends of the Earth & Others v. TotalEnergies* (2019) and *CGT and CFDT v. SNCF* (2024).

60 *Sud PTT v. La Poste* (2021).

61 DT Next., 'Global Luxury's Hidden Supply Chain in India' (2020), https://www.dtnext.in/business/2020/03/14/global-luxurys-hidden-supply-chain-in-india#:~:text=In%202016%2C%20a%20group%20of%20luxury%20houses,of%20labels%20including%20Gucci%20and%20Saint%20Laurent) (last accessed: 30 June 2025).

62 Utthan Framework 2016, p. 4.

'*Nafri* (shift)'[63] system.[64] At the same time, the pact aimed at helping luxury brands meet global sustainability obligations by offering a transparent and accountable production network. The exporters were required to disclose all workshop locations and were prohibited from further subcontracting, curbing middle-level exploitation. This dual focus strengthens ethical sourcing, safeguards craftsmen's welfare, and enhances brand reputation through a traceable, dignified, and law-abiding supply chain.[65]

Although some brands, such as Kering, reported limited progress, the Utthan Pact largely failed due to its voluntary and secretive structure, lack of legal enforcement, and ongoing cost pressures from luxury brands. The pact's goals were undermined by widespread non-compliance, with many subcontractors lacking fire safety, underpaying workers, and falsifying audits. Craftsmen who raised concerns, faced retaliation, exposing the absence of protection and accountability, and highlighting a deep gap between brands' ethical claims and actual practices.[66] Had the pact been properly implemented, it could have enabled luxury brands to meet ESG, human rights, and due diligence obligations under global laws.

The lesson is clear: for CSRD and CSDDD to be effective, they must have a wider scope along with an effective enforcement mechanism. The directives can succeed only if they combine both lessons: robust laws with teeth, but implementation flexible enough to integrate the ground realities of suppliers and workers' voices. It can be a smart mix of regulation, like the DV Act and participatory elements like the Utthan Pact.

---

63 A *nafri* is an eight-hour work shift. However, if the worker does overtime of another four hours, which means a 12 hour shift, this is treated as two *nafris*. There are three grades of workers. The raw worker from the village earns Rs 80–90 ($ 0.92 – 1.03) per *nafri*. The worker with some experience and expertise gets Rs 110 ($ 1.26) per *nafri*. The master artisan gets Rs 250 ($ 2.86) per *nafri* – for further details please *see* http://cec-india.org/libpdf/1437544634Effectiveness-of-the-Eradication-of-Bonded-Labour---Delhi-2007.pdf (last accessed: 23 August 2025).

64 Utthan Framework 2016, p. 7.

65 New York Times, 'Utthan Framework' (2016), https://int.nyt.com/data/documenthelper/6802-utthan-pact-framework-2016/9b9f6b91c036b083e792/optimized/full.pdf#page=1 (last accessed: 30 June 2025).

66 Schultz, 'Luxury's Hidden Indian Supply Chain' (2020).

E. Legal reforms for worker protection and compliance

India has long grappled with fragmented labour laws. It had twenty-nine separate laws governing wages, social security and working conditions. These were mostly a tick-box exercise for employers. These laws failed to improve the conditions of the larger labour force (about 90 per cent unorganised workers)[67] and to make businesses accountable.[68] To simplify this framework, India consolidated them into four Labour Codes in 2020. These codes are: the Code on Wages 2019, covering payment and minimum wages, payment of bonus, and equal remuneration, which were earlier dealt with by four different laws in India;[69] the Code on Social Security 2020, which deals with employee's compensation, insurance, provident fund, compulsory notification of vacancies, maternity benefit, payment of gratuity, cine-workers' welfare, building and other construction workers, and unorganised workers;[70] and the Occupational Safety, Health and Working Conditions Code 2020, which deals with factories, plantation labour, mines, working journalists and other newspaper employees, motor transport, beedi and cigar workers, contact labour, sales promotion employees, inter-state migrant workers, cine and cine theatre workers, dock workers, and construction workers employment conditions.[71] And Industrial Rela-

67 Anonymous, 'New Labour Code for New India' (n.d.), https://labour.gov.in/sites/default/files/labour_code_eng.pdf (last accessed: 02 September 2025), p. 1.

68 Prashant Mara/Devina Deshpande, 'Business and Human Rights under India's New Labour Codes' (2021), https://www.ibanet.org/Business-and-human-rights-under-India%E2%80%99s-new-labour-codes#:~:text=Linking%20regulations%20to%20corporate%20behaviour,BHR%20strategy%20beyond%20technical%20compliance (last accessed: 06 September 2025).

69 Payment of Wages Act, 1936; Minimum Wages Act, 1948; Payment of Bonus Act, 1965; and Equal Remuneration Act, 1976.

70 Employees' Compensation Act, 1923; Employees' State Insurance Act, 1948; Employees' Provident Funds and Miscellaneous Provisions Act, 1952; Employment Exchanges (Compulsory) Notification of Vacancies) Act, 1959; Maternity Benefit Act, 1961; Payment of Gratuity Act, 1972; Cine-Workers Welfare Fund Act, 1981; Building and Other Construction Workers' Welfare Cess Act, 1996; Unorganised Workers' Social Security Act, 2008.

71 Factories Act, 1948; Plantations Labour Act, 1951; Mines Act, 1952; Working Journalists and Other Newspaper Employees (Conditions of Service) and Miscellaneous Provisions Act, 1955; Working Journalists (Fixation of Rates of Wages) Act, 1958; Motor Transport Workers Act, 1961; Beedi and Cigar Workers (Conditions of Employment) Act, 1966; Contract Labour (Regulation and Abolition) Act, 1970; Sales Promotion Employees (Conditions of Service) Act, 1976; Inter-State Migrant Workmen (Regulation of Employment and Conditions of Service) Act, 1979; Cine-Workers

tions Code 2020 deals with industrial dispute, industrial employment dispute, and trade union.[72]

While these codes introduced a progressive element and included gig workers, along with previously included unorganised workers, within the definition of labour, the codes are not without defects, and the issues of the old laws persist.[73] The positive changes, such as gender-neutral wage provisions,[74] national floor wage,[75] penalties for paying lesser wages[76] increasing penalties for non-compliance,[77] along with many others, are included in the code. However, the new law remarkably curbed the bargaining power of the workers and unions by restricting the right to strike (recognised by the Supreme Court of India).[78]

Additionally, the definition of Unorganised Worker under the code remained unchanged and vague, as the previous definition under the Unorganised Workers' Social Security Act 2008. It is defined as 'home-based worker, self-employed worker, or a wage-worker in the unorganised sector'.[79] Unorganised Sector is defined as: 'an enterprise owned by individuals or self-employed workers and engaged in the production or sale of goods or providing services of any kind whatsoever, and where the enterprise employs workers, the number of such workers is less than ten.'[80]

This binary of organised and unorganised acknowledges socio-economic realities that over 90 per cent of India's workforce operates outside formal employment structures. However, the responsibility under the code remains state-centric rather than employer-centric. Moreover the rights under the code are non-justifiable and contingent on workers' registration and the adequacy of schemes. Thus, the codes do not impose any obligations on the employer companies.

---

and Cinema Theatre Workers (Regulation of Employment) Act, 1981; Dock Workers Safety (Safety, Health, and Welfare) Act, 1986; Building and Other Construction Workers (Regulation of Employment and Conditions of Service) Act, 1966.

72 Industrial Disputes Act, 1947; Industrial Employment (Standing Orders) Act, 1946; Trade Unions Act, 1926

73 Rajrishi Ramaswamy/Anuradha Binnuri, 'An analysis of the impact of India's Labour Codes on its organized and unorganized sectors' (2023), https://doi.org/10.1080/23311886.2023.2238458 (last accessed: 06 September 2025).

74 Code on Wages, 2019, s 2(y).

75 Code of Wages, 2019, s 9.

76 Code of Wages, 2019, s 45 and 54.

77 Social Security Code, 2020, s 133 and 134.

78 Syndicate Bank and Ors v. K Umesh Nayak [1994] SCC (5) 572.

79 Social Security Code, 2020 s 2(26).

80 Social Security Code, 2020, s 2(85).

For the EU Directives to achieve meaningful impact in India, complementary domestic reforms are essential. For instance, the Code of Social Security 2020[81] aims to provide security to all the employees and workers (both organised and unorganised), but the duty is imposed on the state and not on employer companies. Security Exchange Board of India (SEBI's) Business Responsibility and Sustainability Reporting (BRSR) imposed a duty on the top 1000 listed Indian companies to report,[82] but CSRD and CSDDD in combination imposed corporate duty to report and also act. Like the EU, India too should mandate not just to report, but also to act.

Additionally, strengthening labour laws can simplify compliance and extend protections to informal workers, such as craftsmen, ensuring better wage security, access to social benefits, and safer working conditions. An amendment in the Company Law that mandates detailed reporting on environmental and social practices within supply chains can align Indian businesses with CSRD requirements. This should also include embedding due diligence processes that identify and mitigate risks, as emphasized by the CSDDD.

Moreover, integrating provisions for blockchain-enabled smart contracts into India's contract law (through amendment) could enhance digital traceability and contribute to improved working conditions for craftsmen.[83] This can be achieved by programming fair labour terms into a smart contract, which is a self-executing agreement on the blockchain. For instance, a smart contract could be programmed to automatically withhold payment if an audit or an IoT (Internet of Things) sensor detects a labour violation in a supplier's workshop. Such automated enforcement provides a stronger, reliable deterrent against abuse. Precedents exist: US law recognises smart contracts under the Uniform Electronic Transactions Act. States like Arizona[84] and Wyoming[85] have laws that explicitly state smart contracts are legally valid and enforceable, and brands like Patagonia are using blockchain to

81 Social Security Code, 2020.

82 SEBI (Listing Obligations and Disclosure Requirements) Regulations 2015, Regulation 34(2)(f).

83 Rosaire Brice Senou/Jules Dégila/Esther Chabi Adjobo/Abigaïl Priscilla M. Djossou, 'Blockchain for Child Labour Decrease in Cocoa Production in West and Central Africa' (2019), 52(13) IFAC, p. 2710, 2715, https://doi.org/10.1016/j.ifacol.2019.11.617 (last accessed: 30 June 2025).

84 The Arizona Electronic Transactions Act, 2017, amended by H.B. 2417.

85 SF0038 – Decentralized autonomous organizations (2021), https://www.wyoleg.gov/Legislation/2021/SF0038 (last accessed: 7 September 2025).

verify the ethical sourcing of raw materials. Thus, these laws provide legal teeth for such contracts to sustain.

Finally, providing technical and financial assistance to SMEs to meet the EU's stringent compliance standards, along with fostering collaboration between government, industry, and worker representatives, can support the development of comprehensive strategies that protect workers' rights while promoting sustainable practices. By implementing these reforms, India can strengthen protections for craftsmen, ensure alignment with international sustainability standards, and preserve its role in the global embroidery supply chain.

F. Conclusion

The EU sustainability directives are reshaping the global supply chain, but the real test lies in whether they reach the most vulnerable workers. Limiting obligations to Tier 1 suppliers and imposing costly compliance without support will exclude small workshops, the very spaces where traditional crafts survive.

The experience of France's DV Act and India's Utthan Pact illustrates the risk of relying solely on either binding law or voluntary agreement. A hybrid approach is needed: enforceable obligations backed by meaningful participation from suppliers and workers. Without this balance and by ignoring unorganised and home-based workers, sustainability governance risks entrenching a two-tier system-formal workers benefiting from compliance visibility while informal workers remain excluded and unprotected.

For India, while these directives aim to enhance transparency and due diligence, their effective implementation requires addressing local complexities, such as the fragmented nature of the industry, the limited resources of SMEs and unorganised sectors, and the lack of domestic laws that align with the directives. To ensure meaningful compliance and protect craftsmen, India must consider legal and policy reforms that align with these directives, including strengthening labour laws, expanding enforceable protections for informal workers, mandating company-level due diligence by amending company law, and harnessing digital tools like smart contracts by amending contract law. These changes can bridge the gap between global directives and local realities. Equally important is providing financial and technical support to SMEs, ensuring they are not priced out of compliance.

In response to the central question, the CSRD and CSDDD can make EU luxury supply chains more transparent and accountable, but their capacity to improve the working conditions of Indian craftsmen depends on two conditions: effective enforcement within the EU, and complementary reforms within India. Only through such joint efforts can sustainability law achieve both accountability and justice.

This study remains preliminary, based on secondary sources. Fieldwork with craftsmen, exporters, and regulators will be essential to test these findings and capture the lived realities of compliance. Future research should investigate the real-world impact of these directives, examining whether they serve as barriers, opportunities, or pathways towards a more equitable global fashion industry.

Rethinking sustainability through pluriculturalism: integrating Indigenous Knowledge into International Environmental Law

*Isadora Camplà Morales**

A. Introduction

'To universalise, it is important for everyone to be involved in the creative work of humanity', suggested Alioune Diop, expressing his call to 'de-Westernise in order to universalise'.[1] In this spirit, pluriculturalism can be understood as the necessity of allowing diverse legal cultures and traditions to shape normative processes, moving beyond a historically Western and monolithic approach to the production of legal norms. This paper examines how the integration of Indigenous knowledge into international environmental law has contributed to rethinking sustainability through a pluricultural lens, while highlighting the structural limits of this devel-

* PhD Candidate in International Law, University of Paris 1 Panthéon-Sorbonne (IREDIES). Teaching Assistant (*Chargée de travaux dirigés*) in Constitutional Law and Public International Law at the same institution. Master's degree in International, European, and Comparative Law, University of Toulouse 1 Capitole. Email: isadora.campla-morales@univ-paris1.fr.

1 Alioune Diop, 'Le sens de ce Congrès (Discours d'ouverture)' (Deuxième congrès des écrivains et artistes noirs, Rome, 26 March to 1st April 1959). This and all further quotes are translated by the author of this paper.

opment, particularly at the intersection with international economic law. Indigenous knowledge is a part of what is referred to as traditional[2] ecological[3] knowledge (TEK)[4], that can be defined as:

> A cumulative body of knowledge and beliefs, handed down through generations by cultural transmission, about the relationship of living beings (including humans) with one another and with their environment. Further, TEK is an attribute of societies with historical continuity in resource use practices; by and large, these are non-industrial (...) societies, many of them Indigenous or tribal.[5]

From an interdisciplinary perspective, there is consensus that such knowledge systems contribute meaningfully to sustainability goals, such as climate action.[6] In particular, the Intergovernmental Panel on Climate Change (IPCC) 'recognises the value of diverse forms of knowledge such as scientific, as well as Indigenous knowledge and local knowledge in understanding and evaluating climate adaptation processes and actions to reduce risks from human-induced climate change.'[7] These considerations influence policymaking and are increasingly incorporated into the development of a legal framework to address climate change. Not only has this shift had consequences for substantive law, but it has also impacted normative pro-

2 'Many scholars prefer to avoid using the term traditional. As well, some purists find the term unacceptable or inappropriate when referring to societies such as Native northern groups whose lifestyles have changed considerably over the years.': Fikret Berkes, 'Traditional Ecological Knowledge in Perspective' in Julian T. Inglis (ed.), Traditional Ecological Knowledge: Concepts and Cases, International Program on Traditional Ecological Knowledge (1993), p.3.

3 'The term ecological knowledge poses definitional problems of its own. If ecology is defined narrowly as a branch of biology in the domain of Western science, then strictly speaking there can be no TEK; most traditional peoples are not scientists. If ecological knowledge is defined broadly to refer to the knowledge, however acquired, of relationships of living beings with one another and with their environment, then the term TEK becomes tenable.': ibid.

4 This paper uses these terms interchangeably, while recognising that they are Western designations which, as noted in the preceding footnotes, raise certain conceptual difficulties.

5 Fikret Berkes, Sacred Ecology (4th edn 2018), p.8.

6 United Nations Sustainable Development Goals (SDGs), are a 17-goal framework aiming to end poverty, reduce inequality, promote environmental protection, and ensure shared prosperity by 2030.

7 IPCC, Climate Change 2022: Impacts, Adaptation and Vulnerability. Contribution of Working Group II to the Sixth Assessment Report of the Intergovernmental Panel on Climate Change' in H-O Pörtner et al (eds.) (2022), p. 7.

cesses themselves at an epistemic and cultural level; as Professor Jacinta Ruru notably argues, 'Indigenous peoples have forcefully challenged the mono-cultural nature of the western legal system, including international law.'[8]

This article is divided into four main parts. Following this introduction (*A*), the first section (*B*) explores the epistemological and ontological shifts in international environmental law, with particular attention to the role of Indigenous knowledge in the biodiversity regime, the legal expression of sustainability's intergenerational dimension, and the ontological paradigms that shape legal relationships with the environment. The second section (*C*) turns to the structural resistance to pluriculturalism at the crossroads of environmental and economic international law. It examines the limited recognition of Indigenous peoples within the economic apparatus, the challenges of transculturation under economic frameworks, the procedural obstacles to recognising Indigenous legal systems, and the functional dissonance between economic and environmental regimes. The final section (*D*) offers some concluding reflections.

B. Epistemological and ontological shifts in Environmental Law

I. Impact of Indigenous Knowledge on the biodiversity legal regime

Although Indigenous peoples are still marginalized in various ways, Indigenous knowledge is being increasingly acknowledged by the international community as a valuable source[9] for rethinking sustainability and environmental governance. Numerous international instruments emphasize the importance of traditional knowledge in this context, from foundational agreements such as the 1992 Convention on Biological Diversity (CBD)[10]

8 Jacinta Ruru, 'Indigenous Peoples', in Lavanya Rajamani/Jacqueline Peel (eds.), The Oxford Handbook of International Environmental Law (2nd edn, 2021), p. 735.

9 Traditional knowledge has its own inherent value, independently of the international community's recognition. Cf. 'J'espère ne pas être accusé de colonialisme mental en attribuant à l'Europe le rôle qui lui revient historiquement : celui du Moi, ce qui nous réserve à nous la position de l'Autre.' (in translation: I hope not to be accused of mental colonialism by attributing to Europe the role that historically belongs to it: that of the Self, which leaves us with the position of the Other): Sergio Paulo Rouanet, 'Regard de l'autre, regard sur l'autre' (2001) Diogène n°193, p. 5.

10 See Art. 8 (j).

and its 2010 Additional Nagoya Protocol,[11] to more recent developments such as the BBNJ Agreement of 2023.[12]

Within the biodiversity legal regime, a striking example of the epistemological and ontological impacts of Indigenous knowledge is the adoption of the Kunming-Montreal Global Biodiversity Framework at the 15th Conference of the Parties (COP 15) to the CBD in 2022. This instrument 'acknowledges the important roles and contributions of Indigenous peoples and local communities as custodians of biodiversity and as partners in its conservation, restoration and sustainable use.'[13] The Kunming-Montreal Framework is an important manifestation of pluriculturalism since it represents a shift from the dominant Western paradigm of the environment and reflects a growing engagement with diverse ontologies. For instance, in the subsection titled 'Different value systems', it mentions 'Mother Earth', which is a reference to the Pachamama of Andean cosmogony. Besides, it states the importance of 'living in harmony with nature and living well in balance and harmony with Mother Earth', referencing the Quechua concept of *sumak kawsay*, which could be translated as 'good living'. This concept envisions an alternative paradigm rooted in collective well-being, reciprocity, and respect for nature.

Admittedly, the participation of Indigenous peoples in the adoption of this instrument was significant. Nevertheless, although manifestations of pluriculturalism are emerging within international environmental law, they do not yet translate into equitable participation in global normative forums. The representation of Indigenous peoples remains limited, uneven, or largely symbolic, even when their knowledge systems actively contribute to reshaping dominant conceptions of sustainability.

---

11 The Nagoya Protocol on Access to Genetic Resources and the Fair and Equitable Sharing of Benefits Arising from their Utilization to the Convention on Biological Diversity. See Preamble, Art. 7 and Art. 12.

12 Agreement under the United Nations Convention on the Law of the Sea on the Conservation and Sustainable Use of Marine Biological Diversity of Areas beyond National Jurisdiction. See Art. 7 (j), Art. 13, Art. 19.3, etc.

13 CBD/COP/DEC/15/4, p. 5.

II. Legal expressions of sustainability's intergenerational dimension

Indigenous legal systems that draw from Indigenous knowledge tend to be considered inherently sustainable,[14] notwithstanding the fact that 'sustainability' itself is a Western concept subject to some critique.[15] The earliest and most widely cited definition emerged with the Brundtland Report 'Our Common Future' of 1987, which defined sustainable development as 'the ability to make development sustainable to ensure that it meets the needs of the present without compromising the ability of future generations to meet their own needs.'[16]

The intergenerational approach to environmental obligations was already embedded in Indigenous legal traditions long before it was articulated by Western legal systems. For instance, the concept of *Ixofil Mongen* of the Mapuche people promotes 'social and intergenerational solidarity'.[17] Similarly, in the case of the Kanaka Ōiwi, the 'knowledge is passed down by *na kapuna* (elders) to *na makua* (the present generation) for the benefit of *na opio* (future generations).'[18]

Since the very notion of sustainability is inseparable from its intergenerational dimension, several international instruments evoke the principle of intergenerational equity, such as the 1992 Rio Declaration,[19] as well as the 2018 Escazú Agreement.[20] Following that logic, the United Nations General

---

14 However, this is not the case in all Indigenous resource management systems. For a critical point of view, see: Peter Ørebech et al., The Role of Customary Law in Sustainable Development (2005), p. 365 et seq.

15 For an example of critique, see: Subhabrata Bobby Banerjee, 'Who Sustains Whose Development? Sustainable Development and the Reinvention of Nature' (2003) 24(1) Organization Studies 143 <https://doi.org/10.1177/0170840603024001341> (last accessed: 22 May 2025).

16 Gro Harlem Brundtland, Our Common Future: Report of the World Commission on Environment and Development (1987) UN Doc A/42/427, ch. I(3), para. 27.

17 Salvador Millaleo Hernández, 'Guarda de la Naturaleza: Conocimientos Ecológicos Tradicionales de los Pueblos Indígenas y Estrategias de Protección' (June 2020) (13) Cadernos de Dereito Actual, p. 210.

18 Maxine Burkett, 'Indigenous Environmental Knowledge and Climate Change Adaptation' in Randall Abate/Elizabeth Ann Kronk Warner (eds.), Climate Change and Indigenous Peoples: The Search for Legal Remedies (2013), p. 115.

19 Rio Declaration on Environment and Development, UN Doc A/CONF.151/26, Principle 3.

20 Regional Agreement on Access to Information, Public Participation and Justice in Environmental Matters in Latin America and the Caribbean (Escazú Agreement) UN Doc LC/PUB.2018/8, Art. 3.

Assembly adopted a Declaration on Future Generations in September 2024, as an annex to the Pact for the Future.[21] The Pact aims to 'protect the needs and interests of present and future generations' and seeks to 'foster synergies between science and technology and traditional, local, Afrodescendant, and Indigenous knowledge, systems, practices, and capacities'[22] in pursuit of that goal. Although this is a soft law instrument, it signals an emerging normative tendency.

Certain jurisdictions have clarified the contours of this trend. Notably, the Inter-American Court of Human Rights – hereinafter, 'the I/A Court' – has shown a tendency to adopt an intergenerational perspective, at least since the 2001 case *Mayagna (Sumo) Awas Tingni Community v. Nicaragua*, where the Court stated that 'for indigenous communities, relations to the land are not merely a matter of possession and production but a material and spiritual element that they must fully enjoy, even to preserve their cultural legacy and transmit it to future generations.'[23] The issue of intergenerational equity became well established in case law with regard to Indigenous or tribal peoples' rights, particularly about land rights, as the ancestral lands represent a connection with future generations.[24]

In the case of *the inhabitants of La Oroya v. Peru*, the I/A Court addressed severe environmental contamination caused by the La Oroya metallurgical complex, including pollution of air, soil, and water. The Court found that this contamination resulted in serious harm to human health, notably dangerously high levels of lead in the blood of local children and adversely affected the surrounding environment. In this case, the Court

---

21 UN General Assembly, A/RES/79/1, 22 September 2024, Action 32.

22 Ibid., para. 56 (a).

23 I/A Court H.R., *Case of the Mayagna (Sumo) Awas Tingni Community* v. *Nicaragua*. Merits, reparations and costs. Judgment of 31 August 2011. Series C nº79, para. 149.

24 See I/A Court H.R., *Case of the Moiwana Community v. Suriname*. Preliminary objections, merits, reparations and costs. Judgment of 15 June 2005. Series C No. 124, para. 131, *Case of the Indigenous Community Yakye Axa v. Paraguay*. Merits, reparations and costs. Judgment of 17 June 2005. Series C No. 125, para. 121, *Case of the Indigenous Community Sawhoyamaxa v. Paraguay*. Merits, reparations and costs. Judgment of 29 March 2006. Series C No. 146, para. 118, *Case of the Saramaka People v. Suriname*. Preliminary objections, merits, reparations and costs. Judgment of 28 November 2007. Series C No. 172, para. 90, *Case of the Garífuna Community of Triunfo de la Cruz and its Members v. Honduras*. Merits, reparations and costs. Judgment of 8 October 2015. Series C No. 305, para. 101.

extrapolated explicitly the 'principle of intergenerational equity'[25] to all components of society, going beyond an Indigenous context, as a general standard linked to the precautionary principle.

In a similar fashion, the European Court of Human Rights in the *Verein Klimaseniorinnen Schweiz* v. Switzerland case of 2024 underlined the issue of 'intergenerational burden-sharing, both in regard to different generations of those currently living and in regard to future generations.'[26] In this case, the Court upheld the application brought by the association *KlimaSeniorinnen Schweiz* (Senior Women for Climate Protection), marking the first time in climate litigation that a State was found to have violated human rights on the basis of inaction. The Court's legal reasoning is particularly noteworthy, as it justified the principle of burden-sharing, despite the fact that 'the legal obligations arising for States under the Convention extend to those individuals currently alive.'[27] It added, in an innovative manner, that 'future generations are likely to bear an increasingly severe burden of the consequences of present failures and omissions to combat climate change' having 'no possibility of participating in the relevant current decision-making processes.'[28] The Court further relied on the fact that, under the United Nations Framework Convention on Climate Change (UNFCCC), States Parties have undertaken the obligation to protect the climate system for the benefit of present and future generations of humankind.[29]

This analysis could suggest a reversal of the traditional direction of legal transplants, from the Global North to the Global South,[30] as some legal transplants now originate in the Global South and are being incorporated into hegemonic systems or, more largely, legal systems of the Global North. As noted, 'environmentalists in the Western world have been much impressed with the idea of intergenerational obligations; it is an idea which

25 I/A Court H.R., *Case of La Oroya Population v. Peru.* Preliminary Objections, Merits, Reparations and Costs. Judgment of November 27, 2023. Series C No. 511, para. 128.

26 ECtHR, *Case of Verein Klimaseniorinnen Schweiz and others* v. Switzerland. Grand chamber judgment of 9 April 2024, 53600/20, para. 419.

27 Ibid., para. 420.

28 Ibid.

29 Ibid.

30 '*Los trasplantes jurídicos usualmente tienen la dirección Norte-Sur* (...)' (in translation: Legal transplants usually follow a North–South direction): Daniel Bonilla Maldonado, Los bárbaros jurídicos: identidad, derecho comparado moderno y el Sur global (2020), p. 18.

speaks to all traditions',[31] a concept that had long existed within many Indigenous legal traditions before being apprehended and reformulated within dominant Western legal systems. This dynamic demonstrates that Indigenous knowledge carries significant implications for law, particularly through the ontological influence it exerts on how legal systems conceptualize their relationship with the environment.

III. Ontological paradigms shaping legal relationships with the environment

Another concept originating in Indigenous legal systems and increasingly extrapolated to broader contexts is the recognition of legal personhood for nature, primarily within domestic legal orders. This can take the form of substantive personification, as exemplified by article 71 of the 2008 Ecuadorian Constitution, which provides: 'Nature, or Pacha Mama, where life is reproduced and occurs, has the right to integral respect for its existence and for the maintenance and regeneration of its life cycles, structure, functions, and evolutionary processes.' Alternatively, it may take the form of procedural personification, as in Colombia, where the Constitutional Court granted legal personality to the Atrato River in 2016.[32]

Both approaches illustrate a profound ontological shift; nature is no longer viewed solely as an object of regulation but as a subject of rights. Significantly, this paradigm is now extending beyond Indigenous contexts, as demonstrated by the recognition of legal personhood for the *Mar Menor* lagoon in Spain.[33] Even in the absence of an international instrument consecrating the personhood of nature, there is evidence of a certain shift away from the hegemonic 'subject–object' dichotomy embedded in the *summa divisio* logic inherited from Roman law.

Nevertheless, an important precedent is the *World Charter for Nature* adopted by the United Nations General Assembly in 1982,[34] which states that 'every form of life is unique, warranting respect regardless of its worth

31 H. Patrick Glenn, Legal Traditions of the World. Sustainable Diversity in Law (2014), p. 80.

32 Constitutional Court of Colombia, Judgment T-622 of 2016.

33 Ley 19/2022, del 30 de septiembre, para el reconocimiento de personalidad jurídica a la laguna del Mar Menor y su Cuenca.

34 A/RES/37/1.

to man'. At the 2010 *World People's Conference on Climate Change and the Rights of Mother Earth* that took place in Cochabamba, Bolivia, a project of a *Universal Declaration of Rights of Mother Earth* was proposed – modelled after the Universal Declaration of Human Rights – although it was ultimately not adopted by the General Assembly. This initiative followed a resolution adopted in 2009 that designates 22 April as International Mother Earth Day.[35]

Extending this logic, the I/A Court first affirmed in its advisory opinion no. 23/17 that 'as an autonomous right, the right to a healthy environment, unlike other rights, protects the components of the environment, (...) even in the absence of the certainty or evidence of a risk to individuals.'[36] Going even beyond, the Court stated in its recent advisory opinion no. 35/25 that 'moving towards a paradigm that recognises ecosystems' own rights is essential for the protection of their integrity',[37] with quite a strong stance suggesting that 'this recognition makes it possible to overcome inherited legal conceptions, which conceived of Nature exclusively as an object of property or an exploitable resource'.[38] In this advisory opinion, the Court particularly insists on the importance of 'local, traditional, and Indigenous knowledge'.[39]

Hence, this tendency reflects both an ontological and an epistemological shift in the legal relationship with the environment, grounded in a pluricultural approach that finds its foundation in Indigenous knowledge, porous even to international law. However, even if provisions referencing traditional knowledge have the merit of triggering a certain epistemological 'openness' when it comes to environmental policies, these are rarely prescriptive. Rather, they tend to serve interpretative or symbolic purposes. At worst, States instrumentalize Indigenous peoples as a form of symbolic capital[40] instead of fostering genuine participation in international forums

---

35 A/RES/63/278.

36 I/A Court H.R., Advisory Opinion OC-23/17 (*Environment and Human Rights*), 15 November 2017 Series A, para. 62.

37 I/A Court H.R., Advisory Opinion AO-32/25 (*Climate Emergency and Human Rights*) Series A No 32, 29 May 2025, para. 279.

38 Ibid., para. 280.

39 Ibid., para. 479 et seq.

40 Jean Foyer/David Dumoulin, 'Objectifying Traditional Knowledge, Re-enchanting the Struggle Against Climate Change' in Stefan C. Aykut, Jean Foyer and Edouard Morena (eds), Globalising the Climate: COP21 and the Climatisation of Global Debates (2017), p. 154.

through a truly pluricultural dynamic, thereby reproducing colonial logics, particularly when economic considerations enter the equation.

This tension points to the limits of the apparent paradigm shift; while discourses of pluralism and Indigenous knowledge gain visibility, structural constraints embedded in international law continue to restrict their transformative potential. It is precisely at the intersection of environmental and economic international law that such resistance becomes most evident.

C. Structural resistance to pluriculturalism at the crossroads of Environmental and Economic International Law

I. Limited recognition of Indigenous Peoples in the economic apparatus

The persistence of colonial logics becomes especially pronounced in the management of natural resources, notably within extractive industries. While international environmental law has made efforts toward integrating pluricultural perspectives, international economic law continues to reflect structural patterns that marginalize Indigenous worldviews. As noted by Hindou Oumarou Ibrahim, 'Indigenous Peoples are still largely ignored by international financial institutions',[41] despite the gradual recognition of Indigenous peoples' structural inequalities and marginalization in specific international economic instruments.

Such is the case of the European Investment Bank (EIB)'s *Environmental and Social Standards* of 2022, whose Standard No. 7 sets objectives specific to projects affecting Indigenous peoples, aiming to 'foster full respect for their rights, identity, culture, and livelihoods' and, *inter alia*, to ensure that 'promoters carry out good faith negotiation with project-affected Indigenous Peoples and obtain their Free, Prior and Informed Consent (FPIC) when required'.[42] However, the EIB has also faced criticism. Before the adoption of this framework, the Special Rapporteur on the rights of Indigenous Peoples reported allegations 'concerning dams and associated infrastructures that were planned or implemented without the consent of

41 Hindou Oumarou Ibrahim, 'Opening Statement at the 23rd Session of the United Nations Permanent Forum on Indigenous Issues' (New York, 15 April 2024), https://cendoc.docip.org/collect/cendocdo/index/assoc/HASH01c2/2ed11719.dir/2_UNPFII%20Chair_Hindou%20Oumarou%20Ibrahim_Opening.pdf (last accessed: 22 July 2025).

42 EIB, Environmental and Social Standards, 2 February 2022, Standard 7, para. 8.

Indigenous Peoples, causing their forced displacement',[43] particularly in relation to a hydropower project in Nepal funded by the EIB.

With respect to trade, a significant example is the partnership agreement between the European Union (EU) and the Southern Common Market (Mercosur) reached in 2024 – hereinafter, 'EU-Mercosur agreement'– that remains yet to be implemented and enter into force. This project, in its current state, contains provisions encouraging the inclusion of Indigenous and forest-based local communities in sustainable supply chains for timber and non-timber forest products, subject to their 'prior informed consent'.[44]

Such provisions are typically found in soft law instruments, but even if incorporated into hard law instruments – as in the latter case, should the EU-Mercosur agreement enter into force – provisions concerning Indigenous peoples are rarely prescriptive. Instead, they tend to serve an interpretative function rather than creating enforceable obligations.

II. Challenges of transculturation under economic frameworks

The corpus of more 'robust' substantive law governing international trade, such as the World Trade Organization (WTO) agreements, is fundamentally built around Western paradigms of market access, private property, and standardization. A similar orientation prevails in international investment law, where principles such as non-discrimination dominate the field. As Sergio Puig observes, 'the focus on nondiscrimination among economic actors results in de facto discrimination against Indigenous peoples and a consequent rise in inequality'.[45]

Supply chains further reinforce this model by relying on uniform standards, such as International Organization for Standardization (ISO) certifications,[46] which rarely accommodate Indigenous land management systems or circular practices – and even less adopt a pluricultural dynamic. By contrast, resource management in Indigenous ancestral lands is grounded in

43 UN Human Rights Council, Report of the Special Rapporteur on the rights of Indigenous Peoples, José Francisco Calí Tzay, 'Green financing – a just transition to protect the rights of Indigenous Peoples', UN Doc A/HRC/54/31, 21 July 2023, para. 43.

44 EU-Mercosur Trade Agreement, chap. on Trade and Sustainable Development, art. 8 'Trade and Sustainable Management of Forests', para. 2(b).

45 Sergio Puig, At the Margins of Globalization: Indigenous Peoples and International Economic Law (2021), p. 5.

46 See, for example, ISO 14001 about Environmental management systems.

communal and restricted land tenure, primarily collective rights, and local particularities inherent to customary legal systems. This divergence highlights the structural limits of pluriculturalism when international economic governance relies on orientations often incompatible with Indigenous legal traditions.

This logic is perpetuated in dominant extractive models, where resources are usually commodified without Indigenous consent, even when some instruments require free, prior, and informed consent (FPIC) or meaningful consultation[47] to be obtained when adopting measures that affect communities. Indeed, there is extensive literature[48] documenting 'inadequate, half-hearted consultation'[49] as the one that resulted in forcible occupation of *U'wa*'s ancestral lands by a petroleum company in Colombia.[50]

III. Procedural obstacles to the recognition of Indigenous legal systems

From a procedural standpoint, investor–state dispute settlement (ISDS) mechanisms tend to systematically overlook customary land tenure systems, primarily because the investment law framework – particularly bilateral investment treaties (BITs) – provides no substantive basis for recognising or incorporating customary law. Although arbitral outcomes may directly affect Indigenous rights and territories, existing procedural regimes rarely afford these communities standing or effective avenues for participation. For instance, in *Bernhard von Pezold and Others v. Republic of Zimbabwe*,[51] the International Centre for Settlement of Investment Disputes (ICSID) tribunal rejected a request by the European Center for Constitutional and Human Rights (ECCHR) and four Indigenous communities to

47 It is important to distinguish FPIC, required, for example, under Art. 16 of the ILO Indigenous and Tribal Peoples Convention 1989 (no. 169), from consultation, which is considerably less constraining from a legal perspective.

48 See, for example, Thierry Rodon et al., 'Inuit Engagement in Resource Development Approval Process:
The Cases of Voisey's Bay and Mary River' in Jennifer Winter (ed.), Protest and Partnership: Case Studies of Indigenous Peoples, Consultation and Engagement, and Resource Development in Canada (2024), p. 83 et seqq.

49 Joshua Kleinfeld, 'The Double Life of International Law: Indigenous Peoples and Extractive Industries' (2016) 129 Harvard Law Review, p. 1755, 1768.

50 Ibid, p. 1767 et seq.

51 ICSID, *Bernhard von Pezold and Others v. Republic of Zimbabwe*, Case No. ARB/10/15 (2010).

participate as *amici curiae*, holding that their submissions did not assist in resolving the dispute under the applicable treaties.

Even when Indigenous peoples have direct *locus standi*, such as in the ongoing *Casino* case[52] brought under France's *Loi sur le devoir de vigilance*,[53] structural obstacles persist. In this litigation, a coalition of Brazilian and Colombian Indigenous communities and NGOs brought a claim in March 2021; the case is now pending before the Paris Judicial Court. The claim alleges that Casino Group, through its subsidiaries in Brazil and Colombia, marketed beef linked to deforestation in the Amazon and to violations of Indigenous land rights. Plaintiffs argue that Casino failed to implement an adequate vigilance plan, as required by the aforementioned law, thereby contributing to environmental destruction and harm to ancestral lands, including those of the *Uru-Eu-Wau-Wau* community.

Despite the granting of formal standing to these communities, they must navigate a legal framework that does not recognize customary land tenure, Indigenous epistemologies, or environmental stewardship. Concerns were raised about 'subtle forms of colonialism [that] continue to be practised against the Indigenous population', underscoring that such proceedings raise fundamental questions about 'epistemological underpinnings, which appear to be very clearly Eurocentric, and remain waiting to be pluralised.'[54] This highlights a broader structural resistance, as international litigation frameworks may allow formal access but only within normative confines still profoundly shaped by Western legal traditions.

IV. Functional dissonance between International Economic and Environmental Law

At the intersection of international economic law and international environmental law lies a conceptual void, where two conflicting interests confront each other: the protection of the environment and the protection of investment. This tension becomes even more complex when Indigenous peoples' human rights are added to the equation.

52 For an overview of the case, see Pierre-Louis Choquet, 'Produire et faire circuler les preuves de la déforestation en Amazonie brésilienne' (2024) 117(2) Droit et Société, p. 266, https://droit.cairn.info/revue-droit-et-societe-2024-2-page-233?lang=fr accessed (last accessed: 2 July 2025).

53 Loi n°2017–399 relative au devoir de vigilance des sociétés mères et entreprises donneuses d'ordre.

54 Ibid., p. 267.

The prevailing dichotomy between these legal regimes, rooted in a Western conception of law that compartmentalizes different branches, can be perceived as artificial. Under the principle of the interdependence and indivisibility of human rights – starting from the premise that certain environmental law provisions can be understood as human rights norms – it becomes increasingly problematic to separate or fragment human rights and environmental protection frameworks. This is especially true given that case law increasingly affirms the interlinkage between environmental protection and Indigenous peoples' rights.[55] For instance, the *European Communities – Measures Prohibiting the Importation and Marketing of Seal Products* dispute under the WTO system[56] demonstrates that, even when Indigenous rights – in this case, traditional hunting practices of Inuit communities – and environmental protection intersect, trade law bodies treat them as distinct justifications and do not address their mutually reinforcing character and interconnection.

D. Conclusion

Indigenous knowledge has thus laid the foundation for a more pluricultural legal approach to environmental governance, particularly by challenging monolithic conceptions of sustainability and encouraging frameworks that reflect diverse human experiences. This shift is contributing to the development of an international legal regime that is increasingly responsive to the normative demands posed by climate change. Although modest, signs of an emerging paradigm shift – both ontological and epistemological – can be observed within international environmental law, as shown by the examples discussed throughout this paper. Nevertheless, it is important to recognize the limits of this progress. Provisions that reference or draw upon Indigenous knowledge remain largely non-prescriptive. For the time being, they represent a symbolic or interpretive shift, rather than a transformation of enforceable obligations.

---

55 See, for example, I/A Court H.R., *Case of the Indigenous Communities of the Lhaka Honhat Association (Our Land) v. Argentina*. Merits, Reparations and Costs. Judgment of February 6, 2020. Series C No. 400, para. 175.

56 Appellate Body Report, *European Communities – Measures Prohibiting the Importation and Marketing of Seal Products* (WTO Dispute DS401), 22 May 2014.

What remains largely unaddressed is the interface between international environmental law and international economic frameworks. Without resorting to a simplistic dichotomy, it is clear that economic law has remained largely resistant to this pluricultural turn. As legal sociologist Boaventura de Sousa Santos argues, these frameworks continue to operate within an 'epistemology of blindness',[57] failing to recognize alternative ways of knowing and relating to the environment – precisely because such epistemologies often conflict with the interests of economic actors. By contrast, international environmental law is gradually moving towards an 'epistemology of seeing',[58] perhaps signalling the early foundations of a pluricultural normative order.

57 This notion illustrates how dominant Western scientific and legal paradigms marginalize or erase alternative ways of knowing, while presenting themselves as universally objective and comprehensive. See: Boaventura de Sousa Santos, *Epistemologies of the South: Justice against Epistemicide* (2016), p. 136 et seqq.

58 By contrast, this concept suggests making visible the forms of knowledge, experience, and reality that have been rendered invisible by dominant epistemologies.

Towards a sustainable consumer law: A preliminary assessment of the French example for Chile

María Elisa Morales[*], *Sara Moreno*[**]

A. Why traditional consumer law falls short in the face of the climate crisis: A comparative perspective to inspire a Chilean proposal

In Chile, the widely circulated image of the 'Atacama Desert clothing cemetery' depicts the massive accumulation of unsold or discarded garments in the country's north, where tonnes of fast fashion and second-hand clothing are dumped annually.[1] It starkly illustrates the consequences of consumer law's failure to integrate sustainability considerations.

* Assistant Professor of Private Law at the Faculty of Law and Social Sciences of Universidad Austral de Chile.
We acknowledge Diego Nichi for his assistance throughout all formal aspects of this work.
** Member of the Faculty of Social and Economic Sciences of Universidad Católica del Maule, Chile.

1 Nicole Iporre, 'El desierto del norte chileno que se convirtió en el basurero de la ropa usada' [The desert in northern Chile that became a dumping ground for used clothing], La Tercera (Santiago, 13 June 2023), https://www.latercera.com/tendencias

This failure reflects the traditional conception of consumer law as a set of rules addressing the structural imbalance between consumers and suppliers. The consumer is seen as the weaker party, justifying state intervention to protect their freedom of choice and reinforce private autonomy. Chilean consumer law largely adheres to this classical view. Although some provisions mention environmental protection, they are limited in scope and rarely enforced – highlighting the need to modernise the legal framework.

This classical conception does not recognise environmental protection or sustainability as autonomous legal interests. By prioritising individual choice and transactional fairness over environmental considerations, this framework implicitly legitimises high-consumption lifestyles, thereby reinforcing unsustainable patterns of production and consumption. Consumer law emerged alongside the rise of consumer society, where consumption beyond basic needs became central to social and economic life. As Howells, Ramsay and Wilhelmsson note,[2] consumer law reflects the structure of consumer society. Consequently, its ecological implications have remained outside the field's normative reach. The focus has been on protecting consumers' so-called basic rights,[3] based on the liberal ideal of rational choice. Yet the climate crisis has shown, this model is insufficient: consumption accounts for nearly two-thirds of global greenhouse gas emissions.[4]

/noticia/el-desierto-del-norte-chileno-que-se-convirtio-en-el-basurero-de-la-ropa-usada/NLUEXOSIAFHCHPO54KXKIKYPHM/); La Tercera, 'El desafío de transformar el desierto de ropa en el norte de Chile' [The challenge of transforming the clothing desert in northern Chile], La Tercera (Santiago, 12 February 2025) https://www.latercera.com/laboratoriodecontenidos/noticia/el-desafio-de-transformar-el-desierto-de-ropa-en-el-norte-de-chile/NGHA3CAFMJC3HLGVEVXGRRB5SY/ (both last accessed 30 August 2025).

2 Geraint Howells/Iain Ramsay/Thomas Wilhelmsson, 'Consumer Law in its International Dimension', in Howells/Ramsay/Wilhelmsson (eds.), Handbook of Research in International Consumer Law, 2nd ed. (2018), p. 1, 4.

3 The basic consumer rights, as first articulated by President John F. Kennedy in his 1962 speech to the U.S. Congress, are: the right to safety, the right to be informed, the right to choose, and the right to be heard.

4 Diana Ivanova et al., 'Quantifying the potential for climate change mitigation of consumption options' (2020), 15, Environ. Res. Lett., p. 1, 1–2. Adding some statistics, the Summary for Policymakers of the *Global Resources Outlook 2019* states that 'the extraction and processing of natural resources accounts for more than 90 per cent of global biodiversity loss and water stress impacts'. Global Resources Outlook 2019: Natural Resources for the Future We Want (International Resource Panel, United Nations Environment Programme, Nairobi, March 2019)(Summary for Policymakers), https://wedocs.unep.org/bitstream/handle/20.500.11822/30797/EGR2019.pdf (Last accessed: 30 August 2025). More recently, it has been noted that consumption-based

Building on this diagnosis, current consumer law aims to empower the weaker contractual party by strengthening their autonomy and market access.[5] Terryn argues that this results in 'unsustainable consumer law':[6] a system centred on consumers as passive holders of economic rights positioned at the end of the supply chain.[7]

A shift towards a more systemic and holistic approach is therefore urgent. One that addresses the social, economic and environmental consequences of consumption. A sustainable consumer law may still protect autonomy, but only if it integrates intergenerational considerations. In this view, autonomy means the right to choose only insofar as those choices do not impair others' well-being or hinder regenerative resource use.[8] This requires not only the transformation but also the redefinition of consumer rights. As Mak and Terryn argue, sustainability policies must be translated into concrete legal norms.[9] Micklitz goes further, calling to wipe the slate clean and design a 'new consumer law'.[10]

In jurisdictions like Chile, where sustainable consumer law remains incipient, the focus is mainly on promoting greener alternatives without regulatory incentives to reduce consumption or encourage less harmful behaviour. The social dimension, such as access to essential goods and the labour conditions of production, also remains largely neglected.

CO_2 emissions are calculated by subtracting the emissions embedded in exports from a country's production-based emissions and adding those associated with imports. This measure attributes responsibility for emissions to domestic consumption rather than territorial production, offering insight into whether a country is a net importer or exporter of CO_2 emissions. It includes emissions from fossil fuel combustion and industrial processes, but excludes land-use change, deforestation, and international aviation and shipping. See Hannah Ritchie and Max Roser, 'Consumption-based CO_2 emissions' Our World in Data (2024) https://ourworldindata.org/grapher/consumption-co2-emissions (last accessed: 30 August 2025).

5 Evelyne Terryn, 'Can Consumer Law Become Sustainable?', in Hans Micklitz/ Christian Twigg-Flesner (eds.), The Transformation of Consumer Law and Policy in Europe (2023), p. 159, 162.

6 Terryn (2023), p. 186.

7 *'Homo oeconomicus passivus'.* Norbert Reich/ Hans Micklitz, 'Economic Law, Consumer Interests and EU Integration', in Norbert Reich et al., European Consumer Law, 2nd ed. (2014), p. 1, 6.

8 Terryn (2023), p. 186.

9 Vanessa Mak/Evelyne Terryn, 'Circular Economy and Consumer Protection: The Consumer as a Citizen and the Limits of Empowerment Through Consumer Law' (2020), Vol. 43, JCP, p. 227, 228.

10 Hans Micklitz, 'Squaring the Circle? Reconciling Consumer Law and the Circular Economy' (2019), JECML, p. 229, 229.

These concerns have begun to shape European consumer law, where sustainability is becoming a transformative domain.[11] The EU has developed a robust sustainable consumption agenda, with France at the forefront.[12] In contrast, such developments are only beginning in most developing countries, like Chile. Given the urgency of the climate crisis, European experience offers valuable lessons, particularly in approaches that have proven to be effective or influential. Chile has previously drawn selectively on European legislation, such as French provisions, not only for their prestige or, as here, for their pioneering character, but also because these jurisdictions share the same civil law tradition.

B. Methodological approach and article structure

This article presents a preliminary comparative study which is intended to be expanded and deepened in future research. It offers a diagnostic step toward a more substantive analysis that may support proposals for the development of Chilean consumer law. Specifically, this study undertakes a *micro-comparison*[13] aimed at fostering a 'better understanding and improvement of national law'.[14] The objective is to extract lessons that may

11 Mateusz Grochowski, 'European Consumer Law after the New Deal: A Tryptich' (2021), Vol. 39, YB of Eur. Law, p. 387, 387.

12 Within the framework of EU law, Member States have progressively incorporated Union guidelines on sustainable consumption. France, however, has emerged as the leading jurisdiction, going beyond EU proposals in this field. Evelyne Terryn, EU Consumer Law and Human Rights (2023), pp. 173–174. Since 2014, the *Loi n° 2014-344 relative à la consommation* ('Loi Hamon') has amended the *Code de la Consommation* to include, inter alia, requirements on the availability of spare parts for repairs. Despite its numerous amendments, the law did not introduce explicit prohibitions on planned obsolescence; Article 8 merely mandated the government to submit a report on the issue, delivered in April 2017: République Française, *Rapport au Parlement sur l'obsolescence programmée* (April 2017), https://www.vie-publique.fr/sites/default/files/rapport/pdf/174000268.pdf (last accessed: 30 August 2025); *Loi n° 2014-344 du 17 mars 2014 relative à la consommation* (2014) JORF n° 0065, 18 March 2014, p 5400 https://www.legifrance.gouv.fr/jorf/id/JORFTEXT000028738036 (last accessed: 30 August 2025).

13 Konrad Zweigert/Hein Kötz, An Introduction to Comparative Law, 3rd ed. (1998), p. 184.

14 René David/Camille Jauffret-Spinosi, Los grandes sistemas jurídicos contemporáneos [The major contemporary legal systems], trad. Alfredo Sánchez/Jorge Sánchez (2010), p. 29.

serve either as inputs for the construction of new regulatory proposals or as the basis for a reinterpretation.

To this end, this article adopts the functional method.[15]

It is widely acknowledged that regardless of the motivation, the guiding principle of functionalism remains constant: only institutions that serve the same function are usefully comparable. In this view, *function* acts as the *tertium comparationis* – the common point of reference for structurally and conceptually distinct legal institutions.[16] This assumption of comparability is rooted in a 'presumption of similarity' or 'universalism', which posits that all legal systems face fundamentally similar problems and arrive at functionally equivalent solutions through diverse legal means.[17] Hence, a functional comparative study must begin with a question framed in non-system-specific, functional terms.[18]

This functional method aligns with the traditional structure of comparative legal research, as outlined by Husa[19] in six steps: (i) formulation of a functional research question, (ii) construction of the comparative framework by identifying the jurisdictions and areas to be compared, (iii) description of the legal institutions under comparison, (iv) enumeration of similarities and differences, (v) analysis and explanation of those findings, and (vi) evaluation of the results of the comparison. This structure guides the analysis that follows.

C. Sustainable consumer law: A micro-comparison between France and Chile

I. Two preliminary clarifications on the concept of sustainable consumer law

Before proceeding with the micro-comparative analysis, two preliminary clarifications are required.

---

15 Ralf Michaels, 'The functional method of comparative law', in Mathias Reimann/ Reinhard Zimmermann (eds.), The Oxford Handbook of Comparative Law (2006), p. 339, 342.

16 Zweigert/Kötz (1998), p. 34.

17 Ibid p. 32.

18 Ibid p. 36.

19 Jaakko Husa, A new introduction to comparative law (2015), p. 140.

First, it must be stated that consumer law does not fit neatly within the traditional boundaries of private law. Rather, it represents a clear manifestation of the crisis of the *summa divisio*. Indeed, it is now possible to argue that consumer law constitutes an autonomous legal discipline, with its own core, foundations, principles, and essential characteristics. Among these, its interdisciplinary nature stands out, as it brings together elements of both private and public law within a single normative framework.[20] A telling example is provided by Chile's Law No. 19.496 on the Protection of Consumer Rights, which operates as the general statute of consumer protection. This Act encompasses a wide variety of provisions: contractual compliance (Article 12, which obliges suppliers to respect the terms and conditions under which goods or services were offered), the control of unfair terms (Articles 16 et seq), regulation of the state agency in charge of enforcement (Articles 57 et seq), and procedural rules for both judicial and administrative redress. Clearly, this body of law demonstrates how consumer protection gathers, within a single normative framework, provisions that belong to both private and public law.

Consumer law thus operates in a domain where autonomy is both regulated and protected and where public law intersects with broader aims of justice. This interaction between public and private norms supports what may be referred to as a binary perspective – one that recognises the 'dual nature' of consumer law.[21] In our view, this dual nature becomes even more evident in what has come to be referred to as sustainable consumer law, as it entails the integration of a supra-individual, and even public interest, namely: the protection of the environment.

Second, in relation to the concept of *sustainable consumer law*, this study closely follows the ideas proposed by Terryn. According to her, sustainable consumer law requires a more systemic and holistic legal approach, one that takes into account not only the economic repercussions of consumption, but also its social and environmental dimensions.[22] While such an

20 María Elisa Morales, 'El lugar del Derecho del Consumo en la summa divisio de las disciplinas jurídicas' [The place of consumer law in the summa divisio of legal disciplines], in Pamela Mendoza/María Elisa Morales (dirs.), Estudios de Derecho Privado. II Jornadas Nacionales de Profesoras de Derecho Privado [Private Law Studies. II National Conference of Women Professors of Private Law] (2020), p. 549, 557–558.

21 Ewoud Hondius, 'The Innovative Nature of Consumer Law' (2012), Vol. 35, JCP, p. 165, 168–170.

22 Terryn (2023), p. 186.

approach may continue to safeguard rights associated with consumer self-determination, it must do so within an intergenerational and intragenerational perspective. As Terryn notes, the right to make consumption choices should be preserved only insofar as those choices do not interfere with others' ability to lead a good life, nor with the sustainable and regenerative management of natural resources.[23]

When considered as a whole, these clarifications provide the conceptual foundation for the micro-comparative analysis. The present study sets out to demonstrate that recognising consumer law as an autonomous and hybrid discipline underscores its capacity to integrate environmental protection as a legally protected interest, traditionally addressed within public law. A sustainable consumer law, therefore, must involve a reconfiguration of classical categories, ensuring that consumer rights are exercised in ways that neither compromise the ability of others to live a good life nor undermine ecological integrity. These considerations will guide the subsequent comparison, the aim of which is to evaluate whether the regulatory frameworks of France and Chile embody this shift towards a consumer law that is both protective and transformative.

II. Formulating the functional research question

The research question is therefore decisive, as it defines both the object and scope of the comparison.[24] A cautious and well-delimited question helps avoid overambitious designs that risk superficial results or a lack of understanding of the foreign legal institutions under review.[25]

Building on this methodological premise, in this study, we follow a micro-comparative approach, understood as a comparison focused on specific legal problems rather than entire legal systems.[26] Accordingly, the research seeks to address the following question: How do the French and Chilean Systems regulate sustainable consumer law? Within this framework, the analysis will focus on three specific areas: the right to information, the reparability of durable goods, and advertising.

---

23 Ibid p. 186.

24 María Elisa Morales, Derecho Comparado. Una primera aproximación [Comparative law. A first approach] (2025), N° 51, Revista de Actualidad Jurídica UDD, p. 147, 157.

25 Husa (2015), pp. 142–143.

26 Ibid p. 145.

III. Construction of the comparative framework: Chile and France

This study is being conducted by Chilean scholars in Chile with the objective of developing a future proposal to enhance Chilean consumer legislation. The study begins with an examination of the Chilean legal system as the primary point of comparison. In accordance with the prevailing tendency in Chilean consumer and private law, the second system selected is of European origin – France. This system offers a particularly advanced example of sustainable consumer law, combining the implementation of key EU directives with ambitious domestic initiatives. France has notably accelerated its regulatory framework since 2020 through the Loi Anti-gaspillage pour une économie circulaire (AGEC) and the Loi Climat et Résilience (LCR), which together illustrate a proactive approach to integrating sustainability into consumer protection.

France was selected not only due to its regulatory advancement in this area, but also because it offers a particularly suitable comparator for Chile. Both countries share a civil law tradition, and Chilean law has been historically shaped by French legal influence, beginning with the Civil Code.[27] This legal compatibility enables more meaningful comparative insights than would be possible with jurisdictions from other legal families. This historical connection makes France a particularly illuminating case through which to observe how sustainability has progressively reshaped European private and consumer law.

Sustainability entered the agenda of European contract law as early as 2004, when the *Manifesto on Social Justice in European Contract Law* declared that 'it is important to align the general principles of social justice governing the market order with rules designed to protect public goods, such as a healthy environment'.[28] Two decades later, private law is increasingly viewed as a space for transformation, with sustainability emerging as a new normative domain.[29]

---

27 Gerardo Caffera/Rodrigo Momberg/María Elisa Morales, 'Legal transplants: A case study of private law in its historical context', in Mathias Siems/Po Jen Yap (eds.), The Cambridge handbook of comparative law (2024), p. 453, 456.

28 Study Group on Social Justice in European Private Law, 'Social Justice in European Contract Law: a Manifesto' (2004), Vol. 10 N° 6, Eur. Law J., p. 653, 666.

29 Grochowski (2021), p. 387. See: Ralf Michaels/Veronica Ruiz Abou-Nigm/Hans van Loon, The Private Side of Transforming our World UN Sustainable Development Goals 2030 and the Role of Private International Law, 1st ed. (2021).

Since 2008, the European Union has pursued a coherent strategy on sustainable consumption, aligned with UN initiatives. Key reforms include the extension of the Ecodesign Directive (2009), revisions of the Ecolabel Regulation (2009) and the Eco-Management and Audit Scheme Regulation (2018), as well as policies on green public procurement, the Roadmap to a Resource Efficient Europe (2011), and the Eco-Innovation Action Plan (2011).[30]

More recently, EU consumer law has placed sustainability at its core through new legislative instruments. Regulation (EU) 2024/1781 introduces ecodesign requirements to ensure product sustainability throughout the lifecycle. Directive (EU) 2024/825 supports the green transition by improving consumer protection and information mandating disclosures on product lifespan, repairability, and protection against greenwashing. Directive (EU) 2024/1799, the 'Right to Repair Directive', promotes repair as a consumer right. Together, these developments mark a shift towards integrating environmental protection as a legal interest in EU consumer law.

Within this broader framework, France stands out for going beyond EU-level proposals in sustainable consumption.[31] Since 2014, the *Loi Hamon* (Law No. 2014–344) has required information on spare part availability in the *Code de la Consommation.* The *AGEC Law* (*Anti-Gaspillage pour une Économie Circulaire*) later introduced reparability and durability indexes for electronic devices. Meanwhile, the *Grenelle 2 Law* (Law No. 2010–788), updated through 2021, mandates carbon footprint labelling on products to involve consumers and businesses in climate action.[32] The *Climat et Résilience Law* (Law No. 2021–1104) further strengthened this framework by adding Articles L541–9–11 to the *Code de l'Environnement*, establishing an environmental impact label for goods and services.

In short, both EU-level reforms and the particularly advanced French case focus on two key areas: the right to information – understood to

30 Elias Van Gool/Anaïs Michel, 'The New Consumer Sales Directive 2019/771 and Sustainable Consumption' (2021), Journal of European Consumer and Market Law, p. 1, 2.

31 Terryn (2023), pp. 173–174.

32 Comisión Económica para América Latina y El Caribe, 'Metodologías de Cálculo de la Huella de Carbono y sus potenciales implicaciones para América Latina' [Carbon Footprint Calculation Methodologies and their Potential Implications for Latin America] (2010), https://repositorio.cepal.org/server/api/core/bitstreams/5475cea4-6e9d-4a76-841b-b71a13b7ac37/content (last accessed: 29 June 2025).

include advertising and the prohibition of greenwashing – and the reparability and durability of consumer goods.

IV. Comparative functional analysis of consumer-information duties and product durability/repairability in France and Chile

1. France

To clarify the analysis, the discussion of France is divided into two parts: first, an overview of the substantive legal framework and key legislative initiatives, and second, an examination of the mechanisms for enforcement and their projected effectiveness.

a) The French approach to sustainable consumer law

France is widely recognised as a frontrunner in sustainable consumer law. As Terryn notes, the country has gone beyond EU requirements, setting more ambitious standards and integrating sustainability more deeply into its national legal framework.[33] France's approach is structured around several key legal instruments. From the perspective of consumer law, the most relevant are the *Loi Anti-Gaspillage pour une Économie Circulaire* (AGEC)[34] and the *Loi Climat et Résilience.*[35]

The AGEC Law aims to shift the French economy from a linear to a circular model by eliminating waste and pollution from the design stage, ending single-use plastics by 2040, combatting planned obsolescence, promoting repair and reuse, and improving consumer information. It applies across a wide range of sectors – including textiles, packaging, electronics, and construction – and to all goods sold in France. Among its innovative

33 Terryn (2023), pp. 173–174.

34 Loi n° 2020–105 du 10 février 2020 relative à la lutte contre le gaspillage et à l'économie circulaire (AGEC) [on the fight against waste and the circular economy], https://www.legifrance.gouv.fr/jorf/id/JORFTEXT000041553759/.

35 Loi n° 2021–1104 du 22 août 2021 portant lutte contre le dérèglement climatique et renforcement de la résilience face à ses effets (1) [combating climate change and building resilience to its effects], https://www.legifrance.gouv.fr/jorf/id/JORFTEXT000043956924.

measures are the Repairability Index,[36] which scores how easy it is to repair a product on a scale of 1 to 10, and the Durability Index,[37] which indicates the expected lifespan of a product. Under this law, France also became the first country in the world to ban the destruction of new but unsold consumer goods.

The *Loi Climat et Résilience* builds upon this framework by introducing new environmental obligations and explicitly classifying greenwashing as a deceptive commercial practice under French consumer law. Article 10 of the law amends Article L121–2 of the *Code de la consommation*, broadening the definition of misleading practices to include:

1. False or misleading claims regarding the properties of a product or service – particularly in terms of environmental impact;
2. Misrepresentation of the scope of a brand's commitments – especially those related to sustainability.

Another major development is the introduction of the French Eco-Score, officially renamed Environmental Cost (*Coût Environnemental*)[38], developed under the *Loi Climat et Résilience* to provide consumers with standardised environmental impact data for clothing and textiles. Although

36 Décret n° 2020–1757 du 29 décembre 2020 relatif à l'indice de réparabilité des équipements électriques et électroniques [on the reparability index for electrical and electronic equipment],https://www.legifrance.gouv.fr/jorf/id/JORFTEXT000042837821.

37 Décret n° 2024–316 du 5 avril 2024 relatif à l'indice de durabilité des équipements électriques et électroniques [on the durability index for electrical and electronic equipment], https://www.legifrance.gouv.fr/jorf/id/JORFTEXT000049375942.

38 Décret n° 2025–957 du 6 septembre 2025 relatif aux modalités de calcul et de communication du coût environnemental des produits textiles, JORF n°0209, 9 September 2025, texte n°84, arts D. 541–240–D. 541–245, https://www.legifrance.gouv.fr/eli/decret/2025/9/6/TECD2515462D/jo/texte, to be read together with *Code de l'environnement* art L541–9–11. The decree defines the environmental cost as a life-cycle impact score expressed in 'points of impact' (art D.541 – 240) and applies to all new or remanufactured textiles placed on the French market (art D.541 – 241). It requires that the cost be made available to consumers at the point of purchase and published on a government-designated portal with a detailed breakdown by impact category and a sustainability coefficient (arts D.541 – 242–243). Manufacturers, importers and other commercialisers must upload the data and are expressly responsible for its accuracy and timely updates (arts D.541 – 243(V)-244). This obligation complements *Code de l'environnement* art L541–9–11, which mandates visible, reliable and easily understandable consumer information on the environmental impacts of goods and services across their entire life cycle, to be provided by marking, labelling or another appropriate means.

it is still commonly referred to as the Eco-Score, the labelling system now displays a numerical value rather than a letter grade, with lower values indicating lower environmental impact.

The methodology is based on life cycle assessments (LCA) and incorporates sixteen environmental indicators, including greenhouse gas emissions, water and land use, energy consumption, and toxicity. In addition to technical factors, the system also evaluates practices such as sustainable agriculture, the release of microfibres, and marketing strategies that may encourage overconsumption – such as extremely low prices or excessive product variety. These criteria allow for differentiation between ultra-fast fashion, conventional, and ethical brands, even when production processes are similar.

The Environmental Cost labelling will apply to all apparel and textile products sold on the French market, including those marketed by foreign companies, with mandatory compliance expected by 2026. Although currently voluntary, brands may already submit their own scores to the public platform. Once enforcement begins, however, third parties will also be permitted to publish scores on a brand's behalf.[39] This creates a strong incentive for companies to report accurate data during the voluntary phase to avoid reputational or regulatory risks.

To support implementation, the French Ministry for Ecological Transition and Territorial Cohesion, in collaboration with other agencies, has launched Ecobalyse,[40] an open-source platform to help companies calculate and disclose their Environmental Cost.

---

39 Décret n° 2025–957 du 6 septembre 2025 relatif aux modalités de calcul et de communication du coût environnemental des produits textiles, JORF n°0209, 9 September 2025, texte n°84, art D. 541–244 https://www.legifrance.gouv.fr/eli/decret/2025/9/6/TECD2515462D/jo/texte 'Art. D. 541–244.-'. Any legal or natural person may calculate and communicate the environmental cost of a textile product reference, based on available data or data estimated from available data, in compliance with all the conditions defined in Article D. 541–243. 'If the manufacturer, importer or any other distributor determines the environmental cost of one of its textile product references themselves or updates it, then this environmental cost is the information used by any person voluntarily communicating on it. Where applicable, the latter shall update the environmental cost on which they previously communicated within a period not exceeding one month. 'Until 1 October 2026, this option shall only apply if the persons referred to in Article D. 541–243 have given their consent or published the environmental cost concerned on the portal referred to in Article D. 541–243.'.

40 Calculez le coût environnemental de vos produits [Calculate the environmental cost of your products], https://ecobalyse.beta.gouv.fr.

In the same sector, France has more recently drawn further attention with the *Proposition de loi visant à réduire l'impact environnemental de l'industrie textile* (Proposed legislation to reduce the environmental impact of the textile industry).[41] This draft law responds to the significant environmental damage caused by fast fashion (*mode éphémère*), which is characterised by mass production, rapid collection turnover, and aggressive pricing strategies. According to the French Environment and Energy Management Agency (ADEME),[42] 'every year, more than 100 billion items are sold worldwide'.[43] Companies such as Shein exemplify this model by offering thousands of new designs daily at ultra-low prices, thereby fuelling the overconsumption of non-essential clothing.

This legislative proposal seeks to go beyond existing regulation. It would require e-commerce platforms to display prominent notices informing consumers of the environmental and social footprint of garments, their geographic origin, and the availability of repair or recycling options. It would also prohibit misleading commercial claims such as *livraison gratuite* (free shipping) and ban advertising for ultra-fast fashion brands across all media channels, including content by influencers.

While the substantive framework outlined above clarifies the functions and objectives of the French provisions, a separate analysis of their enforcement is essential. Distinguishing the mechanisms that ensure compliance highlights the institutional design and practical reach of the system, allowing the reader to see not only what the law requires but also how these requirements are implemented and monitored. This functional separation makes the comparative analysis more transparent and facilitates a clearer assessment of how similar enforcement tools might be adapted to other jurisdictions.

41 Available under: https://www.legifrance.gouv.fr/dossierlegislatif/JORFDOLE000049284718/ (last accessed: 29 June 2025).

42 ADEME is a French agency which participates in the construction of national and local policies for ecological transition. See: https://www.ademe.fr/en/frontpage.

43 Proposition de loi n° 2129 (16e législature), *Proposition de loi visant à réduire l'impact environnemental de l'industrie textile*, Assemblée nationale, déposée le 30 janvier 2024 [Proposed legislation to reduce the environmental impact of the textile industry], https://www.assemblee-nationale.fr/dyn/16/textes/l16b2129_proposition-loi.

b) Enforcement mechanisms and projections of effectiveness

These legal instruments are not only ambitious in their content but also enforceable, as the laws provide concrete mechanisms to ensure compliance. These include financial penalties, product restrictions, and clear obligations for businesses. Moreover, the strong public support for these regulations further enhances their potential effectiveness.

The bill's official explanatory memorandum[44] underscores that the most urgent pressure comes from ultra-fast-fashion imports, highlighting 'the rise of numerous so-called fast-fashion brands [...]. At the forefront of this express fashion, the Chinese ready-to-wear company Shein lists on average more than 7,200 new clothing models per day' and noting that 'Shein's turnover increased by 900 per cent in only three years'. By identifying Shein and similar Asian platforms as emblematic of an unsustainable, high-volume business model, the legislature frames the need for robust enforcement as essential to curb the environmental and social harms of this trade. This context explains the bill's strong focus on border measures and fiscal tools, paving the way for the stringent sanctions and financial penalties that follow.

Significantly, Articles 7 and 8 of the *Proposition de loi visant à réduire l'impact environnemental de l'industrie textile*[45] introduce a dual enforcement strategy that combines trade-border controls with fiscal disincentives. Article 7 requires the Government, within one year of promulgation, to report on 'the implementation of mirror measures at the borders of the European internal market to impose European sanitary, social and environmental standards on the import of *fast and ultra-fast fashion* textile products', and to consider 'reversing the burden of proof so that the exporter must demonstrate that its products were produced in conditions compliant with European standards, with particular vigilance regarding respect for human rights'. This mechanism would make access to the EU market conditional on verifiable sustainable production, shifting the evidentiary burden directly onto exporters. Article 8 complements this approach by creating a 'tax on small parcels of extra-European origin',

44 Available under: https://www.legifrance.gouv.fr/dossierlegislatif/JORFDOLE000049284718/ (last accessed: 02 July 2025).

45 Proposition de loi visant à réduire l'impact environnemental de l'industrie textile, Sénat, Texte n° 136 (2024–2025) modifié le 10 juin 2025 [Draft legislation, aimed at reducing the environmental impact of the textile industry], arts 7–8, https://www.senat.fr/leg/tas24-136.html.

levied on 'every parcel under 2 kg sent to France by marketplaces, platforms or similar operators established outside the European Union and destined for individual consumers'. The tax is calculated per parcel and collected under the same procedures and penalties as value-added tax, with non-EU sellers required to appoint a VAT-registered representative in France to fulfil and guarantee payment obligations. Together, these provisions target the low-cost, high-volume import model characteristic of ultra-fast fashion and provide robust sanctions to ensure compliance.

The bill was passed in the *Assemblée nationale* by an overwhelming majority, with 337 votes in favour and only one against.[46] Although it still awaits validation by the European Commission, it is already seen as one of the most ambitious legislative responses in Europe to the environmental consequences of fast fashion.

Another compelling example is the *Loi Climat et Résilience*. The legislative process behind this law reflected a broad societal consensus, as it incorporated 146 proposals from the Citizens' Climate Convention (*Convention Citoyenne pour le Climat*[47]). In my opinion, this participatory approach not only bolstered the legitimacy of the law but also reinforced its social acceptability and long-term enforceability.

In sum, France's legal framework is not only proactive and technically comprehensive, but also firmly committed to embedding sustainability into consumer law. By combining consumer empowerment, producer responsibility, and robust regulatory mechanisms, France provides a model worth examining in jurisdictions such as Chile.

2. Chile

At the level of public policy, Chile has adopted a 'Long-Term Climate Strategy 2050'.[48] Within this framework, one of the most significant legislative developments has been the enactment of the Framework Law on Climate

46 Sénat, 'Scrutin public n°303 – séance du 10 juin 2025, sur l'ensemble de la proposition de loi visant à réduire l'impact environnemental de l'industrie textile' [Vote No. 303 – Session of 10 June 2025, on the entire draft law aimed at reducing the environmental impact of the textile industry], https://www.senat.fr/scrutin-public/2024/scr2024-303.html.

47 See: https://www.conventioncitoyennepourleclimat.fr/.

48 Instrument designed by the Ministry of Environment. See: https://cambioclimatico.mma.gob.cl/estrategia-climatica-de-largo-plazo-2050/descripcion-del-instrumento/.

Change,[49] published in June 2022. Nevertheless, these policies have had little impact on Chilean consumer law. As will be discussed below, Law No. 19.496 on the Protection of Consumer Rights[50] contains only a few provisions that reflect an emerging concern with environmental matters, most of which have remained largely unenforced, despite being part of the legislation for several years.

Functionally, these provisions aim to safeguard consumers' access to truthful information and to promote sustainable market behavior. Article 3(b) establishes the basic right to 'truthful and timely information' about goods and services, including their price and relevant characteristics, but it does not explicitly mention environmental attributes or impacts, and there is no case law interpreting it in that sense. Article 3(d) goes further by expressly incorporating environmental protection within consumer rights, yet it has likewise not been invoked in judicial decisions.

Several other provisions seek to secure product durability and reliability. Articles 20 and 21 create legal guarantees for durable goods, giving consumers the choice of repair, replacement, or a refund when a product is defective or fails to function properly. This mechanism is widely used in practice and can be enforced directly by consumers against sellers without the involvement of lawyers or state authorities, illustrating how the law functions as a self-help tool for everyday disputes.

Sanctions also have an environmental dimension. Article 24 increases penalties for misleading advertising related to environmental claims, but courts have yet to apply it. Similarly, Article 28(f) prohibits misleading advertising that makes false or ambiguous statements about a product's environmental impact, recyclability, or reusability, yet its judicial application remains minimal. A more recent amendment, Article 1(3), expands the definition of basic commercial information for durable goods to include the product's expected lifespan and the period during which spare parts and technical services will be available, although there are still no reported cases applying this rule.

Taken together, these provisions demonstrate that Chilean consumer law already contains functional mechanisms capable of supporting sustainable consumption, but their potential remains largely untapped in practice.

49 Law No. 21.455, 2022, https://bcn.cl/33ori.
50 Law No. 19.496, 1997, https://bcn.cl/2pv9x.

Beyond the Consumer Protection Act, other Chilean laws also help promote more sustainable consumption by focusing on specific products and supply chains. **Law No. 21.368**[51] (Law on Single-Use Plastics and Plastic Bottles) aims to cut down on disposable items in food services, encourage reuse, and control the use of plastic bottles. It bans all single-use items for eating on site and only allows certified or recyclable materials for takeaway orders when the customer asks for them. The law also requires that certified plastics be easy for consumers to identify and that shops promote the sale of returnable bottles.

The Law No. 20.920[52] (Chile's Recycling Law) sets rules that make manufacturers and importers of products like batteries, electronics, and packaging responsible for managing the waste created after consumers use them. It also supports eco-labelling and organised recycling systems. One example is the voluntary *Elijo Reciclar* ('I Choose to Recycle') label, which shows that a package is at least 80 per cent recyclable and is meant to help consumers choose more environmentally friendly products, even though the label is still in a trial stage.

V. Functional comparison of sustainable consumer law in France and Chile

This section integrates the descriptive and comparative analysis by examining both jurisdictions under the same functional categories. It highlights how each legal system addresses key problems of sustainable consumer law and allows a step-by-step comparison of their approaches.

1. Misleading environmental claims and greenwashing

France. The *Loi Climat et Résilience* explicitly classifies greenwashing as a deceptive commercial practice, amending Article L121–2 of the *Code de la consommation* to prohibit 'false or misleading claims regarding the properties of a product or service—particularly in terms of environmental impact', and to cover misrepresentation of the scope of a brand's sustainability commitments.

Chile. Law No. 19.496 similarly forbids misleading advertising. Article 28(f) prohibits false or ambiguous claims about a product's environmental

51 Law No. 21.368, 2021, https://bcn.cl/2qvub.
52 Law No. 20.020, 2016, https://bcn.cl/2exlx.

impact, recyclability or reusability. Article 24 adds higher penalties for misleading environmental claims, yet neither provision has been meaningfully enforced.

Comparison. Both systems formally address greenwashing, but France provides a direct and enforceable prohibition, whereas Chile's rules remain largely declarative and have seen little judicial application.

2. Consumer information and environmental labelling

France. Environmental information duties are central to the French framework. Article L541–9–11 of the *Code de l'Environnement* establishes an environmental impact label for goods and services. The *Loi Anti-Gaspillage pour une Économie Circulaire* (AGEC) requires detailed disclosure on product durability and reparability, including the Repairability and Durability Indexes, and bans the destruction of unsold consumer goods.
Chile. Article 3(b) of Law No. 19.496 recognises the right to truthful and timely information, but it does not explicitly require environmental data and lacks case law. A 2022 amendment to Article 1(3) requires sellers to inform consumers of a product's expected lifespan and the availability of spare parts and technical services, but there are no reports of enforcement. Voluntary schemes such as the *Elijo Reciclar* label under the Recycling Law (No. 20.920) indicate recyclability but remain in pilot stages.
Comparison. France offers a comprehensive, mandatory labelling regime and measurable indexes, while Chile relies on general information duties and voluntary labels without effective oversight.

3. Product durability and repairability

France. The AGEC Law obliges producers to disclose and, in some cases, ensure product durability and repairability. Consumers can rely on durability and repairability indexes to make informed choices, and producers face clear duties to provide spare parts and repair information.

Chile. Articles 20 and 21 of Law No. 19.496 grant consumers the right to repair, replacement, or refund for defective durable goods. These guarantees are widely used and can be enforced directly by consumers without legal representation, but they do not impose broader obligations to enhance product lifespan. Moreover, Chilean law does not create incentives for consumers to favour repair or long-lasting products. Because they can freely and easily opt for a refund or a new item when a defect occurs, the right to repair remains secondary and less attractive in practice.

Comparison. Both systems recognise durability as a consumer interest, yet France transforms it into enforceable producer duties, while Chile frames it primarily as a post-defect remedy, where the ease of refunds or replacements leaves repair as a less-used option.

4. Waste prevention and fast fashion controls

France. France prohibits the destruction of unsold consumer goods and has introduced the *Proposition de loi visant à réduire l'impact environnemental de l'industrie textile*, which targets ultra-fast fashion with border measures and a tax on small parcels from outside the EU. Article 7 calls for 'mirror measures' to impose EU environmental standards on imports and even proposes reversing the burden of proof so exporters must demonstrate compliance with human-rights and environmental norms. Article 8 establishes a tax on parcels under 2 kg shipped by non-EU platforms, collected under the same procedures as VAT.

Chile. Chilean law contains no equivalent prohibition on destroying unsold goods and no direct regulation of fast fashion. The main waste-reduction instruments are sectoral: Law No. 21.368 bans single-use plastics in food services, while the Recycling Law No. 20.920 creates extended producer responsibility for certain products and encourages eco-labelling and recycling.

Comparison. France adopts targeted measures to reduce textile waste and to curb the environmental impact of fast fashion, while Chile relies on broader waste-management laws that are not consumer-specific.

Moreover, France has initiated the regulation of the fast fashion industry through targeted legal proposals that restrict advertising and impose sustainability-related duties on platforms. Chile has not introduced comparable initiatives.

VI. Reflections and lessons for Chile

This comparison reveals significant differences in legal design, enforceability, and ambition. Chile has introduced some environmental considerations into its consumer law, but these remain modest and rarely applied. In contrast, even within the limits of this preliminary analysis, France offers a more comprehensive and enforceable legal framework—one that places sustainability at the heart of consumer protection.

Several factors may explain why Chile has not yet adopted similarly strict rules. A central reason is the lack of political will, which can be understood in light of the country's status as a developing economy. Policy priorities have tended to focus on issues perceived as more urgent, such as public security, migration, health, and education. Cultural influences also play a role. Chile has long been shaped by strong U.S. cultural and economic influence, particularly since the dictatorship that began in 1973, which reinforced market-oriented, capitalist ideals. These historical and cultural factors help to explain both the limited interest in sustainable consumer law and the weak enforcement of the few environmental provisions that do exist.

For Chile, the implication is clear: integrating sustainability into consumer law requires enforceable duties for producers, rights for consumers, and coherent regulatory mechanisms. While France does not offer a model to be mechanically replicated, its experience provides an inspiring and compatible example of how meaningful legal transformation is both necessary and achievable.

Looking ahead, certain starting points for reform stand out. The most pressing need is to strengthen mandatory environmental labelling and truthful-information duties, ensuring that consumers receive clear, verifiable data on product durability and environmental impact.

France demonstrates the value of moving from aspirational provisions to binding legal standards, supported by measurable tools such as the Repairability and Durability Indexes. It has developed a structured system of environmental labelling, addressed planned obsolescence, introduced waste-prevention measures, and regulated fast fashion. Importantly, these reforms enjoy strong public legitimacy, as shown by the role of the Citizens' Climate Convention in shaping the *Loi Climat et Résilience.*

Nonetheless, any proposal for legal transplantation must be grounded in a more detailed and context-specific analysis. Further research from within France is essential to understand the precise operation and impact of its legal instruments. This article offers only a preliminary perspective intended to guide and encourage future research and policy development.

Nonprofit controlling for profit: the role of 'collective hybrids' in fostering sustainability

*Riccardo Rao**

A. Introduction

Corporate purpose is currently a pivotal topic in business law agendas. There is indeed a growing debate on whether corporations should just serve shareholders or stakeholders as a whole (eg employees, suppliers, customers, the environment).[1] In other words, the question is whether they should only pursue profits or a more holistic balance with social and environmental outputs.

* Post-doc researcher in business law at the University of Parma, Italy.

1 Colin Mayer, 'Prosperity: Better Business Makes the Greater Good' (2018), *passim*; Lucian A. Bebchuk, Roberto Tallarita, 'The Illusory Promise of Stakeholder Governance' (2020), 106 Cornell Law Rev., pp. 91–178; Edward Rock, 'For Whom is the Corporation Managed in 2020? The Debate over Corporate Purpose' (2020), ECGI Law Working Paper no. 515, pp. 1–30.

This is not a new debate, being rather 'as old as corporate law itself'.[2] It arose at least in the Middle Ages,[3] resurfacing from time to time.[4] One might recall: the idea, forged in England during the 17th century, that the corporate form could only be conceded when a public benefit was promoted; then, in the 20th century, the vibrant exchange between American Professors Berle and Dodd, as well as the equally intense dispute among European scholars opposing contractual and institutional views.[5]

Recently, to overcome the inner for profit nature of corporations, alternative legal vehicles have been introduced in various jurisdictions. They are a sort of hybrids in between for profit and nonprofit. An initial prototype may be found in the community interest company or CIC, introduced in the UK in 2004[6] and then implemented by other legal systems too, eg in Canada.[7] Another form is given by the benefit corporation, devised in the US state of Maryland in 2010 and later transplanted with variations in most of the other US states[8] and in foreign jurisdictions, including among others Italy[9] and France.[10]

As an approximation, CICs may be seen as leaning more towards the nonprofit side, while benefit corporations appear to remain closer to the for profit one.[11] Indeed, whereas CICs can distribute profits to their members

---

2 David Kershaw/Edmund-Philipp Schuster, 'The Purposive Transformation of Corporate Law' (2021), 69(3) Am. J. Comp. L., p. 478, 479.

3 Holger Fleischer, 'Corporate Purpose: A Management Concept and its Implications for Company Law' (2021), 18(2) ECFR, pp. 161–189.

4 Jennifer G. Hill, 'Corporations, Directors' Duties and the Public/Private Divide', in Arthur B. Laby/Jacob Hale Russell (eds.), Fiduciary Obligations in Business (2021), pp. 285–300.

5 Martin Gelter, 'Taming or Protecting the Modern Corporation? Shareholder-Stakeholder Debates in a Comparative Light' (2011), 7 NYU J. L. & Bus, pp. 641–730.

6 Joseph S. Liptrap, 'British Social Enterprise Law' (2021), 21(2) J. Corp. L. Stud., pp. 595–630.

7 Community contribution companies or C3s, introduced in the province of British Columbia in 2013.

8 J. Haskell Murray, 'An Early Report on Benefit Corporations' (2015), 118(1) West Virginia L. Rev., pp. 25–57.

9 Marco Speranzin, 'Benefit legal entities in Italy: an overview' (2022), 19(5) Eur. Co. Law, pp. 142–150.

10 Nadège Jullian, 'Sociétés à mission: bientôt 5 ans d'introduction d'une once de non-lucrativité en droit des sociétés' [*Sociétés à mission*: almost five years since the introduction of a hint of nonprofitability into corporate law] (2024), Droit des sociétés, no. 4, pp. 1 et seqq.

11 Dana Brakman Reiser, 'Benefit Corporations – A Sustainable Form of Organization?' (2011), 46 Wake Forest L. Rev., p. 591, 606.

up to a certain percentage (eg 35 %), benefit corporations are allowed to distribute profits up to 100 %.

The overall debate is centred on 'single entity' hybrid models, like those aforementioned. However, a certain degree of hybridization between for profit and nonprofit can be achieved also through separate entities. This is comparatively much less explored in legal scholarship and policymaking.[12]

In fact, rather than setting up a hybrid vehicle, a similar result can be reached by placing a for profit entity (corporation) under a nonprofit one (foundation). In a nutshell, the mechanism works as follows: a foundation owns and controls a corporation that carries out business activities in the market. Thus, the foundation is able to greatly influence how the invested-in corporation is run. On the one side, the foundation aims at preserving the profitability of the controlled corporation; on the other side, as a non-profit organization, it promotes one or more social and environmental purposes. Looking at the whole picture, the structure may be seen as a 'collective hybrid'.

The goal of this work is to argue that – in the same way as single entity hybrids, also – collective hybrids may be a valuable tool in order to foster sustainability. As such, lawmakers should enhance the use of collective hybrids by providing a specific and well-rounded regulatory framework. The work is structured as follows: it starts by depicting the main features of collective hybrids (para. B), before examining the current legal landscape in a selection of jurisdictions (para. C); then, it delves into empirical data on the performance of collective hybrids in terms of sustainability, putting forward on these bases a set of policy proposals (para. D).

B. *'Collective hybrids'*

I. Main features and limitations

A foundation is characterised by certain main features:[13] separate legal personality (full or partial), a charter (which specifies, inter alia, the foundation's purpose), a board of directors (chosen by external institutions

12 Henry Hansmann, 'Foreword', in Anne Sanders/Steen Thomsen (eds.), Enterprise Foundation Law in a Comparative Perspective (2023), p. i, v.

13 Steen Thomsen/Nikolaos Kavadis, 'Enterprise Foundations: Law, Taxation, Governance, and Performance' (2022), 6(4) Ann. Corp. Gov., pp. 227–333.

or through a co-optation regime, in which directors appoint their own successors), oversight by a state authority.

Its creation usually occurs by an irrevocable donation or will. The initial endowment shall encompass sufficient funds, which can also be shares in a corporation. If these shares endow the foundation with a control over the corporation (not necessarily 100 %, usually 51 % of voting rights would be enough), it gives rise to an 'enterprise foundation' plus a 'subsidiary operating corporation', as they are often called in literature. This combination results into a collective hybrid, as it is also referred to herein.

The profits earned by the corporation can be channelled to its shareholder, ie the foundation, by means of distributing dividends. In turn, pursuant to the non-distribution constraint which generally characterises foundation law,[14] the foundation cannot assign these amounts to its founders, members or directors. Rather, they should be used for the altruistic purpose of the foundation, such as the social and environmental common good. Clearly, all the above is net of peculiar provisions across jurisdictions, which are discussed further below.[15]

Before going into the details of the different regulation across jurisdictions, two limitations are here worth pointing out. This work does not deal with 'direct enterprise foundations' and 'subsidiary foundations'. Their differences – compared to enterprise foundations, subject matter of this work – are briefly explained below.

Usually, foundations are allowed to directly run business activities and even gain profits, provided that the non-distribution constraint is fulfilled.[16] So, in order to engage with business activities, a foundation would not strictly need to act through a corporation. But direct enterprise foundations, as they may be called, are not common at all. The major reason is that the foundation form is not designed for directly running a business. Thus, when a foundation intends to engage in business activities, it is way more common to do it by holding participations into a corporation, so resulting into an enterprise foundation's structure.[17]

---

14 Henry Hansmann, 'The Role of Nonprofit Enterprise' (1980), 89 Yale L. J., p. 835, 838.

15 See infra C.

16 Hansmann (1980), p. 838.

17 Austria goes further: therein, direct enterprise foundations are not just rare like in other countries, but explicitly prohibited. The main reason for this ban likely lies in the need to protect the foundation's members from potential claims by business creditors. Indeed, to directly perform business activities is perceived too risky for a foundation; while to hold participations into corporations, as an enterprise founda-

Enterprise foundations shall also be distinguished from another phenomenon: a foundation can be part of a corporate group as the vehicle in charge of promoting philanthropic activities within the group. In this case, there is not a foundation that controls a corporation, but the other way around: the foundation is not at the vertex of the corporate chain, instead it is merely a subsidiary to which part of the group's corporate profits are allocated for philanthropic purposes. Therein, decisions are ultimately assumed by the holding corporation, not by the foundation placed at the bottom. In short, subsidiary foundations have not a say in business decisions, and that is a striking difference compared to enterprise foundations.

II. How widespread are collective hybrids at present?

Once depicted the main features of enterprise foundations, it is useful to explore their quantitative dimension and practical relevance to date. For over a century, enterprise foundations have been common in Denmark;[18] according to a recent study enterprise foundations control about 63 % of Danish capital markets (meaning that, in Denmark, the listed corporations owned by enterprise foundations account for such a share of the entire market capitalization).[19] Renowned examples are Novo Nordisk, A.P. Møller Maersk, and Carlsberg.

Outside Denmark, the model is present in other Scandinavian countries like Sweden (19 %, eg it is used by Ikea) and Norway (8 %), as well as in Luxembourg (62 %) and the Netherlands (14 %).[20] Furthermore, its deployment is not negligible in German-speaking countries like Austria (26 %), Switzerland (6 %, eg Rolex) and Germany (4 %, eg Carl Zeiss).[21]

---

tion, is deemed less risky – given the corporate 'shield' – and so admitted by the law. See Susanne Kalss, 'The Austrian Foundation', in Anne Sanders/Steen Thomsen (eds.), Enterprise Foundation Law in a Comparative Perspective (2023), p. 61, 66–67.

18 Henry Hansmann/Steen Thomsen, 'The Governance of Foundation-Owned Firms' (2021), 13(1) J. Leg. Anal., p. 172, 173.

19 Steen Thomsen, 'Foundation Ownership around the World', in Anne Sanders/Steen Thomsen (eds.), Enterprise Foundation Law in a Comparative Perspective (2023), p. 1, 7 et seq., 15 et seqq.

20 Ibid.

21 Ibid. As a methodological note, the aforementioned figures only refer to listed corporations owned by foundations, for which more reliable data are available. As such, they do not take into account unlisted corporations owned by foundations. This is a significant limitation, due to the difficulty of carrying out empirical analyses on un-

In the rest of the world – with a few exceptions like India (6 %)[22] – enterprise foundations are rare. As a result, at the global level, they account just for an estimated 1.6 % of market capitalization.[23] The different spread is not easy to explain, but it may be due to several factors.

First of all, religion played a role. In Scandinavia and German-speaking countries, having a strong Protestant influence, the sake of profits was not seen in conflict with religious precepts. Profits and the common good could go *pari passu*. On the contrary, in southern Europe, the rooted Catholicism always looked at profits with suspicion:[24] money, the 'devil's excrement',[25] could not be associated with the 'holy' common good.

Secondly, it can be also linked to cultural heritage. In France, during the Revolution – with a powerful echo in neighbouring countries, like Italy or Spain – foundations were viewed as a subtle reinstatement of the feudal type of property. Foundations were indeed seen as tools for perpetual conservation of goods, preventing allocation to the most efficient owners in the market.[26] Another traditional belief in France was that the common good owed to be a prerogative of the state, not of private entities like foundations.[27]

However, religious and cultural values are not the only factors. Protestant precepts have been quite influential in the US as well, but therein enterprise foundations are far less common. Thus, there must be another explanation,

---

listed corporations. But if one considers also the latter, the figures may greatly vary, in particular in relation to countries where firm ownership is not dispersed and capital markets are less wide, because there the vast majority of enterprise foundation-owned corporations may be unlisted.

22 Thomsen (2023), pp. 7 et seq., 15 et seqq.

23 Ibid.

24 Eugenio Barcellona, 'Industrial Foundations under Italian Law', in Anne Sanders/ Steen Thomsen (eds.), Enterprise Foundation Law in a Comparative Perspective (2023), 157, 158 et seq.; Mario Notari, 'Le fondazioni industriali: un nuovo modello di holding no profit per i gruppi quotati?' [Industrial foundations: a new nonprofit holding company model for listed groups?], in Paolo Montalenti, Mario Notari (eds.), La nuova società quotata: tutela degli stakeholders, sostenibilità e nuova governance (2022), p. 59, 69.

25 Old adage attributed to Saint Basil the Great, recalled by Pope Francis a few years ago. See https://www.vatican.va/content/francesco/en/speeches/2015/february/documents/papa-francesco_20150228_confcooperative.html (last accessed: 14 September 2025).

26 Barcellona (2023), pp. 163–164.

27 Pierre-Henri Conac, 'Le fonds de pérennité: the French Privatstiftung?' (2019), RTD Financier, no. 3, p. 29, 29.

a third factor: ie the different regulatory patterns. In the US, a strict legal regime (in particular, tax law) has indeed made enterprise foundations not attractive.[28]

C. Regulatory patterns

The various legislative paths for enterprise foundations are examined herein, focusing on five legal systems: Denmark, Germany, Italy, France and the US. One has been historically permissive (Denmark), one has gone halfway (Germany), while the other three have been hostile (Italy, France and the US).[29] The analysis is accordingly divided in three parts, plus a final comparative outlook.

I. The permissive pattern: Denmark

In Denmark, enterprise foundations 'began their existence (...) with lawyers, utilizing the freedom of contract, drafting bylaws and transferring assets to (...) foundations',[30] including shares in corporations. The first was Carlsberg in 1876.[31] Typically, in Denmark, a foundation controls only one company and such a structure 'is created by the founder of that company at the end of his (or her) life to maintain control of the company in perpetuity'.[32]

The regulatory environment was clarified in 1985 with a double legislation: one applying to ordinary foundations and another one to enterprise foundations (*Erhvervsfondsloven*).[33] A core regulatory point concerns the

28 See especially C.III.

29 For a similar classification (except for France, not examined therein), see Anne Sanders/Steen Thomsen, 'Enterprise Foundation Law in a Comparative Perspective: Concluding Observations', in Anne Sanders/Steen Thomsen (eds.), Enterprise Foundation Law in a Comparative Perspective (2023), p. 221, 240, including table 10.

30 Rasmus K. Feldthusen, 'Denmark: Enterprise Foundations', in Anne Sanders/Steen Thomsen (eds.), Enterprise Foundation Law in a Comparative Perspective (2023), p. 129, 130.

31 Ibid.

32 Hansmann/Thomsen (2018), p. 4. Often, there is a holding company in between the foundation and the operating company: eg in A.P. Møller Maersk, https://apmoller.com/the-a-p-moller-foundation-as-an-owner/ (last accessed: 14 September 2025).

33 Feldthusen (2023), pp. 133 et seqq.

purpose. In principle, a Danish foundation (ordinary or enterprise) can seek any purpose, as long as it is not illegal or *contra bònos mòres*. Of course, this entails the possibility for the foundation to give all the dividends received to charity. However, it may also decide that the subsidiary corporation shall not distribute any dividends: if so, that foundation's purpose would be to run and expand a business (by means of the subsidiary corporation), with no charitable deeds being made.[34]

In addition, Danish enterprise foundations may have a family purpose, meaning to carry out distributions (or 'perpetuities') in favour of the settlor's family members. That was a historical feature, heavily disincentivised by the 1985 legislation, which only applies to foundations established after its entrance into force. As a consequence, in practice, family foundations are not established any longer – while there are older ones which still distribute generous family perpetuities.[35]

In sum, in terms of purpose, Danish enterprise foundations may be distinguished in three categories:

(i) charity (using profits to finance charitable deeds);
(ii) fully business-oriented (keeping all profits within the subsidiary corporation to further develop its business); and
(iii) family (allocating profits, at least partially, to family members).

II. The halfway pattern: Germany

Until the 21st century, freedom of self-regulation in governing foundations was given to each federal state (*Länder*). That led to deep divergences, with some states being very permissive, while others being much stricter.[36]

A unification of the legal regime was achieved in 2002. Then a further reform of foundation law, clarifying the applicable rules, was passed in 2021.[37] A major innovation is the establishment of a federal foundation

34 Although still partially debated, the point can be considered ascertained; cf ibid, pp. 137–140, including fn. 19 therein for further references.

35 Ibid, pp. 146–147.

36 Anne Sanders, 'Enterprise Foundations in Germany', in Anne Sanders/Steen Thomsen (eds.), Enterprise Foundation Law in a Comparative Perspective (2023), p. 25, 28 et seqq.

37 See Rainer Hüttemann/Peter Rawert, 'Das neue Bundesstiftungsrecht – Darstellung und Analyse sowie Vorschläge für notwendige Reformen der Landesstiftungsgesetze'

register, to be kept at the *Bundesamt für Justiz* in Bonn, with effect from 2026.[38]

Yet, the reform did not specifically address enterprise foundations, with the consequence that to date there are still no express rules governing them in Germany. Hence, the question is: are they allowed or not? Overall, a foundation shall not be harmful to the public benefit. This means that, implicitly, enterprise foundations can be deemed permitted. This comes with a limit: according to the majority of scholars and practitioners, there must be a further purpose beyond running and developing a business.[39]

As a result, stricto sensu, in Germany only two categories of enterprise foundations are legitimate: charity and family;[40] while fully business-oriented foundations would risk to be declared unlawful. However, on the latter point, a clarification is needed: in practice, the 'prohibition of foundations with the sole purpose of managing businesses is (...) [not seen] as a major obstacle'[41]. It is simply a matter of finding the right phrasing in the foundation's charter, combining the purpose of managing a business (which can be the major one) with other purposes (which can be designed in a way to remain minor), such as preserving the charitable intentions of the founder or supporting a family.[42] All in all, in terms of purpose, Germany is not significantly different from Denmark, since with the above caveat all three purposes are de facto conceivable.

It remains to be tackled why, albeit the religious and cultural environment is not strongly dissimilar, enterprise foundations are much less widespread in Germany than in Denmark. As previously put forward,[43] an important reason may be found in the legal regime. German entrepreneurs may deem more attractive to use other legal forms, for which rules are

---

[New federal foundation law – presentation, analysis and proposals for necessary reforms of state foundation laws] (2021), ZIP, p. 3.

38 Sanders (2023), pp. 53–54.

39 Ibid, pp. 34–42, including fn. 59 therein for further references.

40 These two purposes are sometimes combined through 'double foundations', where the capital share of the underlying corporation is split between two foundations: a family foundation (set up for the benefit of family members) and a charity foundation (created to finance altruistic deeds). Usually, all or most of voting rights in the underlying corporation are given to the family foundation, so that family members retain control over the corporation. See ibid, p. 37, including fn. 50 therein for further references.

41 Ibid, p. 40.

42 Ibid, including fn. 62 therein.

43 See supra B.II.

more certain (compared to enterprise foundations, on which even after the reform there are no express rules) and the public authority's oversight is less pervasive.[44] Ultimately, the German legal regime for enterprise foundations may be deemed not yet fully satisfactory.[45]

III. The hostile pattern: Italy, France and the US

Historically, Italian law has been hostile to foundations in general. The civil code of 1942, enacted during the fascist era, empowered the government with a strong control over any private institutions and especially foundations (so-called 'police law' or also 'fascist corporatism'). At that time, the prevailing idea was that a foundation could not be involved in business: neither directly, nor indirectly as an enterprise foundation.[46]

With the Italian constitution of 1948, a less strict approach came to light. Foundations were deemed free to engage in business activities, so opening up to enterprise foundations.[47] But this movement was not accompanied by an express set of rules, save for one exception: banking foundations,

---

44 Among others, a more attractive alternative is given by the limited liability company, GmbH. Being the latter compatible with any purpose, it can be shaped in a way to combine business needs, charity or family goals. Here, the holding vehicle would have a GmbH form, in lieu of the enterprise foundation. As an example of its high flexibility, amendments to its articles of associations are much easier to be adopted than to an enterprise foundation's charter. A renowned case is Robert Bosch Stiftung GmbH: https://www.bosch.com/company/ (last accessed: 14 September 2025).

45 For a de lege ferenda view, see Mathias Habersack, 'Stiftungsunternehmen in Deutschland: Gesetzliche Grundlagen, unternehmerische Motive, Reformvorschläge' [Foundation enterprises in Germany: legal bases, entrepreneurial motives, reform proposals] (2021).

46 Barcellona (2023), pp. 160–170.

47 In this development, a crucial role was played by scholars: above all, Pietro Rescigno, 'Fondazione e impresa' [Foundation and enterprise] (1967), Riv. soc., p. 812, and Renzo Costi, 'Fondazione e impresa' [Foundation and enterprise] (1968), Riv. dir. civ., p. 1; for an analysis of their views, Andrea Zoppini, 'Quattro tesi per una rilettura delle norme sulle fondazioni' [Four theses for a reinterpretation of foundation law], in Giulio Ponzanelli (ed.), 'Gli enti "non profit" in Italia' (1994), p. 57, 62 et seqq. On the contrary, courts remained hostile for a while: they kept requalifying enterprise foundations into de facto partnerships (whose members were subject to unlimited liability), see in this regard: Barcellona (2023), pp. 176–177.

governed by a special law issued in the 1990s.[48] Therefore, enterprise foundations – except for those active in the banking sector (a not minor exception, given the importance of banks in the economy, but nevertheless limited in its scope to a sector only) – are still governed by the general provisions of the 1942 civil code, which are rather old, inadequate and incomplete.[49] This regulatory vacuum contributes to explain why enterprise foundations are rarely employed in Italy.

The same uncertainty surrounds their purpose. Clearly, a charitable purpose would not be questioned, but what about a fully business-oriented or a family one? Although various views have been proposed, it seems preferable to maintain that all these purposes would be lawful for an enterprise foundation; after all, the civil code is silent and it does not necessarily require a charity purpose.[50]

Similar to the Italian legislative situation, French law has been traditionally hostile to enterprise foundations. Whereas subsidiary foundations (at the bottom, not at the vertex of corporate groups, see supra B.I.) have been regulated since 1990,[51] enterprise foundations have been governed only recently: with the introduction of *fonds de pérennité* in 2019.[52]

The latter is a special type of foundation, whose distinguishing feature is to acquire and manage participations into corporations as a '*tour de contrôle*', ergo an enterprise foundation. The 2019 law comprehensively regulates its formation, governance and dissolution. Thus, rules on ordinary foundations do not apply.[53]

48 See Vincenzo De Stasio, 'Fondazione (di origine) bancaria (fob) e terzo settore. Appunti' [Banking (originated) foundation (fob) and third-sector. Notes] (2022), Banca Borsa Tit. Credito, p. 523.

49 A new regulation, so-called 'Third-sector reform', was passed in 2017: however, it only applies to foundations whose main activity is not connected to business. Hence, it would be a bit of a stretch to apply it to enterprise foundations, in which business is at the core. See Notari (2022), p. 62. In the same context of the Third-sector reform, the Italian legislator was expected to issue a separate regulation for those foundations that are mainly active in business (directly or indirectly, like enterprise foundations), but such a regulation is yet to be approved, see Barcellona (2023), pp. 193 et seqq.

50 For the same view, see Notari (2022), pp. 63 et seqq. For a reconstruction of the debate and the various opinions held, see Barcellona (2023), pp. 184 et seqq.

51 An example is the Fondation Louis Vuitton, fully owned by the LVMH group led by Bernard Arnault.

52 See Art. 177 of law no. 486, 22 May 2019, so-called '*Loi* PACTE'.

53 Emmanuel Masset, 'L'introduction de nouveaux modèles : Les sociétés à mission et les fonds de pérennité' [Introduction of new models: *sociétés à mission* and *fonds de pérennité*] (2021), Rev. des sociétés, p. 581, no. 21 therein.

In terms of purpose, the paramount aim of a *fond de pérennité* is to preserve and possibly enhance the profitability of invested-in corporations. Additionally, it may promote the social and environmental common good. As such, a *fond de pérennité* has an inner fully business-oriented purpose; optionally, that may be combined with a charity purpose.

Lastly, moving to the US, the general approach has been traditionally hostile too. Whereas it was legally feasible to form enterprise foundations, they were rarely created since heavily discouraged by tax policies,[54] in particular under the reform of 1969.[55]

However, recent tax innovations may increase the popularity of enterprise foundations over time: eg the 2018 'Newman's Own' exception. Pursuant to the latter, a foundation owning 100 % of voting stock in a corporation can enjoy tax benefits. This is subject to the fulfillment of a strict set of conditions, requiring inter alia that the underlying corporation distributes all its profits to the controlling foundation.[56]

Another innovation is worth mentioning. Several US states, such as Delaware, have recently enabled trusts to control corporations. If properly structured (with a non-distribution constraint, which prevents the assets of the underlying corporation from being used for private gain), a trust or more generally a nonprofit entity may work 'in such a way that it is functionally identical or at least similar'[57] to an enterprise foundation. Two examples of corporations having been recently placed under the control of a trust or nonprofit entity are Open AI[58] and Patagonia.[59]

54 Ofer Eldar, 'Are Enterprise Foundations Possible in the United States?', in Anne Sanders/Steen Thomsen (eds.), Enterprise Foundation Law in a Comparative Perspective (2023), p. 201, 219.

55 Joel Fleischman, 'Public policy and philanthropic purpose – foundation ownership and control of corporations in Germany and the United States', in Andreas Schlüter/Volker Then/Peter Walkenhorst (eds), Foundations in Europe: Society, Management and Law (2001), pp. 372–408.

56 Eldar (2023), pp. 212–213.

57 Steen Thomsen, 'Foundation Ownership and Firm Performance: A Review of the International Evidence', in Ciaran Driver/Grahame Thompson (eds.), Corporate Governance in Contention (2018), p. 66, 77; see also Eldar (2023), pp. 204–206, 219.

58 Its legal structure is led by a nonprofit entity (OpenAI, Inc.), which controls a for profit subsidiary. See https://openai.com/our-structure/ (last accessed: 14 September 2025).

59 As of 2022, the voting stock of the corporation (2 % of the capital share) is held by a trust, while the non-voting stock (98 %) by a nonprofit organization (respectively, Patagonia Purpose Trust and Holdfast Collective). See https://www.patagonia.com/ownership/ (last accessed: 14 September 2025).

IV. Comparative outlook: advancements in the regulatory framework (albeit slowly)

The legal landscape for foundations greatly varies across the world.[60] But certain common trends may be identified. First of all, compared to other entities, foundations are not heavily regulated. This is true for any foundation, as well as specifically in relation to enterprise foundations.

Among the jurisdictions herein considered: except for Denmark and recently France, there are no specific rules governing enterprise foundations. Nevertheless, they are everywhere permitted, with general foundation rules applying to fill in the gaps.

In Denmark, where the historical pattern was permissive, the legal landscape is quite stable (save for the restrictions to family foundations dated 1985, which are not recent anymore and should be anyway considered more of an adjustment to prevent abuses than a disruptive change). In all the other examined jurisdictions, the legal landscape is advancing, somehow leaning towards a more permissive approach: ie more liberal interpretation in Italy, express regime in France, new tax exceptions and enabled entities in the US; with respect to Germany, it is true that the reform has not directly governed enterprise foundations, but it has at least contributed to clarify the surrounding regulatory environment (eg with the establishment of a federal foundation register).[61]

Certainly, the gap between Denmark and the other analysed jurisdictions in terms of the spread of enterprise foundations in business practice is likely to survive. However, in light of the above emerging trend, a slight reduction of the distance, albeit slowly, can be predicted (due to an increase in the use of enterprise foundations within the other analysed jurisdictions). Of course, this is merely a theoretical hypothesis that will need to be tested by future empirical analyses.

60 Sanders/Thomsen (2023), p. 241 et seqq.

61 For a similar view (except for France, not examined therein), see ibid, p. 241, including table 11.

D. What role may collective hybrids play in fostering sustainability?

I. Comparatively high ESG (and no worse financial) performance

The growing attention devoted to enterprise foundations by lawmakers, as resulting from the comparative outlook above, raises the question of whether this is desirable. In particular, the dilemma is whether enterprise foundations, as collective hybrids, can or cannot represent a valid model for promoting sustainability. For instance, at least in the intentions, the specific regulation recently passed in France aimed exactly at enabling a scheme '*d'avant-garde*', where the social and environmental common good is taken into account alongside profits.[62]

As a matter of fact, it can be observed in practice that several enterprise foundations have been accused of poor behaviour and associated with bad reputation. The claim is that a foundation-structure may be just employed for tax evasion (eg to escape inheritance taxes) or for social-green washing (declaring to be sustainable, while actually violating human rights and damaging the environment).[63]

In this regard, net of controversial cases and looking at aggregate data, there seems to be a positive correlation between enterprise foundations and environmental-social-governance (ESG) performance. In fact, albeit not yet conclusive, some studies in literature find that enterprise foundation-owned firms have higher ESG rates, compared to other firms.[64] They

62 Nicole Notat/Jean-Dominique Senard, 'L'entreprise, objet d'intérêt collectif' [Enterprise, a subject of collective interest] (2018), p. 1, 8, 75. Moreover, it is not surprising that the same reform (*Loi* PACTE, see fn. 52 supra) has introduced in France both enterprise foundations (*fonds de pérennité*) and benefit corporations (called *sociétés à mission*); thus, both collective and single hybrids, using the expressions coined herein. See Masset (2021), no. 17: '*la philosophie commune (...) transparaît*' [the common vision (...) is evident].

63 Eg see https://www.business-humanrights.org/en/companies/ikea/#associated_allegations (last accessed: 14 September 2025), concerning IKEA. Allegations are made also against structures similar to enterprise foundations: eg see https://www.technologyreview.com/2020/02/17/844721/ai-openai-moonshot-elon-musk-sam-altman-greg-brockman-messy-secretive-reality/, regarding the nonprofit entity OpenAI, Inc.; or https://www.business-humanrights.org/en/companies/tata-group/, concerning Tata, an Indian group owning numerous companies worldwide with a set of trusts at the vertex (both links last accessed: 14 September 2025).

64 David Schröder/Steen Thomsen, 'Foundation Ownership and Sustainability' (2025), 91 J. Corp. Fin., no. 102740, p. 1, 5–14, 18–19; on the relevant methodology and sample, see ibid, pp. 3–4.

appear to be purpose-driven, attempting to holistically balance profits with social and environmental goals; long-term oriented (eg they replace board members less often), in sharp contrast with the often nearsighted short-termism of investor-owned firms;[65] to treat employees and the environment better;[66] to put in place a better governance, in terms of CSR strategies, board representation and stakeholders' engagement;[67] to invest more in research and development (R&D),[68] so being a potential catalyst for sustainable innovation.

Moreover, enterprise foundation-owned firms appear to perform no worse financially than other firms.[69] The latter finding goes against traditional agency theory: one may indeed expect that, without being backed by a for profit motivated shareholder, a firm would perform poorly in financial terms; plus, there would be higher agency costs given that the foundation self-perpetuating board of directors may be inclined to opportunistic behaviours.[70] But this seems not to be the case. A possible explanation is that enterprise foundation-owned firms receive more trust by stakeholders (eg talented employees, loyal consumers), with positive effects on the balance sheet too.[71]

II. Policy proposals: with a focus on charity enterprise foundations

If collective hybrids represent a sustainable tool, they should be adequately regulated by the law. As argued throughout this work, advancements in the regulatory framework are emerging (albeit slowly) and that can be seen favourably. However, the overall legal landscape appears still inadequate,

65 Christa Børsting et al, 'Industrial Foundations as Long-Term Owners' (2018), 26 Corp. Govern. Int. Rev., pp. 180–196.

66 Schröder/Thomsen (2025), p. 8: eg employees of enterprise foundation-owned firms are approximately 6 % more satisfied compared to the average employee satisfaction, and they also show lower injury rates; with respect to the environment, they demonstrate a lower environmental damage cost, both directly and indirectly, so causing less externalities and contributing less to the total environmental harm.

67 Ibid, p. 13: eg enterprise foundation-owned firms are more likely to establish sustainability committees and exhibit a 19 % increase of female directors' representation in their boards compared to other firms.

68 Thomsen (2023), pp. 10–11.

69 Ibid.

70 Hansmann/Thomsen (2018), pp. 4–5.

71 Thomsen (2018), p. 66, 69–70; Feldthusen (2023), p. 133.

with a wide uncertainty on how gaps will be filled in by the relevant national authorities and courts.

As previously pointed out, enterprise foundations may be gathered in three categories, according to the chased purpose: charity, fully business-oriented and family. Even if fully-business oriented and family purposes can be equally deserving, the most suited tool in sustainability terms seems to be an enterprise foundation animated by a charity purpose. This is because the subsidiary's profits would neither be fully reinvested in the business, nor assigned to family members; rather, they would be used to finance charitable deeds for the common good.

It is true that per se a charity enterprise foundation cannot guarantee orientation towards sustainability. After all, sustainability is not about making charity but about running a business in a more balanced way. In theory, a charity enterprise foundation may still be keen on maximising profits through the operating company. However, in practice, it creates an institutional set-up that discourages the above to occur. It removes indeed the incentive to do so, because no profits would be allocated for the benefit of investors or family members. As such, a well-rounded balance may be expected, with the operating company producing a moderate amount of profits, to be later used by the foundation according to the charitable aims precisely identified in the foundation's charter (eg green initiatives, social projects, education or art, etc.).

This conclusion is partially corroborated by some empirical findings, although not final. Charity enterprise foundations demonstrate stronger ESG performance, compared especially to family foundations,[72] but also to foundations that are not animated by meaningful environmental or social goals, ie those called herein fully business-oriented.[73] Such findings somehow match the theoretical assumptions that family foundations may be too focused on personal goals like family legacy and reputation; while fully business-oriented ones may excessively care about pursuing profits, given that the for profit motive (albeit slightly more blurred compared to investor-owned corporations) is still quite profound.

Hence, legislators should pay special attention to charity enterprise foundations, giving them an adequate and complete legal framework, so that they can free all their potential. This is crucial: currently, even the most advanced legal systems (eg Denmark) do not sufficiently differentiate in

72 Schröder/Thomsen (2025), pp. 3–4, 9.
73 Ibid, pp. 13–14.

terms of purpose. There is not a specific set of rules for charity enterprise foundations, as opposed to fully-business oriented and family ones.

Thus, de lege ferenda, it would be advisable to introduce a special regime for charity enterprise foundations.[74] This is the scope of the reform advocated herein, while its exact content may be more conveniently discussed in a future work.[75] In light of their sustainable aptitude – provided that effective mechanisms are in place to prevent abuses – having such foundations at the top of the (corporate) world may hold potential for a real transition.

74 Clearly, the hypothetical law can allow a margin of flexibility: it may also apply to enterprise foundations that combine multiple purposes, provided that charity is prevalent (eg the yearly share of profits reinvested and/or assigned to family members shall be below 50 %).

75 Eg combining valuable features of various jurisdictions: a transparent register (like in Germany), independence of board members, inclusion of employees into the governance trough a co-determination system (like in Denmark), stakeholders' engagement, mandatory auditors at least in bigger foundations beyond certain thresholds (like in France). Moreover, considering the altruistic purpose, a tax benefit would need to be granted; as a general principle, this benefit should not be excessively generous, since it would break neutrality and open up to this form being simply chosen for tax motives.

Regional Economic Communities and corporate water accountability: an ESG perspective

Jebby Romanus Gonza[*]

A. Introduction

In a historical context, multiple examples highlight the catastrophic consequences that can be caused by corporate water unaccountability: The Bhopal disaster in 1989 marked a peak in corporate negligence when Union Carbide's gas leak resulted in over 15,000 deaths and long-lasting soil and groundwater contamination.[1] In the 1993 Hinkley groundwater contamination, Pacific Gas and Electric Company used hexavalent chromium, a toxic chemical linked to cancer, at its gas compressor station, contaminating groundwater for 30 years.[2] In 2011, Chevron-Texaco Petroleum was accused of dumping billions of gallons of crude oil and toxic wastewater into the

---

* Dr. Jebby Romanus Gonza is a Legal Officer at the Office of the Secretary to the Council of the University of Dodoma, Tanzania. She has conducted Postdoctoral research in aspects of International Environmental Law and has completed a PhD in Public International Law (Regional Economic Integration Law) at the University of Bayreuth.

1 Broughton Edward, 'The Bhopal Disaster and its Aftermath: A Review' (2005), 4 Environmental Health No. 6, p. 1.

2 San Bernardino County Superior Court, Barstow Division, 18 March 1993 – No. A055529 – *Anderson and Others v Pacific Gas & Electric Co.*

Amazon rainforest during oil operations in Ecuador from 1964 to 1992.[3] Furthermore, in 2021, Shell Petroleum Development Company was sued before a Dutch Court and the United Kingdom (UK) Supreme Court for oil extraction in the Niger Delta that caused extensive water and soil pollution.[4]

All of these scandals reveal a common challenge for the law. Particularly, international law falls short of providing a binding legal framework that regulates the activities of corporations—including corporate water accountability.[5] At the international level, mechanisms are inadequate to ensure that corporations prevent human rights violations and environmental abuses in their business.[6] While there remains hesitation in recognizing that corporations have direct duties or even legal personality under international law,[7] they are generally regarded as significant actors in pursuing the Sustainable Development Goals (SDGs).

Specific to this context, SDG 6 (Ensure the Availability and Sustainable Management of Water and Sanitation) calls upon all states and stakeholders, including corporations.[8] It encompasses a broader responsibility, not just guaranteeing universal access to safe and affordable drinking water and sanitation, but also to protect and preserve freshwater resources and ecosystems.[9] Corporations contribute to water scarcity by depleting water sources through excessive use in various business and economic activities. These include agriculture, industrial processes, mining, oil extraction, power generation, and the spread of industrial pollution. If not properly managed, these activities can lead to pollution and damage to water sources, ultimately impacting human health and the environment. Additionally, corporate actions contribute to climate change, which worsens water scarci-

---

3 Permanent Court of Arbitration, PCA Case No. 2009–23 – *Chevron Corporation and Texaco Petroleum Corporation v. Ecuador (II).*

4 UK Supreme Court, 12 February 2021 – UKSC/2018/0068 – *Okpabi and others v Royal Dutch Shell Plc and another.*

5 Eghosa Ekhator, 'Multinational Corporations, Accountability and Environmental Justice: The Move towards Sub-Regional Litigation in Africa' (2022), 121(2) ZVglRWiss, p. 118.

6 Ross Fitzpatrick, 'Making Corporate Accountability Mandatory in the EU' (12 March 2022), https://www.iiea.com/images/uploads/resources/Making-Corporate-Accountability-Mandatory-In-The-EU.pdf (last accessed: 18 September 2025), p. 3.

7 Ekhator (2022), p.118.

8 United Nations General Assembly, Transforming our World: The 2030 Agenda for Sustainable Development, 25 September 2015, A/RES/70/1.

9 Ibid.

ty by increasing drought conditions. Yet, the traditional approach in international law regarding corporations' sustainability measures, including corporate water accountability, relies on soft law and voluntary corporate accountability mechanisms.[10]

This chapter argues that Regional Economic Communities (RECs) play a vital role in ensuring their member states not only meet targets under SDG 6 but also establish strong, binding mechanisms for corporate water accountability. Within the scope of this chapter, RECs refer to the cooperation of states established within a specific geographic region, supported through trade agreements aimed at reducing interstate and trade barriers. This chapter suggests that since RECs can regulate legal frameworks related to common markets, they can ensure that corporations are accountable for their water governance in their operations and supply chains by controlling access to the shared market.

On this basis, this chapter examines corporate water accountability as a crucial aspect of sustainability, particularly in Environmental, Social, and Governance (ESG) regulations and regional economic integration. It adopts a comparative legal approach across different RECs to evaluate how they have integrated water stewardship into their legal frameworks. The chapter will assess the regulatory approaches of key regions to determine the extent to which corporate entities are held accountable for their water usage, pollution, and environmental preservation efforts: the European Union, Association of Southeast Asian Nations, and East African Community. It highlights the legal obligations, reporting requirements, and enforcement mechanisms within the RECs while identifying best practices and gaps in current regulatory frameworks.

This chapter contextualizes the central theme of the study by recognizing water as a vital aspect of human life and dignity (B.). It highlights the importance of incorporating corporations into the sustainable development governance framework and provides justifications for corporate accountability in sustainability (ESG) aspects (C.). The Chapter highlights the significant role of RECs in sustainable development, particularly how RECs have established regulatory approaches that ensure corporate water

10 See, for instance, United Nations, Guiding Principles on Business and Human Rights: Implementing the United Nations 'Protect, Respect, and Remedy' Framework, 2011, A/HRC/17/31; OECD, 'Guidelines for Multinational Enterprises on Responsible Business Conduct' (2023), https://doi.org/10.1787/81f92357-en (last accessed: 18 September 2025).

accountability through ESG frameworks (D.), followed by a conclusion (E.).

B. Water security as a significant prerequisite to human life, dignity, and sustainable development

I. Recognition of the right to water

The current epoch has witnessed the concept of water security emerge as a prominent aspect of human well-being. Notably, water is recognized as indispensable for leading a life with human dignity.[11] It has been confirmed as a human right, providing for the entitlement to 'sufficient, safe, acceptable, physically accessible, and affordable water for personal and domestic use'.[12] Since 1976, the right to water has been regarded as implicit within the provisions of certain international covenants.[13] In July 2010, the United Nations General Assembly confirmed, under Resolution 64/292,[14] followed by the Human Rights Council Resolution 15/9 in September 2010,[15] that the right to water is a fundamental human right.

The right to water is considered closely linked and essential for achieving the right to an adequate standard of living, which encompasses the rights to food, the highest attainable standard of physical and mental health, the right to life, and human dignity. Although obligations related to the right to water and sanitation are subject to progressive realization due to resource limitations, many constitutions in both developing and developed countries recognize these rights as fundamental.[16]

---

11 UN Committee on Economic, Social and Cultural Rights (CESCR), 'General Comment No 15: The Right to Water (Art. 11 and 12 of the International Covenant on Economic, Social and Cultural Rights)', 20 January 2003, UN Doc E/C.12/2002/11, para 1.

12 Ibid, para. 2.

13 Chiara Macchi, 'Right to Water and the Threat of Business: Corporate Accountability and the State's Duty to Protect' (2017), 35 Nordic Journal of Human Rights, p. 186.

14 United Nations General Assembly, Resolution 64/292: The Human Right to Water and Sanitation, 28 July 2010, A/RES/64/292.

15 UN Human Rights Council, Resolution 15/9: Human rights and access to safe drinking water and sanitation, 6 October 2010, A/HRC/RES/15/9.

16 Constitution of the Republic of South Africa, 1996, s 27; Constitution of the Republic of Uganda, 1995, art 14; Constitution of Kenya, 2010, art 43(1)(d); Constitution of the Federal Democratic Republic of Ethiopia, 1995, art 90; Constitution of the Republic

Comment 15 by the UN Committee on Economic, Social and Cultural Rights (CESCR) emphasizes the interconnectedness between the right to water and sustainability.[17] Accordingly, the normative elements of the right to water require that it must be adequate for human dignity, life, and health. Similarly, water must be physically and economically accessible and of a safe quality.[18] Comment 15 advocates for a sustainable approach to securing the right to water, ensuring that both current and future generations can benefit from it.

Yet, international law imposes upon states—and not corporations—the obligations to respect, protect, and fulfil the right to water. But, states are accountable, under the responsibility to protect, for failing to prevent third parties—individuals, groups, corporations, and other entities/agents acting under their authority—from interfering with the enjoyment of the right to water.[19] For instance, states have an obligation to adopt the necessary and effective legislative and other measures that restrain third parties, including corporations, from polluting water sources and denying or limiting access to adequate water.[20] Similarly, an extraterritorial reach of the right to water requires states, their citizens, or corporations to refrain from actions that interfere, directly or indirectly, with the enjoyment of the right in other countries.[21] According to Article 2(2)(b) of the Convention on the Protection and Use of Transboundary Watercourses and International Lakes 1992 states must ensure that transboundary waters are used reasonably and equitably and avoid activities that may cause a transboundary impact.[22]

of Guatemala, 1996, art 127; Constitution of the Republic of Panama, 2004, art 114; Constitution of the Kingdom of Thailand, 2015, s 15; Constitution of the Plurinational State of Bolivia, 2009, art 16(1); Constitution of Nepal, 2015, art 35(4); California Water Code § 106.3 (2012).

17 UN Committee on Economic, Social and Cultural Rights (CESCR), General Comment No 15: The Right to Water (Art. 11 and 12 of the International Covenant on Economic, Social and Cultural Rights), 20 January 2003, UN Doc E/C.12/2002/11, paras. 10 et seqq.

18 Ibid, para. 12.

19 Ibid, para. 23.

20 Ibid, paras. 49 et seq.

21 Ibid, para. 31.

22 UN Economic Commission for Europe, Convention on the Protection and Use of Transboundary Watercourses and International Lakes, 6 October 1996, 1936 UNTS 269: Art. 1 defines transboundary impact to mean 'any significant adverse effect on the environment resulting from a change in the conditions of transboundary waters caused by a human activity (…)'. Also see the UNGA, Convention on the Law of the Non-Navigational Uses of International Watercourses, 17 August 2014, 36 ILM 700.

Within the context of sustainability, there has been a call for state parties to adopt comprehensive and integrated strategies to ensure sufficient and safe water for both present and future generations. This leads to an examination of the international community's efforts to achieve sustainable access to safe drinking water and sanitation for the global population.

II. Sustainable development and water

Ensuring access to safe water and sanitation remains one of the most fundamental goals pursued by the international community and the United Nations. Since 1977, particularly with the adoption of the Mar del Plata Plan of Action, there has been a growing emphasis on the need to ensure the orderly management of water resources for economic and social development.[23] Further emphasis on safeguarding water resources from pollution and ensuring sufficient supplies of high-quality water is placed by Chapter 18 of the Agenda 21, which builds upon the Rio Declaration of 1992.[24] Under Goal 7 of the Millennium Development Goals, the world's countries committed to ensuring environmental sustainability. Target 7.C required nations to 'halve, by 2015, the proportion of the population without sustainable access to safe drinking water and sanitation.'[25] While the 2012 statistics proudly reported reaching the target by increasing access to safe drinking water by 90 % compared to 76 % in 1990 globally, progress toward achieving better basic sanitation was regarded as slow.[26] Ensuring the availability and sustainable management of water and sanitation for all (SDG 6) is among the 17 Sustainable Development Goals (SDGs), which were adopted

23 UN Economic and Social Council, United Nations Water Conference, Mar del Plata Action Plan: United Nations Water Conference, 25 March 1977, E/CONF.70/29.C.

24 United Nations, 'Agenda 21: Programme of Action for Sustainable Development' (14 June 1992), https://sustainabledevelopment.un.org/content/documents/Agenda21.pdf (last accessed: 18 September 2025), chapter 18.

25 United Nations General Assembly, United Nations Millennium Declaration, 8 September 2000, A/RES/55/2. Also see United Nations Department of Public Information, Johannesburg Declaration on Sustainable Development and Plan of Implementation of the World Summit on Sustainable Development, 4 September 2002, A/Conf.199/20: which reaffirms Target 7.C of the Millennium Declaration.

26 World Health Organization and United Nations Children's Fund (UNICEF), 'Progress on Drinking Water and Sanitation: 2014 Update', https://iris.who.int/bitstream/handle/10665/112727/9789241507240_eng.pdf (last accessed: 18 September 2025), p. 25.

in September 2015 by the United Nations General Assembly under the 2030 Agenda for Sustainable Development.[27]

However, statistics demonstrate that making progress in access to water and sanitation for the global population under SDG 6 is still challenging. It is estimated that by 2030, approximately 2 billion people will still lack access to safely managed drinking water, 3 billion will be without safely managed sanitation, and 1.4 billion will be without basic hygiene services.[28] The United Nations Sustainable Development Report 2024 stipulates that 'in 2022, about 2.2 billion people still lacked safely managed drinking water, 3.5 billion went without safely managed sanitation (including 419 million who practiced open defecation), and 2 billion still had inadequate basic hygiene services (including 653 million with no facilities at all)'.[29]

The failure to achieve the six targets under Goal 6 of the 2030 Agenda for Sustainable Development is attributed to several factors. Specifically, just to list a few, climate-influenced changes that alter precipitation rates in the water cycles, the inability to meet funding costs for infrastructure and critical water projects (specifically in the Global South), poor water governance policies by governments including lack of coherence and collaboration among governments and private actors, degradation of water quality due to unsafe discharges and poor waste water treatment, and economic activities that result in polluting freshwater resources.[30] Regrettably, the failure to achieve SDG 6 frustrates the achievement of most goals of the 2030 Agenda for Sustainable Development. SDG 6 seems to be at the fulcrum—in a causal nexus manner—of achieving other goals of sustainable development and targets, such as poverty reduction (SDG 1), food security (SDG 2), health (SDG 3), energy (SDG 7), industry (SDG 9), sustainable cities (SDG 11), climate (SDG 13), and responsible consumption and production (SDG 12).

---

27 United Nations General Assembly, Transforming our World: The 2030 Agenda for Sustainable Development, 25 September 2015, A/RES/70/1, p. 18: Targets 6.1 – 6.6.

28 United Nations Department of Economic and Social Affairs, 'The Sustainable Development Goals Report 2024' (June 2024), https://doi.org/10.18356/9789213589755 (last accessed: 18 September 2025), pp. 20 et seq.

29 Ibid.

30 Jaivime Evaristo/Yusuf Jameel/Cecilia Tortajada/Raymond Yu Wang/James Horne/Howard Neukrug/Carlos Primo David/Angela Maria Fasnacht/Alan D. Ziegler/Asit Biswas, 'Water woes: the institutional challenges in achieving SDG 6' (2023), 6 Sustainability Earth Reviews No. 13.

Certainly, achieving the targets[31] set by SDG 6 is impossible without effective water governance policies—including the deployment of smart technology in water management and service delivery, increasing the efficiency of existing financing resources, and developing new financing paradigms.[32] Most importantly, multisector partnerships and cooperations are vital for unlocking potential. This way, actors at the national, regional, and global levels—the public sector, private sectors such as civil society organizations, and academia—can align and optimize resources to unlock the potential for achieving SDG 6.[33] Certainly, the successful achievement of SDG 6 requires integrating corporations into the sustainable development framework, as corporations are vital players in the global economy.

C. Corporations and sustainable water governance

I. Corporations as stewards of water sustainability

Corporations have been recognized since the 1940s as major players in the global economy due to their ability to utilize factors of production and achieve economic efficiency. However, corporations' endeavours to dominate the world economy tend to affect natural resources, including water resources, and cause environmental damage to a greater number of countries. In light of the foregoing, corporations are recognized as key actors that can contribute to achieving the SDGs, including those related to water sustainability.

The Preamble to the Stockholm Declaration of 1972 emphasizes the necessity for corporations to accept the responsibility of defending and

31 The six targets of SDG 6 advocate for achieving universal and equitable access to safe and affordable drinking water, sanitation, and hygiene for all, and end open defecation, taking into consideration the needs of women and girls and the vulnerable; improve water quality and safety by reducing pollution, and curtailing the release of hazardous chemicals, and increasing treatment of wastewater, recycling, and re-use; protection and restoration of water-related ecosystems.

32 United Nations, Sustainable Development Goal 6: Synthesis Report 2018 on Water and Sanitation (July 2018), https://www.unwater.org/sites/default/files/app/uploads/2018/12/SDG6_SynthesisReport2018_WaterandSanitation_04122018.pdf (last accessed: 18 September 2025), p. 181.

33 Ibid.

improving the environment for present and future generations.[34] From the foregoing, it is possible to infer that corporations are required to be responsible by incorporating environmental concerns into their decision-making processes, including paying due regard to the intergenerational principle—the needs of water by future generations.

Chapter 30 of the Agenda 21, regarding 'strengthening the role of business and industry', is one of the most substantial soft laws, stipulating corporate responsibility in the area of sustainable development by the UN General Assembly.[35] Accordingly, the policies and operations of businesses and industries, including transnational corporations, are encouraged to play a significant role in mitigating their impacts on resource use and the environment.[36] The Chapter 30 introduces the concept of corporate responsibility and 'responsible care' by emphasizing the need for (transnational) corporations to recognize environmental management as a priority and a key determinant of sustainable development.[37] One may regard corporate accountability in water management as emphasised by Chapter 30, when it encourages the provision of annual reports on environmental records, particularly the use of energy and natural resources.[38] Regarding health and sustainable development, the World Summit on Sustainable Development, held in Johannesburg in 2002,[39] highlights the importance of corporations participating in public-private multisector partnerships to secure international funding and technologies for safe water, sanitation, and waste management in rural and urban areas of developing countries and transition economies.

The 2030 Agenda for Sustainable Development explicitly encourages private businesses to contribute to achieving the SDGs by using their creativity and innovation to solve sustainable development challenges.[40] SDG 6 does

---

34 United Nations, Report of the United Nations Conference on the Human Environment, 1973, A/CONF.48/14/Rev.1, p. 3.

35 Elisa Morgera, Corporate Environmental Accountability in International Law, 2nd ed. (2020), p. 9.

36 United Nations, Agenda 21: UN Conference on Environment and Development, 12 August 1992, A/CONF.151/26, para 30.2.

37 Ibid, para. 30.3.

38 Ibid, para. 30.10.

39 United Nations Department of Public Information, Johannesburg Declaration on Sustainable Development and Plan of Implementation of the World Summit on Sustainable Development, 4 September 2002, A/Conf.199/20, p. 32.

40 See United Nations General Assembly, Transforming our World: The 2030 Agenda for Sustainable Development, 25 September 2015, A/RES/70/1, para 67.

not explicitly define the role of corporations or the private sector. However, the importance of corporations can be inferred from the various targets. For instance, Target 6.4 can be interpreted as highlighting the adoption of water-efficient processes by corporations, especially in agriculture and manufacturing, to enhance water use efficiency.

II. Integrating Sustainability Practices in Corporate Water Governance

The traditional view of corporate purpose is seen to focus on maximizing the company's value by considering the interests of its shareholders. Corporate water governance is regarded as a comprehensive framework and process for decision-making and implementing policies related to the use and management of water resources.[41] Accountability is considered one of the key attributes of water governance, as it aims to ensure that the entity responsible for water services and resources is answerable to its stakeholders for its actions and omissions.[42] The United Nations Framework on Business and Human Rights, 2011, identifies essential principles for fulfilling corporate accountability.[43] It regards business enterprises as 'specialized organs of society' with the responsibility (i) to respect all human rights and avoid causing or contributing to adverse human rights impacts through their activities; (ii) to establish policies and processes that embed the corporates' responsibility to protect; (iii) conduct human rights due diligence to identify, prevent, mitigate, and address their adverse human rights impacts; (iv) communicate how they handle these impacts; and (v) cooperate in the remediation process through legitimate means if they have caused or contributed to adverse impacts.[44] This framework does not create a direct legal obligation for corporations under international law; yet, it provides a basis for public and governments to regulate corporations' impacts on water resource allocation decisions.

41 James Hazelton, 'Developments in Corporate Water Accounting and Accountability', in David Crowther/Muhammad Azizul Islam (eds.), Modern Organisational Governance (2015), pp. 28, 30.

42 Alejandro Jiménez/Panchali Saikia/Ricard Giné/Pilar Avello/James Leten/Birgitta Liss Lymer/Kerry Schneider/Robin Ward, 'Unpacking Water Governance: A Framework for Practitioners' (2020), 12 Water No. 827, p. 12.

43 United Nations, Guiding Principles on Business and Human Rights: Implementing the United Nations 'Protect, Respect, and Remedy' Framework, 2011, A/HRC/17/31.

44 Ibid, pp. 1, 13–26.

A new approach to corporate governance highlights the importance of considering all stakeholders. Consistent with the three pillars of sustainable development—environmental protection, social development, and economic development—integrating sustainability into corporate governance involves monitoring the company's financial performance, as well as its commitment to advancing ESG factors in investment decisions. Incorporating ESG factors into investment decisions is viewed as a means to create more stable and predictable markets, ultimately benefiting market participants and supporting the sustainable growth of global society.[45]

The Global Compact Report, a 2004 UN Report, promulgated guidelines and recommendations on how to integrate better environmental, social, and corporate governance issues in corporations' overall management.[46] The integration of ESG factors in investment decisions is viewed as 'falling within the scope of the fiduciary duty of trustees, financial advisers, asset managers and intermediary institutions.'[47] The UN Global Compact Report outlines principles that focus on human rights, labour, environment, and anti-corruption, which corporations are expected to follow. Principles 7 to 9 of the UN Global Compact Report emphasize that businesses should support a precautionary approach to environmental challenges, undertake initiatives to promote greater environmental responsibility, and encourage the development and diffusion of environmentally friendly technologies.

ESG is recognized as a crucial element of corporate accountability and water governance. Effective water governance is essential for ensuring the sustainable and efficient use of water, addressing water-related challenges, and promoting fair access to water services.[48] ESG reporting enhances transparency for investors, regulators, and consumers regarding environ-

45 Katrin Hummel/Dominik Jobst, 'An Overview of Corporate Sustainability Reporting Legislation in the European Union' (2024), 21 Accounting in Europe, pp. 320, 322 et seqq.

46 United Nations Global Compact Office, 'The Global Compact Leaders' Summit: United Nations Headquarters, 24 June 2004: Final Report' (24 June 2004), https://d306pr3pise04h.cloudfront.net/docs/news_events%2F8.1%2Fsummit_rep_fin.pdf (last accessed: 18 September 2025).

47 UN Global Compact, 'Who cares Wins: Connecting Financial Markets to a Changing World' (December 2004), https://documents1.worldbank.org/curated/en/280911488968799581/pdf/113237-WP-WhoCaresWins-2004.pdf (last accessed: 18 September 2025), p. 3.

48 Gabriel Minea/Elena Simina Lakatos/Roxana Maria Druta/Alina Moldovan/Lucian Marius Lupu/Lucian Ionel Cioca, 'The Role of ESG in Driving Sustainable Innovation in Water Sector: From Gaps to Governance' (2025), 17 Water No. 2259, pp. 3 et seq.

mental risks, particularly those associated with water resources. ESG reports accurately depict companies' efforts in water management, including measures to reduce water usage, improve wastewater treatment, and lower their environmental footprint. The Global Reporting Initiative (GRI) and the Sustainability Accounting Standards Board (SASB) provide essential frameworks for meeting reporting requirements.

D. RECs and sustainable development

Within the framework of International Law, RECs are established under the WTO Agreement—Article XXIV of the General Agreement on Tariffs and Trade, and Article V of the General Agreement on Trade in Services—which permits its members to create regional trade agreements, such as free trade areas (FTAs) and customs unions (CUs), outside the multilateral system.

While the 2030 Agenda acknowledges that the implementation of the SDGs must occur through multi-stakeholder engagement and participation, it also recognizes the significant role of RECs in sustainable development:

> We acknowledge the importance of the regional and subregional dimensions, regional economic integration, and interconnectivity in sustainable development. Regional and subregional frameworks can facilitate the effective translation of sustainable development policies into concrete action at the national level.[49]

RECs play a vital role in promoting sustainability through developing and enforcing both binding and non-binding legal instruments, harmonizing policy frameworks, and establishing institutional mechanisms for sustainable development at the regional and national levels. Agenda 21 emphasizes the significance of RECs in promoting trade, economic growth, and environmental sustainability. Additionally, Principle 12 of the Rio Declaration, 1992, emphasizes the significance of RECs by stating that 'States should cooperate to promote a supportive and open international economic system that would lead to economic growth and sustainable development.'

From a perspective where most instruments related to sustainable development are established under soft law, RECs are crucial actors in trans-

49 United Nations General Assembly, Transforming our World: The 2030 Agenda for Sustainable Development, 25 September 2015, A/RES/70/1, para. 21.

forming sustainability from mere soft law—political ambitions—into legal obligations or enforceable frameworks. These frameworks not only guide member states but also hold them accountable for their acts or omissions related to implementing the SDGs.

I. European Union (EU)

It is worth noting that member states of the European Union[50] emphasize their commitments to achieve sustainable development as a key objective in the European Treaties. Based on this commitment, the EU positions itself as a leading REC in promoting corporate water accountability through its ESG frameworks and regulations. The EU Green Deal from 2019 is a policy incentive that advocates for EU member states to promote water-efficient technologies, reduce industrial water pollution, and invest in nature-based solutions and resilient water systems.[51] In aligning with the Green Deal the EU enhances corporate water accountability by implementing mandatory corporate reporting systems. The Corporate Sustainability Reporting Directive (CSRD) requires EU and non-EU companies operating within the EU with an average of more than 500 employees[52] to report detailed, high-quality ESG data related to water use and marine resources. Specifically, companies must disclose information on all significant environmental factors, including impacts on and dependencies on climate, air, land, water, and biodiversity.[53] To ensure the standardization of reporting, the EU

50 Established by the Maastricht Treaty (also known as the Treaty on European Union) but initially founded by the European Coal and Steel Community (ECSC) in 1951 and composed of 27 states, namely Austria, Belgium, Bulgaria, Croatia, Cyprus, Czech Republic, Denmark, Estonia, Finland France, Germany, Greece, Hungary, Ireland, Italy, Latvia, Lithuania, Luxembourg, Malta, the Netherlands, Poland, Portugal, Romania, Slovakia, Slovenia, and Spain, Sweden.

51 European Commission, The European Green Deal 2019, 11.12.2019, COM (2019) 640 final, pp. 9, 11, 14.

52 Directive (EU) 2022/2464 of the European Parliament and of the Council of 14 December 2022 amending Regulation (EU) No 537/2014, Directive 2004/109/EC, Directive 2006/43/EC and Directive 2013/34/EU, as regards corporate sustainability reporting, 16 December 2022, OJ L 322, para. 17.

53 Ibid, para. 46.

has established the European Sustainability Reporting Standards (ESRS), which formulates strict guidelines for ESG information disclosure.[54]

Additionally, the EU Taxonomy for Sustainable Activities[55] complements the Green Deal and the CSRD by providing a classification system for sustainable economic activities. Corporate activities are considered environmentally sustainable if they meet the six environmental objectives set by the European Commission,[56] one of which includes the sustainable use and protection of water and marine resources. To comply with the water-related objective, corporate activities must significantly contribute to achieving or maintaining the good status of, or preventing the deterioration of, water bodies and marine waters.[57]

The Corporate Sustainability Due Diligence Directive (CSDDD) requires companies to make meaningful contributions to the sustainability transition by conducting due diligence to identify and address water-related risks across supply chains.[58] The Directive adopts a negative obligation approach by prohibiting corporate actions that cause measurable environmental degradation, such as water pollution, excessive water consumption, or other impacts on natural resources that deny a person access to safe and clean drinking water or make it difficult for a person to access sanitary facilities.[59] The Sustainable Finance Disclosure Regulation (SFDR) mandates financial institutions to disclose how they incorporate ESG risks, including water, into their investment decisions.[60] This encourages companies to manage water use effectively to remain attractive to investors.

---

54 Commission Delegated Regulation (EU) 2023/2772 of 31 July 2023 supplementing Directive 2013/34/EU of the European Parliament and of the Council as regards sustainability reporting standards, 22 December 2023, OJ L 2023/2772.

55 Regulation (EU) 2020/852 of the European Parliament and of the Council of 18 June 2020 on the establishment of a framework to facilitate sustainable investment, and amending Regulation (EU) 2019/2088, 22 June 2020, OJ L 198, pp. 13 et seq.

56 Ibid, para. 23: the six objectives include climate change mitigation; climate change adaptation; the sustainable use and protection of water and marine resources; the transition to a circular economy; pollution prevention and control; and the protection and restoration of biodiversity and ecosystems.

57 Ibid, Art 12.

58 Directive (EU) 2024/1760 of the European Parliament and of the Council of 13 June 2024 on corporate sustainability due diligence and amending Directive (EU) 2019/1937 and Regulation (EU) 2023/2859, 13 June 2024, OJ 2024/1760, paras. 15 and 32.

59 Ibid, para. 32.

60 Regulation (EU) 2019/2088 of the European Parliament and of the Council of 27 November 2019 on sustainability-related disclosures in the financial services sec-

Overall, the EU has strengthened corporate water accountability through ESG by requiring detailed water-related disclosures, setting standards and thresholds for sustainable water practices, embedding water as a critical metric in financial and sustainability regulations, and enforcing supply chain due diligence obligations.

II. Association of Southeast Asian Nations (ASEAN)

The members of the Association of Southeast Asian Nations (ASEAN)[61] have committed themselves under Article 1(9) of the ASEAN Charter 2008 to promoting sustainable development, ensuring the protection of the region's environment, and the sustainability of its natural resources. In an attempt to promote sustainability, ASEAN has established the ASEAN Taxonomy for Sustainable Finance (Version 3).[62] The ASEAN Taxonomy for Sustainable Finance aims to harmonize the classification of sustainable activities and assets across ASEAN states. Specifically, it provides guidance to potential users (ie corporations, investors, and governments) on whether an activity can be classified as sustainable under the ASEAN Taxonomy, demonstrating that it contributes to at least one of the environmental objectives.[63] The environmental objectives include climate change mitigation, adaptation, protection of healthy ecosystems and biodiversity, resource resilience, and the transition to a circular economy.[64] Thus, activities intended to promote aspects of protecting healthy ecosystems and biodiversity include undertakings that conform to the principles of safety, preservation, or restoration of water bodies.[65] ASEAN has introduced voluntary but influential ESG standards. It identifies sustainable activities, including wa-

tor, 9 December 2019, OJ L 317: See the definition of 'sustainable investment' under Art 2.

61 Established in 1967 and composed of 10 Southeast Asian countries: Brunei Darussalam, the Kingdom of Cambodia, the Republic of Indonesia, the Lao People's Democratic Republic, Malaysia, the Union of Myanmar, the Republic of the Philippines, the Republic of Singapore, the Kingdom of Thailand, and the Socialist Republic of Vietnam.

62 ASEAN Taxonomy Board, 'ASEAN Taxonomy for Sustainable Finance, Version 3' (20 December 2024), https://asean.org/wp-content/uploads/2024/12/ASEAN-Taxonomy-Finalised-Version-3-4.pdf (last accessed: 18 September 2025).

63 Ibid, p. 28.

64 Ibid, pp. 28, 53.

65 Ibid, p. 30.

ter and wastewater management, as priorities for green investment.[66] The ASEAN Corporate Governance Scorecard (ACGS),[67] although not explicitly focused on water, evaluates transparency and sustainability practices that intersect with environmental management. Consequently, corporations seeking investment or improved credit ratings are now incentivized to report on water use, risks, and pollution control to align with taxonomy guidelines and ESG scoring systems.[68] Within the context of cross-border water and pollution initiatives, ASEAN has promoted transboundary water cooperation and shared pollution standards, especially for the Mekong River Basin and industrial water discharges.[69] ASEAN member states coordinate to harmonize pollution thresholds.

III. East African Community (EAC)

The EAC Treaty 1999 emphasizes an endeavour of member states to achieve sustainable development as a fundamental principle of the Community.[70] The EAC[71] member states commit to cooperating in fostering joint, efficient, and sustainable management and utilization of natural resources.[72] ESG frameworks are not yet fully institutionalized in the EAC; however, specific key initiatives and policy trends have indirectly enhanced water accountability.

66 Ibid.

67 ASEAN Capital Market Forum, 'ASEAN Corporate Governance Scorecard Self Assessment (2023–2024)' (2024), https://www.theacmf.org/initiatives/corporate-governance/-2024-asean-corporate-governance-scorecard (last accessed: 18 September 2025).

68 Ibid (n 17).

69 See ASEAN Member States, ASEAN Declaration on Environmental Sustainability (20 November 2007), https://cil.nus.edu.sg/wp-content/uploads/2019/02/2007-ASEAN-Declaration-on-Environmental-Sustainability.pdf (last accessed: 18 September 2025), para. 6.

70 See Treaty for the Establishment of the East African Community, 30 November 1999: Art 5.

71 The EAC is a regional intergovernmental organization composed of Kenya, Tanzania, Uganda, Rwanda, Burundi, South Sudan, the Democratic Republic of Congo, and Somalia.

72 See EAC Protocol on Environment and Natural Resources Management, 29 April 2006, Art 111 to 114 (not yet in force).

The EAC Protocol on Sustainable Development of Lake Victoria (2003)[73] and the EAC Protocol on Environment and Natural Resources Management (2006) emphasize the member states' commitment to promoting transboundary water governance frameworks aimed at protecting shared water resources, particularly in the Lake Victoria Basin.[74] Article 4(2) of the Basin Protocol stipulates that member states will adhere to the principle of equitable and reasonable utilisation of water resources in the management of the Victoria Basin resources. Similarly, Article 45 of the Lake Victoria Basin Protocol requires member states to report on the measures they have taken to implement the Protocol's provisions for the sustainable development of Lake Victoria, as well as their effectiveness in achieving the objectives. The member states have established the Lake Victoria Basin Commission (LVBC),[75] which compels governments to regulate industrial discharges, water abstraction, and water quality—particularly in high-pollution sectors such as agriculture, mining, and manufacturing. Companies operating near key water basins face stricter oversight and compliance is increasingly linked to licensing, taxation, and access to financing.[76]

Furthermore, the EAC member states have been pressured by multilateral donors (eg, World Bank, International Finance Corporation, African Development Bank) to incorporate ESG reporting mechanism in donor-funded projects.[77] These initiatives by multilateral donors have played a significant role in advancing water accountability through ESG-aligned funding in the regional blocks. For instance, water infrastructure and sani-

73 See ibid, Art 45.

74 See ibid, preamble.

75 See the organizational structure and functions of the Lake Victoria Basin Commission and other institutions under the Protocol for Sustainable Development of Lake Victoria Basin, 29 November 2003, Art 33 and 34. Also see Global Environment Facility's (GEF), Lake Victoria – Results, https://www.iwlearn.net/iw-projects/basins/908/results (last accessed 18 September 2025).

76 See Protocol on Sustainable Development of Lake Victoria, 29 November 2003, Artt 6, 14, 16, 25, 29, 33.

77 See, for instance, World Bank, 'Environmental and Social Framework' (2020), https://www.worldbank.org/en/projects-operations/environmental-and-social-framework (last accessed: 18 September 2025); United Nations Development Programme, 'UNDP Social and Environmental Standards (UNDP 2021)' (2021), https://www.undp.org/publications/undp-social-and-environmental-standards (last accessed: 18 September 2025); African Development Bank, 'Environmental, Social and Governance (ESG)' https://www.afdb.org/en/topics-and-sectors/topics/environmental-social-and-governance-esg (last accessed: 18 September 2025).

tation projects often require corporate ESG alignment and reporting via the International Finance Corporation Performance Standards.

E. Conclusion: Evaluation and synergy

Yet, the real test is whether regional integration law has created binding legal frameworks to regulate corporate activities, including water accountability. This chapter suggests that RECs have made progress in establishing harmonized standards that guide sustainability practices at the regional level.

Notably, RECs have achieved important milestones in advancing corporate water accountability. The European Union (EU) stands out by eliminating voluntary mechanisms of corporate water accountability and replacing them with binding frameworks that mandate Environmental, Social, and Governance (ESG) reporting. In doing so, the EU sets a benchmark for other RECs. It demonstrates that regional legal frameworks can go beyond guidance and deliver enforceable obligations in corporate water accountability. By contrast, RECs such as the Association of Southeast Asian Nations (ASEAN) and the East African Community (EAC) continue to rely largely on voluntary mechanisms. While this reflects recognition of the importance of sustainability, reliance on voluntary water disclosures risks inconsistent implementation, as corporations may not always adopt rigorous accountability practices. Nevertheless, both ASEAN and the EAC have shown progress by creating legal and institutional mechanisms to safeguard transboundary water resources. In the case of the EAC, donor-funded projects, regional trade, and cooperation with international organizations have further strengthened corporate water accountability.

Overall, RECs contribute to regional policy harmonization and standardization by establishing region-wide frameworks and directives that align environmental standards with water use and pollution control among member states. Through RECs, it becomes easier to enforce ESG standards and prevent companies from exploiting regulatory loopholes across borders. RECs help standardize and set ESG Reporting Requirements, making it simpler for companies to report consistently on water use, pollution, and conservation efforts.

The ambivalent promise of the abyss: Deep-seabed mining, governance gap and the race for critical minerals

Sanjeet Ruhal

A. Introduction: the ocean's dilemma

The deep ocean, once conceived as a silent, lifeless abyss, is now recognised as the planet's largest habitable space, a realm of staggering biodiversity and critical ecosystem services.[1] It is also the Earth's final frontier for resource extraction. Beneath the crushing pressure and perpetual darkness of the abyssal plains lie vast, untapped deposits of polymetallic nodules—potato-sized concretions rich in cobalt, nickel, copper, and manganese alongside cobalt-rich crusts and polymetallic sulphides.[2] These are the very metals and minerals essential for the twenty-first century's clean-energy technologies, from electric-vehicle batteries to wind turbines and solar panels,[3] as well as indispensable components of advanced electronics, defence

1 Samuel Georgian/Sarah Hameed/Lance Morgan/Diva J. Amon/U. Rashid Sumaila/David Johns/William J. Ripple, 'Scientists' Warning of an Imperilled Ocean' (2022), 272 Biological Conservation, p. 1.
2 International Seabed Authority, 'Polymetallic Nodules' (2022), https://www.isa.org.jm/exploration-contracts/polymetallic-nodules/ (last accessed: 6 October 2025).
3 Ryan Murdock, 'Deep Sea Mining and the Green Transition' (16 October 2023), https://hir.harvard.edu/deep-sea-mining-and-the-green-transition/ (last accessed: 6 October 2025).

systems, and aerospace industries.[4] As the world intensifies its pursuit of a low-carbon future, these deep-sea deposits are increasingly viewed as a strategic solution to the limitations and harms of land-based mining.[5]

Yet, this new frontier is not without formidable legal, ecological, and political challenges. The very notion of extracting resources from one of the planet's most pristine and poorly understood ecosystems raises difficult questions about sustainability, equity, and governance.[6] At stake is not only the health of the ocean floor but the credibility of the international legal frameworks designed to manage humanity's shared resources.

The convergence of ecological fragility and industrial necessity has created an oceanic dilemma with profound legal, environmental, and geopolitical implications. Global decarbonisation has sharply increased demand for critical minerals, with the International Energy Agency predicting demand will triple by 2030. Yet, terrestrial mining, which currently supplies these minerals, is marked by severe environmental damage, political instability, and human rights abuses.[7] The Democratic Republic of the Congo, for example, produces around 70 per cent of global cobalt in conditions linked to conflict and labour exploitation.[8] Concentration of resources has also generated bottlenecks, leaving supply chains exposed to disruption and geopolitical manipulation.[9]

4 European Parliament, 'Commission Must Tackle China's Export Restrictions on Rare Earth Elements' (4 July 2025), https://www.europarl.europa.eu/news/en/press-room/20250704IPR29456/commission-must-tackle-china-s-export-restrictions-on-rare-earth-elements (last accessed: 6 October 2025).

5 United Nations Environment Programme, 'Critical Energy Transition Minerals' (2024), https://www.unep.org/topics/energy/renewable-energy/critical-energy-transition-minerals (last accessed: 6 October 2025).

6 Lisa Depraiter/Stéphane Goutte/Thomas Porcher, 'Geopolitical risk and the global supply of rare earth permanent magnets: Insights from China's export trends' (2025), 146 Energy Economics, no. 108496, p. 4.

7 International Peace Information Service, 'Mineral Extraction, Environmental Harm, and Conflict: The Role of EU Due Diligence in Promoting Sustainable Practices in Conflict Hotspots' (16 April 2025), https://ipisresearch.be/weekly-briefing/mineral-extraction-environmental-harm-and-conflict-the-role-of-eu-due-diligence-in-promoting-sustainable-practices-in-conflict-hotspots/ (last accessed: 6 October 2025).

8 Sasha Lezhnev, 'Testimony of Sasha Lezhnev – Democracy and Human Rights in the Democratic Republic of the Congo' (29 November 2016), https://enoughproject.org/reports/testimony-sasha-lezhnev-democracy-and-human-rights-democratic-republic-congo (last accessed: 6 October 2025).

9 European Parliament, 'Commission Must Tackle China's Export Restrictions on Rare Earth Elements' (4 July 2025). https://www.europarl.europa.eu/news/en/press-room/2

Against this backdrop, deep-seabed mining (DSM) is promoted as a strategically less damaging alternative,[10] securing minerals for renewable technologies without deforestation, child labour, or biodiversity loss in terrestrial hotspots.[11] Its legal foundation lies in the United Nations Convention on the Law of the Sea (UNCLOS),[12] which declares resources of "the Area" the common heritage of mankind (CHM),[13] to be managed by the International Seabed Authority (ISA) for the benefit of all, particularly developing States, and with environmental safeguards. Properly regulated, DSM could support UN Sustainable Development Goals[14] by supplying materials for climate action while reducing harmful land-based extraction.[15]

Yet, this rationale faces strong opposition. Scientific knowledge of the deep sea remains limited, and mining may cause irreversible biodiversity loss,[16] disrupt carbon sinks, and damage ecosystems[17] that recover only over millennia. This has led to a growing global chorus of scientists, governments, and corporations calling for a moratorium,[18] invoking UNCLOS

02507041PR29456/commission-must-tackle-china-s-export-restrictions-on-rare-earth-elements (last accessed: 12 February 2026).

10 Pedro Madureira/Dale Squires/Luísa Pinto Ribeiro, 'The International Seabed Authority and the United Nations 2030 Agenda for sustainable development' (2023), 86 Resources Policy, no. 103166.

11 Ibid., pp. 4 et seq.

12 United Nations, Convention on the Law of the Sea, 10 December 1982, 1833 UNTS 397.

13 Ibid, Art. 136.

14 International Seabed Authority, 'ISA's contributions to the achievement of the 2030 Agenda' (November 2021), https://www.isa.org.jm/isa-and-the-2030-agenda/ (last accessed: 6 October 2025).

15 Madureira/Squires/Ribeiro (2023), pp. 3 et seqq.

16 Wenbin Ma/Kairui Zhang/Yanlian Du/Xiangwei Liu/Yijun Shen, 'Status of Sustainability Development of Deep-Sea Mining Activities' (2022), 10 Journal of Marine Science and Engineering, no. 1508, p. 14.

17 European Commission, Joint Communication to the European Parliament, the Council, the European Economic and Social Committee and the Committee of the Regions Setting the Course for a Sustainable Blue Planet – Joint Communication on the EU's International Ocean Governance Agenda, 24 June 2022, JOIN (2022) 28 final.

18 Matteo Bedendi/Lorenzo Schiano di Pepe, 'A New Chapter of Ocean Governance and the European Union: Codification Efforts and Prospects of a Moratorium at the International Seabed Authority' (2025), 40(2) The International Journal of Marine and Coastal Law, p. 403, 413.

Article 145 and the precautionary principle, or an outright ban on DSM until its consequences can be fully understood.[19]

Geopolitical competition compounds the issue.[20] Critical minerals are indispensable for defence, renewables and advanced electronics. China now controls the lion's share of rare earths,[21] controlling over ninety per cent of certain rare earth elements[22] and has used export restrictions in trade disputes,[23] revealing Western vulnerabilities and spurring a search for alternative supply chains.[24] This has ignited a desperate search for alternative and more secure supply chains, with DSM emerging as a potential new frontier.[25] Nations are investing heavily in DSM capabilities, including the U.S., which, despite not being a party to UNCLOS, has recently issued a controversial Executive Order supporting unilateral seabed mining initiatives beyond national jurisdiction.[26] This position, grounded in domestic law, has raised alarm about a possible breach of international law and a direct challenge to the CHM regime, undermining the legitimacy of the ISA and threatening to fracture the shared legal framework in favour of national self-interest.[27]

At the heart of this maelstrom lies a critical legal vacuum. While the ISA has issued regulations for exploration, it has yet to finalise the comprehen-

19 United Nations, Convention on the Law of the Sea, 10 December 1982, 1833 UNTS 397.
20 Nik Martin, 'How China wields rare earths as a strategic weapon' (23 June 2025), https://www.dw.com/en/how-china-wields-rare-earths-as-a-strategic-weapon/a-72868760 (last accessed: 6 October 2025).
21 Depraiter/Goutte/Porcher (2025).
22 John Liu/Simone McCarthy, 'US, China formalize deal on rare earth shipments in trade breakthrough', (27 June 2025), https://edition.cnn.com/2025/06/27/business/us-china-trade-deal-agreement-signed-intl-hnk (last accessed: 6 October 2025).
23 Depraiter/Goutte/Porcher (2025), p. 2.
24 Tiago Tecelão Martins, 'A Brief History of US-China Rare Earth Rivalry' (8 December 2023), https://www.geopoliticalmonitor.com/a-brief-history-of-us-china-rare-earth-rivalry/ (last accessed: 6 October 2025).
25 The White House, 'Unleashing America's Offshore Critical Minerals and Resources' (24 April 2025), https://www.whitehouse.gov/presidential-actions/2025/04/unleashing-americas-offshore-critical-minerals-and-resources/ (last accessed: 6 October 2025).
26 ibid.
27 Leticia Reis de Carvalho, 'Statement on the US Executive Order: "Unleashing America's Offshore Critical Minerals and Resources"' (30 April 2025), https://www.isa.org.jm/news/statement-on-the-us-executive-order-unleashing-americas-offshore-critical-minerals-and-resources/ (last accessed: 6 October 2025).

sive 'Mining Code', the legally binding rules for commercial exploitation.[28] While the regulatory landscape for deep-seabed mining was evolving,[29] the nation of Nauru initiated a procedural step to prompt the ISA to prioritise the finalisation of comprehensive regulations.[30] The activation of the 'two-year rule' under the Implementation Agreement of UNCLOS put pressure on the ISA to either finalise these regulations promptly or to consider mining applications under existing provisions.[31] This has created pressure to establish a robust framework where environmental, economic, and other impacts are thoroughly assessed to ensure sustainable development.

This article argues that deep-seabed mining governance is at a critical juncture, navigating the complex interplay of sustainability, equity, and geopolitical competition. It posits that the framework must urgently reconcile these pressures through the finalisation and robust implementation of a comprehensive, science-based, and enforceable legal framework within the Mining Code. This framework is essential to balance marine environmental protection, equitable benefit distribution as envisioned by UNCLOS, and the demands of the global resource race. Without it, the potential of the

28 International Seabed Authority, 'FAQs about the International Seabed Authority and deep-sea mining' (2025), https://www.isa.org.jm/faq-for-media/ (last accessed: 6 October 2025).

29 International Seabed Authority, 'The Mining Code: Draft exploitation regulations' (2025), https://isa.org.jm/the-mining-code/draft-exploitation-regulations-2/ (last accessed: 6 October 2025): ISA has undertaken work since 2014 to develop regulations for the exploitation of mineral resources in the Area. The process began with preliminary work in expert workshops, involving the preparation of a number of expert studies, discussion papers and open stakeholder consultations. It culminated in the development of draft regulations submitted by the Legal and Technical Commission for consideration by the Council in 2019.

30 Government of the Republic of Nauru, 'Nauru requests the International Seabed Authority Council to adopt rules and regulations within two years' (2021), https://www.nauru.gov.nr/government/departments/department-of-foreign-affairs-and-trade/faqs-on-2-year-notice.aspx (last accessed: 6 October 2025).

31 Annex Section 1(15) of the Agreement Relating to the Implementation of Part XI of the United Nations Convention on the Law of the Sea (New York, 28 July 1994, in force 28 July 1996) 1836 UNTS 42. The 'two-year rule' was inserted as a pragmatic mechanism to prevent indefinite delays in the finalisation of the deep seabed mining regulatory framework. It reflects a compromise between states advocating for the rapid exploitation of resources and those prioritising the establishment of comprehensive environmental protections. Essentially, it was designed to create a definitive timeline, compelling the ISA to conclude its regulatory work or face the potential for exploitation applications to proceed under a less complete legal regime, thereby providing a pathway forward in the absence of full consensus.

deep-sea risks becoming unsustainable, undermining the common heritage for potentially short-term gains.

B. Legal foundations of deep-seabed mining

The legal architecture governing the deep seabed stands as one of the most ambitious and idealistic constructs in modern international law. Envisaged in the mid-twentieth century,[32] it represents a profound vision of global co-operation and shared stewardship over areas beyond national jurisdiction.[33] The doctrine of CHM's centrepiece sought to transcend traditional notions of State sovereignty by declaring the resources of the international seabed Area as the collective property of all nations, to be managed for the common good.[34] The translation of this principle into a functional legal regime through UNCLOS and the establishment of the ISA represent a landmark achievement in global governance.[35] However, contemporary challenges highlight the difficulties of implementing such a visionary concept amid the practical realities of State interests and commercial pressures.

I. Historical development: From mare liberum to a common heritage

For centuries, the law of the sea was dominated by the Grotian doctrine of *mare liberum*—the freedom of the seas—which primarily governed navigation and fishing on the high seas.[36] This principle, famously expounded by Hugo Grotius in 1618 and asserted earlier by figures like Queen Elizabeth I in 1580 that the oceans and their resources were open to all and incapable of appropriation.[37] The deep seabed itself, however, remained

32 Sanjeet Ruhal, 'India and Global Maritime Commons', in Shashikala Gurpur/Aakarsh Banyal (eds.), International Law in Pursuit of Global Justice (2025), pp. 61 et seq.

33 Ibid.

34 Yoshifumi Tanaka, The International Law of the Sea, 3rd ed. (2019), pp. 25 et seq.

35 International Seabed Authority, 'Secretary-General Annual Report 2024' (28 June 2024), https://www.isa.org.jm/wp-content/uploads/2024/06/ISA_Secretary_General_Annual_Report_2024.pdf (last accessed: 6 October 2025), p. 16.

36 Satya N. Nandan/Michael W. Lodge/Shabtai Rosenne, 'The Development of the Regime for Deep Seabed Mining' (11 April 2002), https://www.isa.org.jm/wp-content/uploads/2022/06/regime-ae.pdf (last accessed: 6 October 2025), p. 3.

37 Ibid.

largely outside the explicit scope of international law, often viewed as a *terra nullius* theoretically open to appropriation by any State with the requisite technological capacity.[38]

This status quo was dramatically challenged in 1967 when Arvid Pardo, Malta's Ambassador to the United Nations, delivered a seminal address to the UN General Assembly.[39] Pardo warned of an impending technological gold rush to the seabed, foreseeing that it would benefit only a handful of wealthy, technologically advanced nations.[40] He cautioned that such unchecked exploitation could reignite colonial-style competition, lead to the militarisation of the oceans, and inflict irreversible environmental harm.[41] To prevent this outcome, Pardo advanced a revolutionary proposal: that the seabed and its mineral resources beyond national jurisdiction be designated the 'common heritage of mankind.'[42]

This was not merely a call for shared access but for collective ownership and management. Under this principle, the Area could not be subject to sovereign claims; its resources were to be managed by an international body, and the financial benefits derived from their exploitation were to be shared equitably, with a particular focus on benefiting developing countries. This vision resonated powerfully in a post-colonial era, and in 1970, the UN General Assembly adopted the Declaration of Principles Governing the Sea-Bed and the Ocean Floor (Resolution 2749 (XXV)), formally enshrining the CHM principle in international law.[43]

II. Part XI of UNCLOS: codifying the common heritage

The CHM became the cornerstone of the protracted negotiations that ultimately culminated in Part XI of the Convention. As the longest, most complex, and politically contentious section, Part XI is devoted entirely

38 Ibid, p. 60.
39 Ruhal (2025), p. 62.
40 Ibid.
41 Nandan/Lodge/Rosenne, 'The Development of the Regime for Deep Seabed Mining' (11 April 2002), p. 17.
42 Ibid.
43 United Nations General Assembly, Declaration of Principles Governing the Sea-Bed and the Ocean Floor, and the Subsoil Thereof, beyond the Limits of National Jurisdiction, 17 December 1970, A_RES_2749(XXV).

to the Area and establishes the legal and institutional framework for operationalising the CHM principle.[44] Its key provisions establish:

- *Legal status of the Area and its resources:* Article 136 unequivocally states: 'The Area and its resources are the common heritage of mankind'. Article 137 follows logically, stipulating that no State shall claim or exercise sovereignty over any part of the Area or its resources, and no State or person can appropriate any part thereof. The rights to the resources are vested in humankind as a whole, on whose behalf the International Seabed Authority shall act.[45]
- *Institutional management:* The ISA is established as a treaty-based autonomous international organisation with its own legal personality, mandated to serve as a trustee for humanity. As a specialized intergovernmental body, its mandate encompasses: adopting regulations for prospecting, exploration, and exploitation in the Area; approving and overseeing mining contracts; ensuring marine environmental protection (Article 145); equitably distributing monetary and non-monetary benefits to all States, with priority given to developing nations (Article 140); and operating the Enterprise—its commercial arm intended to carry out mining on behalf of the international community. This institutional arrangement is designed to ensure non-appropriation, equitable access, and environmentally responsible resource management.
- *The parallel system of exploitation:* Reflecting the influence of the New International Economic Order (NIEO) movement of the 1970s,[46] the original Part XI envisaged a 'parallel system' for exploitation. Under this system, private and state-sponsored contractors seeking mining licences were required to submit two sites of equivalent commercial value. One would be allocated to the contractor; the other would be reserved for the Enterprise, which was to act on behalf of developing States. This system was coupled with provisions for mandatory technology transfer from contractors to both the Enterprise and developing countries, and financial obligations to support the Enterprise's operations.

---

44 Part XI is the longest and most complex part of the Convention, consisting of 58 out of its 320 Articles and an associated Annex.

45 Art. 137(2) UNCLOS.

46 John E. Noyes, 'The Common Heritage of Mankind: Past, Present, and Future' (2011), 40 Denver Journal of International Law and Policy, p. 447, 459.

This ambitious framework quickly became a source of major controversy. Industrialised nations—most notably the United States under the Reagan administration—criticised the original Part XI as economically impractical and ideologically incompatible with free-market principles. Their objections focused on the mandatory technology transfer regime, production controls intended to protect land-based mining, and the perceived over-representation of developing countries within ISA decision-making structures.[47] As a result, the United States refused to sign UNCLOS in 1982, citing Part XI as the principal obstacle, and instead adopted domestic legislation to govern the deep-seabed mining activities of U.S. nationals.[48]

This impasse threatened the universality and effectiveness of the Convention.[49] To resolve it, a series of informal consultations, initiated by the UN Secretary-General in 1990, led to the 1994 Agreement Relating to the Implementation of Part XI.[50] The Agreement fundamentally altered the deep-seabed mining regime to make it more palatable to industrialised nations.[51] It eliminated mandatory technology transfer, revised the Council's voting structure to give greater weight to States with significant economic interests, and scaled back the operational ambitions of the Enterprise, stipulating that it would initially operate through joint ventures.[52] This compromise paved the way for near-universal ratification of UNCLOS, although the United States remains a notable outsider, having not ratified the treaty to this day.[53]

III. The role and regulations of the International Seabed Authority

As mentioned before, the ISA's primary function is to develop the rules, regulations, and procedures—collectively known as the 'Mining Code' to

47 Nandan/Lodge/Rosenne, 'The Development of the Regime for Deep Seabed Mining' (11 April 2002), p. 2.

48 United States, Deep Seabed Hard Mineral Resources Act 1980.

49 Michael W. Lodge, 'The Deep Seabed', in Donald R. Rothwell/Alex G. Oude Elferink/Karen N. Scott/Tim Stephens (eds.), The Oxford Handbook of the Law of the Sea (2015), p. 277, 277.

50 Ambassador Nandan served as Special Representative of the Secretary-General and Under-Secretary-General for Oceans and the Law of the Sea from 1984 to 1993.

51 Lodge (2015), p. 227.

52 Noyes (2011), p. 464.

53 National Ocean Service, 'Deep Seabed Hard Minerals Mining' (9 August 2025), https://oceanservice.noaa.gov/deep-seabed-mining/ (last accessed: 6 October 2025).

govern prospecting, exploration, and exploitation of deep-seabed minerals.[54] This must be done in accordance with its dual mandate: promoting the development of the Area's resources while ensuring the effective protection of the marine environment from harmful effects.[55]

To date, the ISA has successfully established regulations for the first two phases of mining. The ISA has issued separate regulations for the exploration of polymetallic nodules (adopted in 2000, updated in 2013), polymetallic sulphides (2010), and cobalt-rich ferromanganese crusts (2012).[56] Under these rules, the ISA has entered into 15-year contracts for the exploration of polymetallic nodules (PMN), polymetallic sulphides (PMS) and cobalt-rich ferromanganese crusts (CFC) in the deep seabed with 22 contractors.[57] These contracts grant exclusive rights to explore vast tracts of the seabed, primarily in the Clarion-Clipperton Zone (CCZ) in the Pacific Ocean, but also in the Indian and Atlantic Oceans.

However, the crucial third piece of the Mining Code—the *exploitation regulations*—remains in draft form.[58] The finalisation of these rules has been the subject of intense and often contentious negotiations for years, delayed by the complexity of the issues and deep divisions among member States on key questions.

IV. Current legal challenges and the regulatory gap

The paramount legal challenge confronting the DSM regime remains the absence of a finalised Mining Code, perpetuating significant regulatory un-

54 Nandan/Lodge/Rosenne, 'The Development of the Regime for Deep Seabed Mining' (11 April 2002), p. 57.

55 Art. 145 UNCLOS.

56 Michael W. Lodge, 'International Seabed Authority (ISA)' (September 2020), https://opil.ouplaw.com/display/10.1093/law:epil/9780199231690/law-9780199231690-e1180 (last accessed: 6 October 2025).

57 International Seabed Authority, Exploration Contracts (2025), https://www.isa.org.jm/exploration-contracts/ (last accessed: 6 October 2025): Nineteen of these contracts are for the exploration for polymetallic nodules in the Clarion-Clipperton Fracture Zone (17) and Central Indian Ocean Basin (1), and Western Pacific Ocean (1). In addition, there are seven (7) contracts for exploration for polymetallic sulphides in the South West Indian Ridge, Central Indian Ridge and the Mid-Atlantic Ridge and five (5) contracts for exploration for cobalt-rich crusts in the Western Pacific Ocean.

58 International Seabed Authority, 'The Mining Code: Draft Exploitation Regulations' (2022).

certainty. Since 2014, the International Seabed Authority (ISA) has undertaken the complex task of developing this comprehensive regulatory framework.[59] Progress, however, has been consistently impeded by substantive disagreements among member States concerning requisite environmental safeguards, equitable benefit-sharing mechanisms, and appropriate fiscal terms. A critical procedural juncture was reached in June 2021 when Nauru, acting as the sponsoring State for the contractor The Metals Company (TMC), invoked the 'two-year rule' stipulated in Section 1(15) of the 1994 Agreement relating to the Implementation of Part XI of UNCLOS.[60] This invocation triggered a formal requirement for the ISA Council to finalise the exploitation regulations by 9 July 2023. The Council's failure to meet this deadline activated the rule's secondary obligation: the Council must now 'consider and provisionally approve' any exploitation contract application submitted to it, irrespective of the ongoing regulatory gaps. This development has substantially intensified pressure on the ISA and amplified widespread concerns regarding the potential for premature mining approvals, the influence of commercial entities within the regulatory process,[61] and the attendant risk of significant and potentially irreversible harm to the marine environment due to the lack of fully operational safeguards.[62]

The current state of the regulatory framework is embodied in the *Revised Consolidated Text* of January 2025, further advanced by the ISA Council's second reading in July 2025.[63] This draft represents the most substantial progress towards codification, establishing foundational governance architecture, although numerous critical provisions remain subject to negotia-

---

59 Ibid.

60 Ryan Murdock, 'Deep Sea Mining and the Green Transition' (16 October 2023).

61 Ibid. In March 2023, Michael Lodge, then Secretary-General of ISA, faced criticism from diplomats and officials of Germany, France, and Costa Rica for allegedly exceeding his mandate as an impartial facilitator. Critics argued that Lodge advocated for expediting the regulatory drafting process, aligning with interests favouring accelerated deep-sea mining. Concurrently, discussions between the ISA and The Metals Company (TMC), a Canadian mining corporation, dating back to 2007, have raised concerns. These communications, focused on identifying optimal mining exploration areas, are permitted but have been criticised as inconsistent with the ISA's mandate to engage directly with states rather than multinational corporations.

62 Georgian/Hameed/Morgan/Amon/Sumaila/Johns/Ripple (2022), p. 1.

63 International Seabed Authority, 'Draft regulations on exploitation of Mineral resources in the Area' (10 January 2025), https://www.isa.org.jm/wp-content/uploads/2025/01/10012025-Revised-Consolidated-Text-2.pdf (last accessed: 6 October 2025).

tion and refinement. On environmental protection, the draft codifies a multi-tiered framework.

Regarding liability, the draft provisions aim to clarify responsibilities across key actors: contractors, sponsoring States, and the ISA itself.[64] Contractors are expressly required to carry financial insurance sufficient to cover potential environmental risks and liabilities,[65] while sponsoring States retain their overarching due diligence obligations[66] and related jurisprudence.[67]

The draft operationalizes the UNCLOS standard of preventing serious harm and requires contractors to systematically identify risks, assess scientific uncertainties, and adopt mitigation measures, underpinned by a mitigation hierarchy prioritising avoidance, minimisation, mitigation, and remediation where feasible.[68] Furthermore, an Environmental Compensa-

64 The draft regulations are designed to provide a comprehensive legal framework for mineral exploitation, clarifying the distinct responsibilities of contractors, sponsoring States, and the Authority itself. For example, specific duties of contractors are set out in Part IV, while the obligations of sponsoring States and the Authority are detailed in Part I and Part VII, respectively.

65 International Seabed Authority, 'Draft regulations on exploitation of Mineral resources in the Area' (10 January 2025), reg. 36.

66 Art. 139 UNCLOS.

67 Request for an Advisory Opinion submitted by the Commission of Small Island States on Climate Change and International Law Advisory Opinion, 21 May 2024, ITLOS Rep 2024, paras. 210–221, 233–240; Ghana/Côte d'Ivoire (Provisional Measures) (Order, 25 April 2015) ITLOS Rep 2015, p. 146, paras 84–89, 102; Responsibilities and Obligations of States Sponsoring Persons and Entities with respect to Activities in the Area (Advisory Opinion, 1 February 2011) ITLOS Rep 2011, p. 10, paras 110–122, 230–235; Land Reclamation by Singapore in and around the Straits of Johor (Malaysia v Singapore) (Provisional Measures, 8 October 2003) ITLOS Rep 2003, p. 10, paras 99–106, 121; MOX Plant (Ireland v United Kingdom) (Provisional Measures, 3 December 2001) ITLOS Rep 2001, p. 95, paras 82–89, 106; Southern Bluefin Tuna Cases (New Zealand v Japan; Australia v Japan) (Provisional Measures, 27 August 1999) ITLOS Rep 1999, p. 280, paras 70–77; Obligations of States in respect of Climate Change (Advisory Opinion, 23 July 2025) ICJ Rep, paras 158–170, 254–270; Pulp Mills on the River Uruguay (Argentina v Uruguay) (Judgment) [2010] ICJ Rep 14, paras 197–205, 204, South China Sea Arbitration (Philippines v China) (Award, 12 July 2016) PCA Case No 2013–19, paras 947–991, 992–1011; Guyana v Suriname (Award, 17 September 2007) PCA Case No 2004–04, 30 RIAA 1, paras 445–454, 465.

68 International Seabed Authority, 'Draft regulations on exploitation of Mineral resources in the Area' (10 January 2025), regs. 2, reg. 44, 46, 47, 49.

tion Fund is established to address irremediable residual harm, enforcing the polluter-pays principle.[69]

Concurrently, the draft regulations propose key institutional reforms to improve governance and transparency. These reforms include the establishment of a Compliance Committee[70] and new inspection powers to monitor and report on activities.[71] The draft also enhances transparency by mandating public access to environmental data[72] and requiring stakeholder consultations.[73]

The draft regulations outline the financial architecture, but key elements remain unresolved and highly contested. While proposals for royalty structures, payment mechanisms, audit requirements, and penalties for non-compliance are included, their final details, which are critical for the economic viability of projects and equitable benefit-sharing, are still under negotiation. Similarly, the specific methods for distributing financial and other benefits, a core obligation under CHM,[74] have not been finalised. Therefore, the *Revised Consolidated Text* marks a critical transition from aspirational principles to concrete rules, yet it remains incomplete.

Simultaneously, the regime faces significant external pressures challenging its universality from the non-parties of UNCLOS. Recent activities by U.S. government entities, exploring pathways to engage in DSM exploitation under the authority of domestic legislation,[75] specifically the Deep Seabed Hard Mineral Resources Act of 1980 raises substantial legal and

69 International Seabed Authority, 'Draft regulations on exploitation of Mineral resources in the Area' (10 January 2025), reg. 54 establishes the Environmental Compensation Fund as a last-resort mechanism for addressing unforeseen or unmitigated environmental damage. In alignment with the 'polluter-pays' principle, contractors are primarily responsible for financing measures to mitigate and remedy any harm caused by their activities. The fund serves as a backstop, financing these measures only when a contractor is unable to fully meet its liability for unlawful environmental damage that was not anticipated in the Plan of Work or resulted from a breach of a condition of approval.

70 Ibid., reg. 102.

71 Ibid., regs. 96 et seqq.

72 Ibid., reg. 92 bis.

73 Ibid., regs. 93 bis, 93 ter.

74 Art. 140 UNCLOS.

75 United States Congress, 'Seabed Mining in Areas Beyond National Jurisdiction: Issues for Congress' (15 July 2025), https://www.congress.gov/crs-product/R47324 (last accessed: 6 October 2025).

political concerns.[76] Any unilateral move by the U.S. to authorize exploitation outside the ISA framework would constitute a direct challenge to the Authority's exclusive mandate under UNCLOS and the foundational CHM principle.[77] Such action risks triggering broader disregard for the international regime, potentially leading to uncoordinated exploitation by other States, thereby undermining decades of multilateral efforts dedicated to ensuring environmental protection and the equitable sharing of benefits from the international seabed.[78]

C. DSM: necessities v. uncertainties

The debate over deep-seabed mining (DSM) is ultimately a contest between necessity and uncertainty. On one side, proponents emphasise the indispensable role of DSM in securing the critical minerals required for the global energy transition. On the other, critics highlight the profound environmental risks and economic doubts that continue to shadow the industry. This tension has come to define one of the most significant natural resource debates of the twenty-first century.

Proponents of DSM advance three principal arguments. First, they point to the mineral demands of decarbonisation.[79] The technologies underpinning the transition to renewable energy—electric vehicles, batteries, wind turbines, and solar panels—are intensely mineral-dependent.[80] Global demand for nickel, cobalt, copper, and manganese is projected to rise sharply over the coming decades.[81] At present, the supply chains for these minerals

76 United States, Deep Seabed Hard Mineral Resources Act, 28 June 1980, Pub. L. No. 96–283, 94 Stat. 553.

77 United States Congress, 'Seabed Mining in Areas Beyond National Jurisdiction: Issues for Congress' (15 July 2025) https://www.congress.gov/crs-product/R47324 (last accessed: 12 February 2026).

78 Leticia Carvalho, 'Thirty-Fifth Meeting of States Parties to the United Nations Convention on the Law of the Sea: Agenda item 9: Information reported by the Secretary-General of the International Seabed Authority' (23 June 2025), https://www.isa.org.jm/wp-content/uploads/2025/06/SG_Statement-Thirty-fifth-meeting-of-State-Parties-to-UNCLOS_Agenda-Item-9.pdf (last accessed: 6 October 2025).

79 Oliver Ashford/Jonathan Baines/Melissa Barbanell/Ke Wang, 'What We Know About Deep-Sea Mining — and What We Don't' (23 July 2025), https://www.wri.org/insights/deep-sea-mining-explained (last accessed: 6 October 2025).

80 Ibid.

81 Kirsten Hund/Daniele La Porta/Thao P. Fabregas/Tim Laing/John Drexhage, 'Minerals for Climate Action: The Mineral Intensity of the Clean Energy Transition' (2020),

are highly concentrated, with over 70 per cent of cobalt production located in the Democratic Republic of Congo,[82] nearly 40 per cent of copper output concentrated in Chile and Peru,[83] and the refining of rare earths and other critical minerals dominated by China.[84] This geographical concentration creates acute supply risks, exposing importing States to political instability and, in the case of China, to the potential for deliberate supply-chain manipulation.[85] DSM, its advocates contend, could mitigate such vulnerabilities by providing access to resources located in the international seabed,[86] thereby diversifying supply away from terrestrial chokepoints.

Second, the terrestrial mining industry carries with it significant social and environmental costs.[87] Land-based mining has been closely linked with deforestation, water pollution, biodiversity loss, displacement of local communities, and in some cases, child labour and other human rights violations.[88] By contrast, DSM would occur thousands of metres below the ocean surface and far from human settlements, eliminating risks of deforestation and displacement. It is argued that, if properly regulated, DSM could be designed to avoid the most egregious social harms associated with terrestrial mining, offering a cleaner and more ethically acceptable alternative.[89]

Third, terrestrial deposits are increasingly of lower grade, meaning that more earth, water, and energy must be expended to yield the same amount

https://documents1.worldbank.org/curated/en/099052423172525564/pdf/P16627806f5aa400508f8c0bdcba0878a3e.pdf (last accessed: 6 October 2025), pp. 71 et seqq.

82 Natural Resources Canada, 'Cobalt Facts' (2023), https://natural-resources.canada.ca/minerals-mining/mining-data-statistics-analysis/minerals-metals-facts/cobalt-facts (last accessed: 6 October 2025).

83 Carla Selman/Veronica Retamales Burford/Johanna Marris, 'Chile and Peru's copper for energy transition' (5 April 2023), https://www.spglobal.com/sustainable1/en/insights/special-editorial/chile-and-peru-s-copper-for-energy-transition (last accessed: 6 October 2025).

84 International Energy Agency, 'Executive summary: the role of critical minerals in clean energy transitions' (5 May 2021), https://www.iea.org/reports/the-role-of-critical-minerals-in-clean-energy-transitions/executive-summary (last accessed: 6 October 2025).

85 Depraiter/Goutte/Porcher (2025), p. 2.

86 Murdock, 'Deep Sea Mining and the Green Transition' (16 October 2023).

87 Madureira/Squires/Ribeiro (2023), pp. 3 et seqq.

88 Ibid.

89 Ibid.

of metal.[90] By comparison, polymetallic nodules on the abyssal plains contain high concentrations of multiple metals within a single ore body.[91] This, proponents argue, provides efficiencies unavailable on land. Industry projections suggest that a single DSM operation could supply a substantial share of annual cobalt demand, thereby reducing pressure on terrestrial sources.

Yet, these claims are strongly contested. Critics argue that DSM carries environmental and economic uncertainties of a scale that cannot be ignored. The deep seabed is not barren, but rather the largest and least explored biome on Earth, hosting fragile ecosystems adapted to conditions of extreme pressure, darkness, and low temperatures.[92] Polymetallic nodules themselves are slow-forming substrates that provide habitat for unique organisms, many of which have only recently been discovered. Mining would entail the direct removal of nodules, along with the organisms attached to or inhabiting them, resulting in irreversible habitat destruction. Sediment plumes generated by seabed vehicles and discharge from surface vessels could spread for tens or even hundreds of kilometres, smothering benthic communities, releasing toxic metals, and disrupting filter-feeding species.[93] In addition, DSM operations would introduce light and noise pollution into an environment evolved in silence and darkness,[94] with potential impacts on deep-sea fauna and even on migratory megafauna such as whales. Perhaps most troubling, disturbing deep-sea sediments could interfere with

---

90 Daina Paulikas/Steven Katona/Erika Ilves/Saleem H. Ali, 'Deep-sea Nodules versus Land Ores: A Comparative Systems Analysis of Mining and Processing Wastes for Battery-metal Supply Chains' (2022), 26 Journal of Industrial Ecology, p. 2154, 2155 et seq.: The study suggests nodule exploitation may yield less waste with lower severities, potentially alleviating terrestrial mining's intensification, but caveats include uncertain plume effects and the need for comprehensive life-cycle assessments. It advocates balanced policymaking under the International Seabed Authority, emphasising scientific safeguards to minimise ecological harm while meeting sustainable development goals.

91 Aurora Cato/Philippe Evoy, 'Exploring plausible future scenarios of deep seabed mining in international waters' (2025), 24 Earth System Governance, no. 100249.

92 Ashford/Baines/Barbanell/Wang, 'What We Know About Deep-Sea Min-ing — and What We Don't' (23 July 2025).

93 Lamjahao Sitlhou/Parthasarathi Chakraborty, 'Comparing deep-sea polymetallic nodule mining technologies and evaluating their probable impacts on deep-sea pollution' (2024), 206 Marine Pollution Bulletin, no. 116762, pp. 13 et seqq.

94 Kathryn A. Miller/Kirsten F. Thompson/Paul Johnston/David Santillo, 'An Overview of Seabed Mining Including the Current State of Development, Environmental Impacts, and Knowledge Gaps' (2018), 4 frontiers in Marine Science, no. 418, p. 15.

the ocean's role as a carbon sink, undermining global climate regulation and creating a paradox where mining undertaken to advance the energy transition may in fact exacerbate climate risks.[95]

The critics also highlight that economic viability adds another layer of uncertainty.[96] The costs of seabed metals are unlikely to be competitive given market fluctuations and the rapid evolution of battery technology, which increasingly favours lithium, iron, phosphorus, and sodium over cobalt, nickel, copper, and manganese—the very minerals targeted by DSM.[97]

DSM technologies designed for large-scale seabed mining have yet to demonstrate their feasibility in the harsh deep-sea environment. The collapse of Nautilus Minerals' Solwara 1 project in Papua New Guinea, which ended in bankruptcy before extraction began, illustrates the significant financial risks for both investors and host States.[98] Investor scepticism has only grown, as major early participants, including Lockheed Martin and Maersk, have exited the sector, citing market volatility and regulatory risk.

Furthermore, DSM's economic case is weakened by the rapid rise of alternatives. The circular economy promises significant reductions in demand for virgin minerals, with the International Energy Agency estimating that recycling could meet a quarter of cobalt demand and nearly 40 per cent of copper and nickel demand by 2050.[99] At the same time, technological innovation is shifting markets away from cobalt and nickel altogether, as evidenced by the widespread adoption of lithium iron phosphate (LFP) batteries and the development of sodium-ion technologies.[100] In light of these competing trends, DSM's necessity for the energy transition may be less compelling than its advocates suggest.

---

95 Ibid., pp. 15 et seq.

96 Bobbi-Jo Dobush/Maddie Warner, 'Deep Seabed Mining Isn't Worth the Financial Risk' (2024), https://oceanfdn.org/wp-content/uploads/2024/02/dsm-finance-brief-2024.pdf (last accessed: 6 October 2025), p. 1: The report highlights that DSM remains an unproven industrial venture, marked by profound technological, financial, and regulatory uncertainties. Its business cases often rely on unrealistic assumptions about future metal demand and ignore the volatility of mineral markets; for instance, cobalt prices fell by 10 per cent between 2016 and 2023 despite a 2,000 per cent increase in electric vehicle production.

97 Ibid., p. 2.

98 Justin Alger/Jessica F. Green/Kate J. Neville/Susan Park/Stacy D. VanDeveer/D. G. Webster, 'The false promise of deep-sea mining' (2025), 4 njp ocean sustainability, no. 21, p. 2.

99 Ashford/Baines/Barbanell/Wang, 'What We Know About Deep-Sea Mining — and What We Don't' (23 July 2025).

100 Dobush/Warner, 'Deep Seabed Mining Isn't Worth the Financial Risk' (2024), p. 19.

D. Geopolitics as the new battleground

Although framed primarily in environmental and economic terms, the DSM debate is increasingly geopolitical. The race for critical minerals has transformed supply chains into arenas of strategic competition, with access to resources now equated with national power. The most striking precedent lies in China's dominance of rare earth elements.[101] Controlling roughly 70 per cent of global production and over 90 per cent of processing, Beijing has repeatedly demonstrated its willingness to use resource leverage as a geopolitical tool,[102] most notably during a dispute with Japan in 2010[103] and in the context of trade tensions with the United States.[104] This pattern has spurred Western States to diversify supply through domestic mining, recycling, and partnerships, but rebuilding supply chains is costly and slow. Against this backdrop, the deep seabed is increasingly perceived as a potential buffer against Chinese dominance.[105]

This resource geopolitics is producing fractures in the multilateral regime. Although the United States is not a Party to UNCLOS, the prohibition on unilateral mining activities in the Area is widely accepted, binding upon all States. The issuance of the Executive Order,[106] coupled with The Metals Company's submission of applications to the National Oceanic and Atmospheric Administration (NOAA) for deep-sea mining licences,[107]

---

101 Tom LaTourrette/Fabian Villalobos/Elisa Yoshiara/Zohan Hasan Tariq, 'The Potential Impact of Seabed Mining on Critical Mineral Supply Chains and Global Geopolitics' (9 April 2025), https://www.rand.org/content/dam/rand/pubs/research_reports/RRA3500/RRA3560-1/RAND_RRA3560-1.pdf (last accessed: 6 October 2025), pp. 1 et seq.

102 Ibid.

103 Martin, 'How China wields rare earths as a strategic weapon' (23 June 2025).

104 Reuters, 'Trump Says China Will Supply Rare Earths, US to Allow Students' (11 June 2025), https://www.reuters.com/world/china/trump-says-china-will-supply-rare-earths-us-allow-students-2025-06-11/ (last accessed: 6 October 2025).

105 Craig Hart, 'Mapping China's strategy for rare earths dominance' (13 June 2025), https://www.atlanticcouncil.org/in-depth-research-reports/issue-brief/mapping-chinas-strategy-for-rare-earths-dominance/ (last accessed: 6 October 2025).

106 The White House, 'Unleashing America's Offshore Critical Minerals and Resources' (24 April 2025).

107 The Metals Company, 'The Metals Company to Apply for Permits under Existing U.S. Mining Code for Deep-Sea Minerals in the High Seas in Second Quarter of 2025' (27 March 2025), https://investors.metals.co/news-releases/news-release-details/metals-company-apply-permits-under-existing-us-mining-code-deep/ (last accessed: 6 October 2025).

under the Deep Seabed Hard Mineral Resources Act of 1980,[108] has intensified concerns that the U.S. may seek to circumvent the ISA framework. However, the U.S. cannot credibly claim persistent objector status, as it has consistently acknowledged the core principles of the seabed regime and even signed the 1994 Implementing Agreement.[109] These developments have led the ISA to reaffirm that the Area's resources form part of the common heritage of mankind and that no State may unilaterally exploit them.[110]

Within the ISA, divisions are equally stark. Over twenty States, including Germany, France, Spain, Canada, Brazil, and numerous Pacific Island nations, support a precautionary pause or moratorium.[111] They are opposed by a pro-mining bloc including China, Russia, and small island States sponsoring contractors such as Nauru and Tonga. This polarisation has slowed consensus-building within the Council and highlights the fragility of the cooperative vision underpinning UNCLOS.

Equity remains another unresolved fault line. The promise of the common heritage principle was that seabed resources would be managed and shared equitably, especially for the benefit of developing countries. Yet, proposals for payment regimes have been criticised for disproportionately benefiting contractors and sponsoring States, leaving minimal returns for distribution among the wider membership. Practices of 'sponsorships of

---

108 United States, Deep Seabed Hard Mineral Resources Act, 28 June 1980, Pub. L. No. 96–283, 94 Stat. 553.

109 Vienna Convention on the Law of Treaties, 23 May 1969, 1155 UNTS 331, art. 18(a). By signing the 1994 supplementary agreement to the United Nations Convention on the Law of the Sea (UNCLOS), the United States incurred a legal obligation under Article 18(a) of the Vienna Convention on the Law of Treaties (VCLT) to refrain from acts that would defeat the object and purpose of the treaty. Although the U.S. is not a party to the VCLT, this principle is widely considered customary international law. The core purpose of the UNCLOS deep-seabed mining framework is to regulate activities in 'the Area' as the 'common heritage of mankind' through the International Seabed Authority (ISA). Therefore, the U.S. remains under an international obligation to not undermine the ISA or the principle that the seabed is a global commons.

110 Eileen Travers, 'Deep-sea must not turn into 'Wild West' of rare minerals exploitation, agency head says' (24 July 2025), https://news.un.org/en/story/2025/07/1165482 (last accessed: 6 October 2025).

111 Kathy-Ann Brown, 'The Draft Regulations on Exploitation of Mineral Resources in the Area: "A Work in Progress"', in Alfonso Ascencio-Herrera/Myron H. Nordquist (eds.), The United Nations Convention on the Law of the Sea, Part XI Regime and the International Seabed Authority: A Twenty-Five Year Journey (2022), p. 328.

convenience', where companies based in developed economies operate under the sponsorship of small, economically vulnerable island States, have drawn sharp criticism.[112] These arrangements risk exposing developing States to liability without corresponding benefits, replicating extractive patterns familiar from terrestrial mining.

The geopolitics of deep-seabed mining is thus a complex tapestry of strategic anxiety, national ambition, and systemic inequity. The race for rare earths and critical minerals has not only created the impetus for DSM but is also shaping its development in ways that threaten to undermine the cooperative, equitable vision upon which its legal framework was built. The seabed, far from being a peaceful commons, is becoming a new frontier where the enduring struggles over resources, power, and justice are being played out in the dark depths of the ocean.

E. Conclusion: Charting a sustainable course

The prospect of deep-seabed mining has brought the international community to a critical juncture, one defined by the intersecting pressures of resource demand, ecological vulnerability, and geopolitical rivalry. At the heart of this debate lies the principle of the *common heritage of mankind*, originally envisioned as a framework for multilateral cooperation and equitable benefit-sharing. Yet, that principle is now under strain, threatened by the accelerating push to commercialise the seabed. At the same time, the deep ocean is emerging as a theatre of strategic competition among States, amplifying the danger that short-term geopolitical imperatives will override both ecological prudence and international legal commitments.

Therefore, the governance gap for deep-seabed mining is now the decisive legal issue. The Mining Code remains unfinished, scientific knowledge of deep-sea impacts is incomplete, and geopolitical pressures are increasing the risk of unilateral action. These facts create a clear legal and policy choice: either complete a robust multilateral framework before any commercial exploitation proceeds or accept the likelihood of fragmented practice that will weaken the authority of the international regime.

A practical roadmap follows from this assessment. First, finalise the exploitation rules in the Mining Code on the basis of the precautionary approach, with clear thresholds and mandatory, peer-reviewed environmental

112 Cato/Evoy (2025), p. 6.

assessments. Second, require continuous, independent monitoring and a liability and compensation mechanism based on strict liability and an operational compensation fund. Third, maintain a pause on the grant and exercise of exploitation licences until these safeguards are in place and key scientific uncertainties are narrowed. Fourth, reform ISA governance to improve transparency, wider stakeholder participation, and equitable benefit-sharing so that sponsorship arrangements cannot be used to evade obligations. These measures are necessary to reconcile resource needs with environmental protection and distributive fairness.

If States adopt this course, the international regime can remain the primary vehicle for managing the Area and for distributing benefits in an orderly way. If not, the result will be legal fragmentation, reduced investment security, and a higher risk of irreversible harm to a unique global ecosystem. The choice is therefore institutional and legal rather than purely technical: it requires States to align short-term interests with a rules-based approach to a shared global resource.

Sustainability through incentives: unravelling the effects and hidden deficiencies of the European 'right to repair'

Marlon Luca Dreisewerd, Melina Schleef***

A. *The European 'right to repair'*

The European Green Deal[1] is one of the most ambitious sustainability programmes in the world, aiming to combine environmental sustainability with economic growth. To achieve the goals of the Green Deal, the EU has drawn up an action plan for the circular economy.[2] The circular economy concept follows three strategies: reduce the input of materials and output of waste, keep resources within the system, and reintegrate products into the system at the end of their lives.[3] These strategies can be achieved through design, maintenance, repair, reuse, remanufacturing, refurbishing,

* Doctoral Student at the Chair of Civil Law and Law of Digitalisation and Innovation, Faculty of Law, Bielefeld University.

** Postdoctoral Researcher at the Chair of Innovation and Technology Management, Faculty of Business Administration and Economics, Bielefeld University.
We would like to thank Prof. Dr. Paul Tobias Schrader (Chair of Civil Law and Law of Digitalisation and Innovation, Faculty of Law, Bielefeld University) for supporting this research.

1 European Commission, Commission Communication – The European Green Deal, 11 December 2019, COM (2019) 640 final.

2 European Commission, Commission Communication – A new Circular Economy Action Plan. For a cleaner and more competitive Europe, 11 March 2020, COM (2020) 98 final.

3 Valerio Elia/Maria Grazia Gnoni/Fabiana Tornese, 'Measuring Circular Economy Strategies through Index Methods: A Critical Analysis' (2017), 142(4) J Clean Prod, p. 2741, 2742; Yuliya Kalmykova/Madumita Sadagopan/Leonardo Rosado, 'Circular

and recycling.[4] Herein, the repair option is deemed to play a pivotal role in the efforts to achieve sustainability. In view of these insights, the EU has designated the promotion of repair over replacement as one of the key pillars for fostering sustainable growth, framing this decision under the concept of the 'Right to Repair'.

One of the central problems identified by the EU is the prevalence of a throwaway society. This term describes a societal tendency in which products are no longer valued for long-term use and maintenance, but instead are disposed of prematurely, even when they could easily be repaired.[5] In many cases, consumers replace goods as soon as a defect occurs rather than considering sustainable alternatives such as repair or refurbishment. This behavioural pattern has contributed significantly to increasing resource consumption and electronic waste.[6] The EU has recognised that the widespread reluctance to repair is not merely a consequence of individual preferences but a structural problem. It reflects a market environment in which repair options are often inaccessible, opaque, or economically unattractive compared to the purchase of new goods.

A striking example of this throwaway mentality can be observed in the use of electronic devices: there are billions of smartphone users worldwide. Against the background of this incredibly high number, it is alarming that 87 % of the smartphone owners use their smartphones for less than two years.[7] As many of the smartphones' precious resources end up in landfills, there is huge potential and urgency to act.[8] When it comes to the 'Right to Repair', the EU is targeting electronic devices such as smartphones, laptops and tablets in particular. These contain important raw materials that could be reintroduced into the economic cycle through recycling.[9] The EU sees huge potential for repair and recycling due to the thousands of tonnes of electronic devices on the internal market.

Economy: From Review of Theories and Practices to Development of Implementation Tools' (2018), 135 RCR, p. 190, 194.

4 Martin Geissdoerfer et al., 'The Circular Economy: A New Sustainability Paradigm?' (2017), 143 J Clean Prod, p. 757, 759.

5 Collins Dictionary, 'the throwaway society' (n.d.), https://www.collinsdictionary.com/dictionary/english/the-throwaway-society (last accessed: 14 July 2025).

6 Christian Rasquin/Julia Möller-Klapperich, 'Das Recht auf Reparatur ("Right to Repair") in der Europäischen Regulierung' (2024), 78(2) NJ, p. 58, 59.

7 Margot Möslinger et al., Towards an Effective Right to Repair for Electronics (2022), p. 1, 5.

8 Möslinger et al. (2022), p. 5.

9 Rasquin/Möller-Klapperich (2024), p. 59.

Recognising that many consumers discard defective goods prematurely,[10] the EU has adopted a legislative bundle consisting of three legislative acts: First, the Ecodesign Regulation[11] requires manufacturers to incorporate reparability into the product design process. For a repair to be simple and straightforward, the product must first be designed to be repairable. Second, a new Consumer Rights Directive[12] obliges sellers and manufacturers to inform consumers about the option, conditions, and costs of repairs. Third, the Repair Directive[13], as the core of the 'Right to Repair' initiative establishes a direct obligation on manufacturers and sellers to repair defective goods for consumers. If the consumer has no warranty rights—for example, because the warranty period has expired—they must bear the costs of the repair themselves. For these cases, which lie outside warranty law, the Repair Directive creates new rules for the relationship between consumers and manufacturers.[14] Manufacturers are obliged to offer repair outside the statutory warranty and to provide transparent information about repair conditions.[15] They may charge a reasonable fee or offer repair within the scope of a commercial guarantee.[16] In addition, an EU-wide online repair platform will help consumers find and compare repair services based on standardised information.[17] The EU also establishes a European repair information form and a voluntary European quality standard for repair

10 Susanne Augenhofer/Rebecca Küter, ‚Gedanken zum Vorschlag für eine RL über gemeinsame Vorschriften zur Förderung der Reparatur von Waren‘ (2023), 38(7) VuR, p. 243.

11 Regulation (EU) 2024/1781 of the European Parliament and of the Council of 13 June 2024 establishing a framework for the setting of ecodesign requirements for sustainable products, amending Directive (EU) 2020/1828 and Regulation (EU) 2023/1542 and repealing Directive 2009/125/EC [2024] OJ L89/1.

12 Directive (EU) 2024/825 of the European Parliament and of the Council of 28 February 2024 amending Directives 2005/29/EC and 2011/83/EU as regards empowering consumers for the green transition through better protection against unfair practices and through better information [2024] OJ L16/1.

13 Directive (EU) 2024/1799 of the European Parliament and of the Council of 13 June 2024 on common rules promoting the repair of goods and amending Regulation (EU) 2017/2394 and Directives (EU) 2019/771 and (EU) 2020/1828 [2024] OJ L20/1.

14 Johanna Croon-Gestefeld, ‚Das Recht auf Reparatur – Vorschläge aus Brüssel‘ (2024), 32(2) ZEuP, p. 379, 387; Stefanie Jung/Magdalene Back, ‚Die Förderung der Wahl der Nachbesserung im Mängelgewährleistungsrecht‘ (2025), 78(9) NJW, p. 537, 538.

15 Art. 5, Art. 6 Repair Directive.

16 Art. 5(2)(a) Repair Directive.

17 Art. 7 Repair Directive.

services to harmonise repair conditions and improve transparency and consumer trust.[18]

While the Repair Directive contains its own provisions – in particular regarding the obligations of manufacturers beyond the warranty period – it also amends the existing Sale of Goods Directive[19].[20] This amendment directly affects the contractual relationship between buyers and sellers under the Sale of Goods Directive.[21] In this contribution, the focus will be placed on this revised framework and, more specifically, on the new incentive mechanism introduced by the Repair Directive. This mechanism aims to influence consumer behaviour by rewarding the choice of repair with an extended warranty period. However, as will be discussed, this approach also entails hidden deficiencies, which may affect its effectiveness in practice.

B. The warranty rights of the Sale of Goods Directive

Consumers in the EU already benefit from harmonised warranty rights under the Sale of Goods Directive. The Sale of Goods Directive aims to achieve a balanced allocation of rights and obligations between the contracting parties by establishing fair and harmonised rules across the internal market.[22] For the warranty rights to arise, it is decisive that the consumer and the trader have concluded a sales contract.[23] The subject matter of this contract must be a good, defined broadly to encompass any tangible movable item.[24] However, goods with digital elements,[25] such as smart devices, are also subject to special provisions. These provisions apply where the content or services are integrated into or interconnected with

18 Art. 4 Repair Directive.

19 Directive (EU) 2019/771 of the European Parliament and of the Council of 20 May 2019 on certain aspects concerning contracts for the sale of goods, amending Regulation (EU) 2017/2394 and Directive 2009/22/EC, and repealing Directive 1999/44/EC [2019] OJ L136/28.

20 Art. 16 Repair Directive.

21 Anna Kirchhefer-Lauber, 'Nachhaltigkeit im deutschen Kaufrecht zwischen Verbraucherschutz, Ökodesign-VO und Warenreparatur-RL' (2024), 64(10) JuS, p. 915, 915 et seq.

22 Art. 1 Sale of Goods Directive.

23 Art. 2(1) Sale of Goods Directive.

24 Art. 2(5)(a) Sale of Goods Directive.

25 Art. 2(5)(b) Sale of Goods Directive.

the goods in such a way that their absence would prevent the goods from performing their functions.

The Sale of Goods Directive establishes a comprehensive system of remedies, including repair, replacement, price reduction and termination, all embedded in a harmonised framework that aims to reconcile consumer protection objectives with the legitimate interests of traders in a proportionate manner.[26] At the core of the Sale of Goods Directive is the right of the consumer to have defective goods brought into conformity free of charge.[27] The consumer has the right to choose between repair and replacement as primary remedies, unless the remedy chosen is impossible or would impose costs on the seller that are disproportionate compared to the alternative remedy.[28] A lack of conformity exists where the good deviates negatively either from the subjective requirements or from the objective requirements.[29] In other words, any defect that impairs the conformity of the good with the contractually agreed characteristics or with the reasonable expectations of an average consumer constitutes a lack of conformity. The liability of the seller requires that the lack of conformity already existed at the time when the risk passed to the consumer, which is regularly the moment of the handover of the good.[30]

If the consumer exercises the right of choice between replacement and repair and opts for a replacement, the seller is obliged to take back the defective good.[31] In the past, consumers have frequently preferred the replacement to the repair.[32] This preference is mainly attributable to the perception that receiving a new good is more beneficial.[33] Consumers expect a longer product lifespan and anticipate that any signs of wear and tear associated with the previous good will also be eliminated by obtaining a replacement. Currently, warranty rights under the Sale of Goods Directive expire two years from the date of handover of the good.[34] In principle, the

26 Art. 13 Sale of Goods Directive.

27 Art. 14 Sale of Goods Directive.

28 Art. 13(2) Sale of Goods Directive.

29 Art. 6, Art. 7 Sale of Goods Directive.

30 Art. 10(1) Sale of Goods Directive.

31 Art. 14(2) Sale of Goods Directive.

32 European Commission, Proposal for a Directive of the European Parliament and of the Council on common rules promoting the repair of goods and amending Regulation (EU) 2017/2394, Directives (EU) 2019/771 and (EU) 2020/1828, 22 March 2023, COM (2023) 155 final, p. 1; Augenhofer/Küter (2023), p. 243.

33 Augenhofer/Küter (2023), p. 243.

34 Cf figure 1 below; Art. 10(1) Sale of Goods Directive.

limitation period does not restart because of a replacement or a repair.[35] Consequently, where a lack of conformity becomes apparent outside this period, the trader is no longer liable, and the consumer cannot invoke the remedies provided under the Directive.

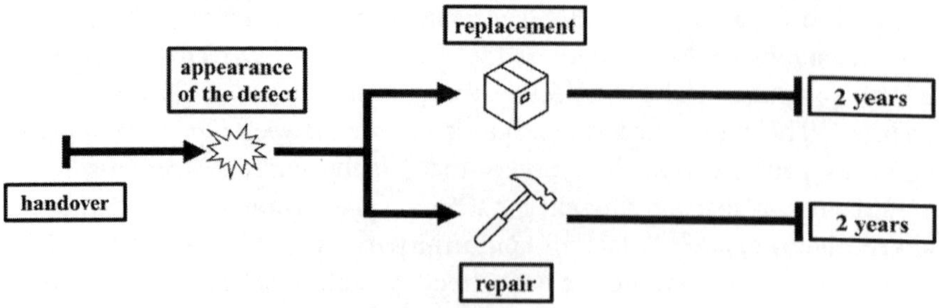

Figure 1: The primary warranty rights of the Sale of Goods Directive

In Germany, the provisions of the Sale of Goods Directive have been implemented primarily through §§ 434 et seqq. of the German Civil Code (Bürgerliches Gesetzbuch, BGB).[36] According to § 434 BGB, goods are deemed to be free from defects if they possess the agreed quality and, in the absence of any such agreement, if they are suitable for the customary use and exhibit the quality which is usual in goods of the same kind. § 437 BGB provides the consumer with a catalogue of remedies in the event of non-conformity. These rights include the right to demand repair or replacement, to withdraw from the contract, to reduce the purchase price and to claim damages. The right to have the goods brought into conformity is further specified in § 439 BGB, according to which the buyer may, at their discretion, demand a repair or a replacement.[37] The seller bears all expenses necessary to bring the goods into conformity, including transport, labour and material costs. Notably, § 439(1) BGB embodies the consumer's right to choose between repair and replacement in alignment with Article 13(2) Sale of Goods Directive, subject to the seller's right to refuse the chosen remedy if it would entail disproportionate costs within the meaning of § 439(4)

35 Stefan Arnold in Beate Gsell et al. (eds.), beck-online.GROSSKOMMENTAR (1 May 2025), § 438 BGB, para. 138, 154 et seqq.
36 Stephan Lorenz, 'Die Umsetzung der EU-Warenkaufrichtlinie in deutsches Recht' (2021), 74(29) NJW, p. 2065.
37 Rasquin/Möller-Klapperich (2024), p. 60.

BGB.[38] In practice, replacement is often less costly and therefore more common, yet it comes with the peculiarity that the consumer effectively receives a new product. Under §§ 439(6), 346(1) BGB, the seller could in principle demand the return of the defective item together with compensation for use. However, in the case of consumer sales this right is restricted by § 475(3) BGB. While the consumer must return the defective good, they are not obliged to pay compensation for use. As a result, the 'newness advantage' of replacement is not fully offset, but this outcome reflects the Directive's underlying consumer protection rationale.

C. The incentive mechanism of the Repair Directive

As already outlined, many consumers so far prefer replacement over repair.[39] In view of the fact that most carbon emissions are released during the production of a product, the EU considers consumer preference for a new product to be problematic from a sustainability perspective. In the initial legislative proposal, the EU had planned to restrict the consumer's right to choose by introducing a cost-based limitation: according to Article 12 of the Repair Directive Proposal, the option to choose replacement would have been excluded if the costs of replacement were equal to or higher than the costs of repair.[40] This proposal attracted significant criticism, as it was perceived to contradict the EU's assurances that consumer rights would not be curtailed.[41]

In light of these concerns, the EU ultimately abandoned this approach and instead adopted a reward-based mechanism intended to promote repair as the preferred remedial measure. Specifically, Article 16(2)(a) of the Repair Directive amends Article 10 of the Sale of Goods Directive by inserting a new paragraph. Under the newly introduced Article 10(2a) of

38 Rasquin/Möller-Klapperich (2024), p. 60.

39 European Commission, Proposal for a Directive of the European Parliament and of the Council on common rules promoting the repair of goods and amending Regulation (EU) 2017/2394, Directives (EU) 2019/771 and (EU) 2020/1828, 22 March 2023, COM (2023) 155 final, p. 1; Augenhofer/Küter (2023), p. 243.

40 Kirchhefer-Lauber (2024), p. 918; Jung/Back (2025), p. 539.

41 Augenhofer/Küter (2023), p. 245 et seq.; Tim Hülskötter, 'Auswirkungen der Pflicht zur Reparatur auf das Verhältnis von Umwelt- und Verbraucherschutz im Europäischen Verbrauchervertragsrecht: Die neue Abwägung zwischen drei Polen' (2024), 39(4) VuR, p. 130, 131 et seq.

the Sale of Goods Directive, where the consumer opts for repair as the remedy to bring the good into conformity and the seller has completed the repair, the limitation period is extended once by twelve months. Put simply, consumers who choose repair will receive an additional year of warranty, extending the limitation period for defects from two to three years.[42] Recital 40 of the Repair Directive clarifies that this extension is designed to create an incentive for consumers to choose repair voluntarily, rather than choosing replacement, by offering a tangible advantage in the form of prolonged protection against defects.[43] The approach thus seeks to reward environmentally preferable consumer behaviour, rather than to compel it by limiting options. The Repair Directive leaves it to the discretion of the Member States to provide for a longer extension of the limitation period than the one-year extension laid down in Article 16(2)(a). According to Article 16(2)(b) of the Directive, Member States may adopt or maintain provisions stipulating that, if the consumer opts for repair, the limitation period is extended by a period longer than twelve months. This measure is accompanied by further regulatory changes to strengthen the attractiveness and transparency of repairs. For instance, Article 16(1) amends Article 7(1) of the Sale of Goods Directive by specifying that goods must possess not only durability but also repairability as part of their objective conformity requirements. Additionally, Article 16(3) of the Repair Directive introduces new information obligations: Before providing a remedy, the seller must inform the consumer of their right to choose between repair and replacement and of the possibility that the limitation period will be extended if repair is selected.

---

42 Cf figure 2 below; Art. 16(2)(a) Repair Directive; Arun Kapoor/David Leucuta, 'Das neue Recht auf Reparatur – Was ändert sich im digitalen Verbrauchergewährleistungsrecht?' (2024), 40(11) CR, p. 728, 732.

43 Jung/Back (2025), p. 540.

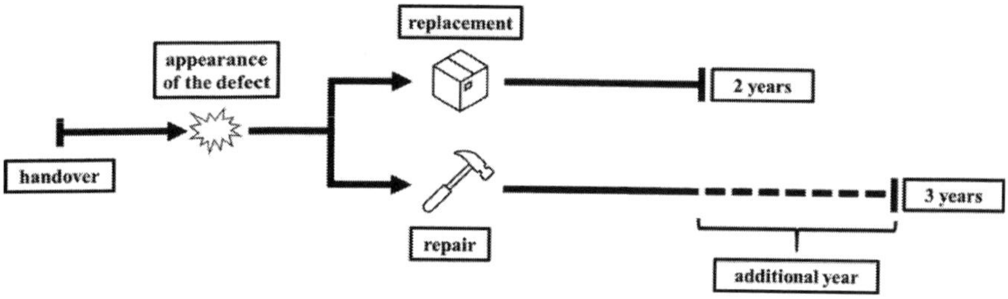

Figure 2: The new incentive mechanism of the Repair Directive

The Member States must transpose these amendments into their national legal orders by the deadline of 31 July 2026.[44] In Germany, this will require targeted adjustments to the rules on conformity and remedies in §§ 434, 438, 439 BGB. Given the Directive's focus on consumer protection, these changes are likely to be implemented within the special regime for consumer sales law pursuant to §§ 474 et seqq. BGB, rather than extending to B2B and C2C transactions, unless the German legislator decides on an implementation which applies the new rules beyond consumer contracts. It is important to note that the Repair Directive lays down fully harmonised rules in this area, meaning that Member States are, in principle, not permitted to maintain or introduce national provisions deviating from the Directive's requirements.[45] One exception is the optional extension of the limitation period beyond twelve months.[46] Within this context, the question emerges as to whether, and to what degree, the incentive mechanism is capable of steering consumer behaviour toward repair rather than replacement.

D. Interdisciplinary research on the effectiveness of the incentive mechanism

Assessing whether the newly introduced incentive actually achieves its intended objectives requires an interdisciplinary perspective that combines legal analysis with behavioural and economic research. The EU already conducted certain studies during the legislative process, forecasting a 12 %

44 Art. 22(1) Repair Directive.
45 Art. 3 Repair Directive.
46 Art. 16(2)(b) Repair Directive.

increase in consumers' willingness to opt for repair over a 15-year period.[47] Based on signalling theory[48] and the current literature on repair intentions,[49] investigating behavioural effects of an additional year of warranty shows that offering an extra year of warranty can, in principle, influence consumer behaviour. However, important questions remain regarding the practical effectiveness of this incentive, in particular whether consumers sufficiently perceive, comprehend and trust the extended liability period as a credible benefit. Interdisciplinary research into the effectiveness of the European 'Right to Repair' thus illustrates a broader trend: scholarship increasingly transcends the traditional boundaries of doctrinal legal analysis to integrate insights from consumer psychology and behavioural economics. Such approaches do not merely examine the legal framework conditions in the abstract. Rather, they seek to understand how consumers actually respond to regulatory measures in practice, for example, when faced with the choice between a replacement and a repair.

Interdisciplinary studies are frequently carried out in collaborative, cross-disciplinary settings, enabling legal scholars, economists and social scientists to jointly address complex research questions. One central issue that emerges concerns the allocation of the burden of proof. This challenge becomes apparent in the design of a specific experimental setting, in which it is necessary to determine what information consumers would be presumed to have regarding the legal framework conditions. In order to approximate realistic conditions as closely as possible, participants should be informed about those framework conditions that will form part of the new information obligations. However, the rules governing the allocation of the burden of proof do not belong to the scope of the information obligation. These insights form the basis for examining in greater depth the hidden deficiencies of the incentive mechanism and information obligation, to which the following section will now turn.

---

47 European Commission, Study to support the Commission's policy development on promoting repair of consumer goods and contracts in the data economy (2023), pp. 92 et seqq.

48 Michael Spence, 'Job Market Signaling' (1973), 87(3) Q J Econ, p. 355, 356 et seqq.

49 Nataliia Roskladka/Anicia Jaegler/Giovanni Miragliotta, 'From "right to repair" to "willingness to repair": Exploring consumer's perspective to product lifecycle extension' (2023), 432 J Clean Prod, p. 1, 5 et seqq.

E. The hidden deficiencies of the incentive mechanism

At first glance, the extension of the liability period by an additional year appears to be a promising legal incentive to encourage repairs and thus promote sustainable consumption. However, its effectiveness critically depends on the consumer's understanding of the legal framework in which this incentive is embedded. Under the Repair Directive, the seller is obliged to inform the consumer merely of the existence of the right to choose between repair and replacement and of the possibility that the liability period will be extended in the event of a repair.[50] Yet, no obligation exists to inform the consumer about several additional framework conditions, some of which can be decisive for the enforceability of warranty rights in practice. Such framework conditions include the allocation of the burden of proof, the duration of the repair, and the (un)availability of replacement devices during the repair period. In this respect, it is noteworthy that the Repair Directive does not require traders to inform consumers about these hidden framework conditions. From the perspective of maximising the incentive effect, this omission may be advantageous, as consumers are not confronted with information that could diminish the perceived value of repair. Yet, at the same time, this approach stands in tension with the principle of informed consumer decision-making: If essential contextual factors are withheld, the consumer's decision to choose repair over replacement risks being shaped by incomplete information rather than genuine preference.

These disadvantages are not caused by the extension of the liability period itself, but they may considerably weaken its incentive effect if consumers are aware of them, since replacement may then be perceived as the more advantageous option despite the longer liability period. In some cases, the consumer may only become aware of the existence of the right to choose between repair and replacement because of the new information obligation and, as a result, may for the first time consciously decide in favour of replacement delivery rather than repair. Moreover, the incentive effect may erode over time as these disadvantages become more widely known among consumers, thereby reducing the effectiveness of the liability extension as a tool to promote repair.

50 Art. 16(3) Repair Directive.

A particularly crucial legal framework condition concerns the allocation of the burden of proof.[51] Under the Sale of Goods Directive, any lack of conformity that becomes apparent within the first year after delivery is presumed to have existed at the time of the transfer of risk, unless this presumption is incompatible with the nature of the goods or the defect itself.[52] This presumption significantly eases enforcement, as it relieves the consumer of the need to provide evidence regarding the origin of the defect.[53] However, the new incentive mechanism under the Repair Directive does not extend this presumption to the additional year granted as a reward for choosing repair.[54] Accordingly, if a defect arises during this third year, the consumer once again bears the burden of proving that the defect already existed at the time of delivery—a task that is likely to be substantially more challenging after such an extended period has elapsed.[55] Furthermore, under German law, the situation is even more complex. In cases of replacement delivery, the one-year reversal of the burden of proof recommences in full for the entire product, as has been argued in the German literature.[56] Conversely, when a repair is carried out, only a six-month reversal applies, and this is limited exclusively to the parts actually repaired.[57] As a result, the choice of replacement delivery is clearly privileged in terms of evidentiary facilitation.

This discrepancy in the burden of proof allocation undermines the intended incentive effect of the Repair Directive. Even if the consumer is aware of the additional year of liability, the risk of evidentiary failure during this period remains substantial. It is therefore questionable whether a rational consumer, who is properly informed about these conditions, would indeed prefer repair to replacement. Since they are neither laid down in the statutory text nor generally known, but rather discussed only in specialised legal literature, a rational choice would presuppose their inclusion in the seller's information obligation. Particularly in cases where the defect occurs

---

51 Christoph Hanecker /Martin Schmidt-Kessel, 'Die Änderung des Warenkaufs durch die Reparaturrichtlinie (EU) 2024/1799' (2024), 21(6) GPR, p. 236, 238; Jung/Back (2025), p. 540.

52 Art. 11(1) Sale of Goods Directive.

53 Susanne Augenhofer in Beate Gsell et al. (eds.), beck-online.GROSSKOMMENTAR (1 June 2025), § 477 BGB, para. 2 et seq.

54 Hanecker/Schmidt-Kessel (2024), p. 238.

55 Jung/Back (2025), p. 540.

56 Stephan Lorenz in Jürgen Säcker et al. (eds.), Münchener Kommentar zum Bürgerlichen Gesetzbuch (2024), § 477 BGB, para. 18.

57 Ibid.

one year after the handover of the product, the consumer's rational calculus will often favour replacement delivery, which not only provides a functioning product but also restarts the burden of proof reversal for another full year. This imbalance may explain an increase in repair intentions, especially when the defect arose early in the product's lifecycle. In this respect, the incentive mechanism appears fragile and susceptible to erosion over time.

F. Conclusion

The "Right to Repair" legislative bundle marks a recent, though incremental, attempt by the EU to promote sustainable economic development within the internal market. By adjusting warranty rights and their legal preconditions, the EU has established a new incentive structure designed to influence consumer behaviour in favour of repair rather than replacement. In particular, Article 16(2)(a) of the Repair Directive extends the liability period by an additional twelve months if the consumer opts for repair as the remedial measure to bring goods into conformity. While this additional year of warranty is intended to make repair a more attractive choice, its practical benefit for many consumers remains limited. The burden of proof continues to shift back to the consumer after the first year pursuant to Article 11(1) of the Sale of Goods Directive, irrespective of the extended liability period. Consequently, consumers may still perceive replacement as the less risky and more convenient option, especially when the evidentiary requirements of demonstrating a pre-existing defect become decisive.

From a sustainability perspective, the Repair Directive is a step forward, as it signals the EU's willingness to incentivise more resource-conserving consumption behaviour. However, it cannot be regarded as a transformative intervention capable of fundamentally altering established consumer preferences or the throwaway culture that prevails in many product segments. The effectiveness of the Directive will therefore largely depend on the practical implementation of its provisions in national laws, the transparency of information obligations imposed on sellers, and the degree to which consumers are made aware of both the advantages and disadvantages associated with repair. Experimental studies based on signalling theory have shown that extending the liability period can indeed increase consumers' intentions to choose repair. Yet, these positive effects are not uniform across all product categories and may depend on factors such as the elapsed time of use and the perceived durability of the product.

Moreover, the asymmetry of information concerning the burden of proof poses a significant risk that consumers will overestimate the security afforded by the extended warranty period. While such overestimation may, in the short term, strengthen the Directive's incentive effect and increase the likelihood of repair, it does so at the expense of the principle of informed consumer decision-making. This hidden deficiency may therefore undermine the Directive's broader objective to reconcile sustainability with transparency and autonomy in consumer choice. In sum, the success of this incentive mechanism hinges on whether it can overcome structural and behavioural barriers in practice. Should the Directive fail to substantially increase the frequency with which consumers select repair over replacement, further legislative refinements may be necessary. Interdisciplinary research is indispensable to monitor the impact of the incentive structure and to identify any unintended consequences. It can also support the development of comprehensive measures that align consumer decision-making more consistently with the overarching goals of the European Green Deal.

Neuro-legal nudging and sustainable economics: a behavioural approach to sustainability law

Sameh Mansour[*], *Maha Balbaa*[**]

A. Introduction

Modern sustainability law operates under the fundamental economic principle that market actors are rational, driven by legal incentives and the rules that govern (and regulate) economic and social relations. Traditional environmental regulation, such as carbon taxes, emissions trading and mandatory corporate sustainability reporting, are built on the assumption that people and organisations will rationally weigh up costs and benefits of their actions when they take decisions that impact the environment.[1] Yet, this model of the rational actor is increasingly found wanting in the face of growing evidence from behavioural economics and neuroscience of the degree to which human decision-making is significantly 'bounded' by

* Doha Institute for Graduate Studies.
** The American University in Cairo.

1 Richard H. Thaler/Cass R. Sunstein, Nudge: Improving Decisions About Health, Wealth, and Happiness (2008), p. 45.

cognitive biases, heuristic processing and neurological processes that run counter to narrow rational calculation.[2]

In sustainability contexts, the lack of correspondence between legal expectations and actual human behaviour causes considerable problems for the effectiveness of environmental policies. Notwithstanding decades of regulatory evolution, as well as increasingly sophisticated legal systems, levels of compliance remain unsatisfactory, economic inefficiency persists, and public resistance to sustainability measures continues to undermine policy objectives.[3] This gap is indicative of the fact that the traditional legal understanding, at least in theory, leaves very little space for the psychological and neurological facts about how the human decision-making process works and eventually shapes human behaviour in terms of individual and organisational compliance with sustainability regulations in our society.

Recent developments in cognitive neuroscience have started to shed light on the intricate neural machinery that underlies environmental decision-making, showing that sustainable decisions are mediated by the recruitment of a constellation of brain networks including the amygdala (responsible for fear and risk processing), the prefrontal cortex (site of rational planning and executive control), and the ventral striatum (involved in reward processing and motivational drive).[4] These findings imply that good sustainability law cannot just serve to increase the material incentives or costs of harmful or beneficial behaviour but must engage the real cognitive structure of human reason-making, as opposed to abstract rational choice assumptions.

In addition, research in behavioural economics has shown that cognitive biases, such as present bias, loss aversion, and social proof, have a significant impact on environmental decisions.[5] For example, people tend to underestimate the positive effects of long-term environmental benefits in comparison to short-term costs, a phenomenon known as temporal discounting that significantly reduces the effectiveness of policy approaches aimed at encouraging sustainable behaviour. Additionally, environmental

---

2 Daniel Kahneman, Thinking, Fast and Slow (2011), p. 267.

3 Ameya Patil et al., 'Behavioral Economics and Environmental Sustainability—The Complicated Nexus', in Pardeep Singh/Shikha Daga/Kiran Yadav (eds.), Nudging Green: Behavioral Economics and Environmental Sustainability (2024), p. 123.

4 Letizia Richelli/Maria Arioli/Nicola Canessa, 'Neurosustainability: A Scoping Review on the Neuro-Cognitive Bases of Sustainable Decision-Making' (2025), 15(7) Brain Sci., p. 678.

5 Thaler/Sunstein (2008), p. 78.

loss-frame messages have been demonstrated to be more effective in promoting motivation than equivalent gain-frame messages; thus, how regulatory information is conveyed psychologically can have a significant impact on the extent of compliance.[6]

This article presents a theoretical framework that systematically integrates findings from brain research, economic theory, and legal theory to enhance the effectiveness of sustainability law. The core contention is that we can help design better legal and regulatory architectures by strategically embedding 'neuro-legal nudging' strategies—regulatory design standards shaped by the cognitive and neuropsychological dimensions of human thinking about the environment. Instead of trying to subvert or bypass these psychological realities, the approach advances the idea of using them to promote sustainability.

This work has three research aims. First, to construct a comprehensive theoretical framework consolidating neuroscience, behavioural economics, and legal analysis in the context of sustainability regulation. This interdisciplinary synthesis aims to contribute to a deeper understanding of how legal compliance is achieved in the context of individual and organisational decision-making. Second, to propose an applied three-tier legal model that operationalises neurobiological and behavioural findings into specific regulatory design principles. This model considers cognitive bias attenuation, social norm incorporation and default optimisation as orthogonal strategies to improve compliance with the law. Third, to provide empirical research and policy innovation with a groundwork by stating transparent hypotheses about how neuro-legal approaches could enhance sustainability.

The implications of this study are not only theoretical but also far-reaching in the policy formulation and implementation. By delivering evidence-based approaches to improving compliance with the law through behavioural optimisation to policymakers, this framework has the potential to strengthen the impact of existing sustainability policies, while also reducing the social and economic costs of enforcement. Furthermore, the interdisciplinary methodology developed in this paper makes a contribution to the fledgling field of neurolaw by demonstrating how neuroscientific insights can inform regulatory design in complex policy fields.

6 Eric Johnson/Daniel Goldstein, 'Do Defaults Save Lives?' (2003), 302 Science, p. 1338.

B. Literature review and theoretical background

I. Behavioural economics and environmental law

The convergence of behavioural economics and environmental law has become an area of significant scholarly inquiry, raising fundamental questions about what drives individuals and organisations to respond to sustainability regulations. Conventional economic theories of environmental policy-making assume that decision makers will always rationally balance costs against benefits in their decisions about whether to comply or not comply with environmental regulations.[7] Yet research in behavioural economics reveals that the rational choice framework does not adequately account for the psychological forces that influence environmental decision making.

Thaler and Sunstein's classic work on nudge theory proposes a framework for developing an environmentally effective yet freedom-preserving way of influencing environmental behaviour.[8] Their study reveals that seemingly minor changes to the presentation of options can sustainably alter decision outcomes, a finding with profound implications for the design of sustainability regulations. Several studies have shown that messages framed in terms of what can potentially be lost as a consequence of an activity (loss-framed messages) are more effective in inducing pro-environmental behaviour than their gain-framed counterparts.[9]

Another behavioural economics insight directly relevant to sustainability law is the phenomenon of temporal discounting. This 'temporal discounting' of future benefits, or equivalently, the tendency to focus on present rather than future costs, has been shown conclusively in many experimental settings, where it constitutes a strong bias and is problematic for policies involving environmental challenges, particularly when there is a divergence between immediate costs and long-term benefits.[10] This bias also serves to explain the resistance generated around carbon taxing schemes, even when they are in the potential best interest of the country in the long run, both in terms of economy and environment.

---

7 Gary Becker, 'Crime and Punishment: An Economic Approach' (1968), 76(2) JPE, p. 169.

8 Thaler/Sunstein (2008), p. 6.

9 Amos Tversky/Daniel Kahneman, 'The Framing of Decisions and the Psychology of Choice' (1981), 211 Science, p. 453.

10 Shane Frederick/George Loewenstein/Ted O'Donoghue, 'Time Discounting and Time Preference: A Critical Review' (2002), 40(2) JEL, p. 351.

Loss aversion, another well-documented cognitive bias, has significant consequences for how we frame environmental rules. Prospect theory, developed by Kahneman and Tversky, reveals that people perceive losses as equivalent to gains about twice as intensely, suggesting that environmental policies framed in terms of avoiding losses may be more effective than those focused on potential benefits.[11] Social proof and conformity effects are another mechanism through which behavioural insights can increase the effectiveness of environmental law, with evidence demonstrating that people are significantly influenced by information on what others are doing.[12]

II. Neuroscience of environmental decision-making

The new field of environmental neuroscience is just beginning to shed light on the brain systems involved in pro-environmental action, with potential implications for creating more effective policies for sustainability. Functional magnetic resonance imaging (fMRI) and electroencephalography (EEG) studies have shown that environmental decision-making involves complex interactions between multiple brain networks, including regions associated with emotional processing, cognitive control, and social cognition.[13]

Recently, Richelli, Arioli, and Canessa summarised the role of the neurocognitive substrates underlying sustainable decision-making. However, the crucial brain circuits that contribute to pro-environmental behaviour remained an open question.[14] Their observed results further indicate that sustainable decision-making activates brain structures associated with mentalising and moral cognition, which may partly reflect the implication of these areas in integrating the personal and contextual dimensions of environmental choices. Furthermore, their findings suggest that sustainable choices are processed by brain regions related to attentional monitoring and affective motivation, as well as by circuits commonly engaged in value generation for decision making in general.

The temporoparietal junction (TPJ) has been identified as a key brain area in the study of environmental decision-making. Previous research indicates

---

11 Daniel Kahneman/Amos Tversky, 'Prospect Theory: An Analysis of Decision under Risk' (1979), 47 Econometrica, p. 263.

12 Robert Cialdini, Influence: The Psychology of Persuasion (2006), p. 116.

13 Richelli/Arioli/Canessa (2025), p. 680.

14 Richelli/Arioli/Canessa (2025), p. 678.

that pro-environmental and prosocial choice decisions share neural substrates, with the TPJ being centrally involved in both types of decision-making.[15] This convergence lends support to the idea that environmental decision-making might be intrinsically social, necessitating reflection about what effects one's actions have on other people and the future. Research on the prefrontal cortex has demonstrated its key role in prioritising long-term benefits over short-term advantages in the environment. In contrast, the amygdala's role reflects the emotional nature of choices related to sustainability.[16]

III. Legal compliance and behavioural insights

The influence of behavioural insights on legal scholarship has led to significant developments in understanding how and why individuals obey the law. According to traditional deterrence theory, compliance is primarily determined by the anticipated costs and benefits of legal violations. However, behavioural research has demonstrated that a broader range of psychological constructs strongly influences compliance.[17]

Social norms are a critical aspect of legal compliance, with research demonstrating that individuals are more likely to comply with legal requirements when they believe that compliance is widespread and socially expected.[18] This has profound implications for sustainability law, where it implies that policies that render compliance visible (and hence socially salient) might be more effective than those, even if formally sanctioned, that do not. Another important factor in legal obedience is the notion of legitimacy—people are more likely to comply with the law when they consider it to be legitimate and fair.[19]

Neurolaw is a nascent field that has begun to examine how neuroscience can illuminate legal theory and practice. Preliminary developments in neuroimaging have had a profound impact on doctrine regarding criminal

15 Mauricio Delgado, 'Reward-Related Responses in the Human Striatum' (2007), 1104(1) Ann. N.Y. Acad. Sci., p. 70.
16 Kevin Ochsner/James Gross, 'The Cognitive Control of Emotion' (2005), 9(5) Trends Cogn. Sci., p. 242.
17 Tom Tyler, Why People Obey the Law (2006), p. 45.
18 Tyler (2006), p. 67.
19 Tyler (2006), p. 103.

responsibility—above all, on notions of guilt and dangerousness.[20] These changes present crucial challenges to the fields of forensic psychology and forensic psychiatry concerning the reformulation of knowledge about mental disorders and their consequences in legal contexts.

C. The neuro-legal framework for sustainability

I. Theoretical foundation

This neuro-legal sustainability framework is a methodologically innovative approach that integrates knowledge from neuroscience, behavioural economics, and legal scholarship to improve the effectiveness of environmental regulation. Compliance with the law is, in essence, a psychological process that operates within the cognitive and neural substrates of human decision-making. Rather than viewing these psychological facts as barriers to be overcome, the approach aims to integrate regulatory design with the way people and organisations process information and make decisions about the natural environment.

This framework is based on three fundamental principles. First, human cognition about the environment is systematically skewed by cognitive biases and neural processes that, a priori, are not consistent with rational choice theory. Second, we can understand and predict these psychological mechanisms through science and use this knowledge for evidence-based regulatory design. Third, legal systems can be 'cognitively and neuronally' optimised, if cognitive and neural processes are taken into account when legal rules are created and enforced.

The psychological and neural architecture of environmental decision-making integrates the activities of several interacting brain systems, which contribute different types of information and processing toward the choice.[21] Emotional processing centres (based around the amygdala and associated structures) compute the affective meaning of information from the environment and generate motivational responses that may either facilitate or subvert pro-environmental activity. The cognitive control systems, including regions of the prefrontal cortex (pfC), allow individuals to over-

20 Eric García-López/Cristina Nombela/Eduardo Demetrio Crespo, 'Editorial: Law and neuroscience: justice as a challenge for neurorights, neurolaw, and forensic psychology' (2025), 16 Front. Psychol., p. 1615234.

21 Richelli/Arioli/Canessa (2025), p. 681.

ride immediate impulses and choose long-term environmental benefits, even when doing so entails short-term costs. The social cognition network, for example, the TPJ and medial prefrontal cortex (mPFC), is involved in encoding culturally specific information about social norms, expectations, and the repercussions of local actions on others in the environment.

Knowledge of these neural mechanisms is crucial for effective regulation. Policies that tap into emotional processing systems through relatable content or vivid imagery may be more effective at motivating behaviour change than those based on abstract statistical information. On the other hand, to the extent that these systems have evolved to promote efforts at decision-making, less taxing policies aimed at lowering demands on the cognitive control system through simplified choice architectures or default options may more effectively facilitate alternative decision-making approaches rather than interfering with these natural processes.

II. Framework Components

The neuro-legal infrastructure consists of three interacting model components which address aspects of the psychology of environmental decision-making: cognitive bias correction, social norm incorporation and default enhancement. Each module addresses specific psychological processes and helps regulate the overall system.

Cognitive bias mitigation involves the systematic identification and correction of cognitive biases that interfere with accurate environmental decision-making. Present bias is especially central as a target for intervention because the tendency to put a lower value on future benefits creates systematic barriers to policies with long-term environmental payoffs. Regulations that address present-bias environmental decision-making include providing immediate information on consequences to increase the saliency of long-term outcomes, framing the costs and benefits of environmental behaviour in daily (rather than yearly) terms, and offering immediate rewards for pro-environmental behaviour.

Another means of reducing cognitive bias is through the mediation of temporal framing effects. It has been shown that the exact cost or benefit for the environment can be perceived very differently depending on how it is presented in time. For example, £365 per year is probably way more expensive than £1 per day, even though they are mathematically the same.[22] Such legal frameworks that utilise psychological pricing mechanisms systematically can increase the attractiveness perception of sustainable options without compromising economic efficiency.

Social norm integration is based on the recognition that environmental decision-making is essentially social—that what others are doing and what is expected or accepted by others is taken into account. The framework we introduce is aimed at utilising social norm information for regulatory creation by systems such as peer comparison forces, public disclosure needs, and reputational incentives that render environmental performance visible to interested constituents.

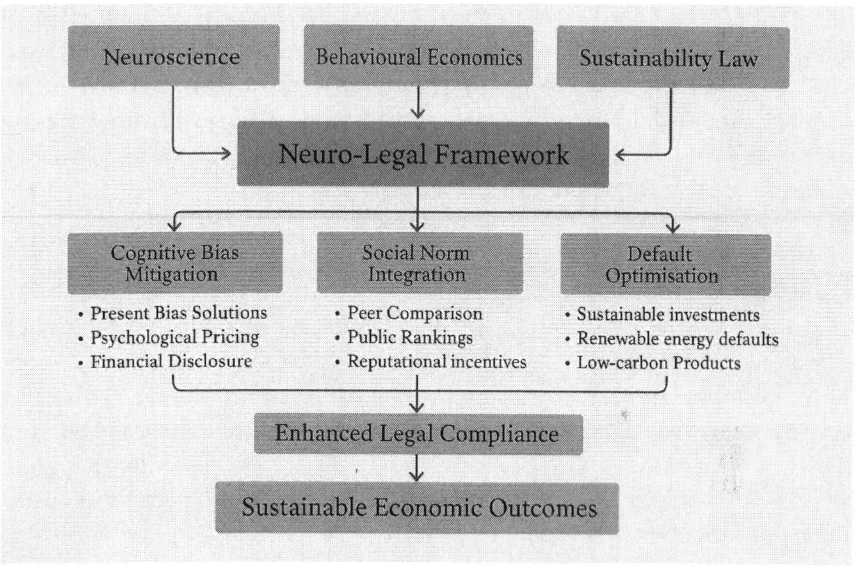

Figure 1: Theoretical model for neuro-law sustainability

Default optimisation is the final pillar of the model, dealing with the potent role of default settings in determining choice. The psychological literature has overwhelmingly shown that people have a strong bias towards defaulting and that even when changing a default is the best course of action, most people will

22 Thaler/Sunstein (2008), p. 89.

still stick with the default.[23] This default effect can be harnessed to encourage sustainable behaviours by designing choice architectures such that environmentally better options are taken as the default.

Figure 1 illustrates the intersection of neuroscience, behavioural economics, and sustainability law in a holistic framework to improve legal compliance by focusing on how to mitigate cognitive bias, integrate social norms, and optimise the default strategy.

D. The three-tiered legal model

For the proposed three-tiered legal model, the theoretical contributions of the extrajudicial neuro-legal framework are applied to specific regulatory design principles that can be effectively implemented within existing legal regimes. These tiers each target psychological mechanisms, making an independent contribution to the success of sustainability law through the use of coordinated and mutually reinforcing strategies to increase compliance and improve environmental performance.

I. Tier one: cognitive bias mitigation

The model's first tier involves the systematic detection and control of cognitive distortions that undermine ecological decision-making. This level acknowledges that traditional regulatory approaches are ineffective because they are not grounded in structures of rational decision-making that align with the psychology of how individuals (including firms) process environmental information and make decisions.

The most serious cognitive bottleneck in the development of effective environmental policy is present bias. 'This systematic bias in the overweighting of immediate costs vis-à-vis remote gains implies a natural resistance to environmental policies in which investments by a generation today translate into external benefits for a range of time in the future.'[24] The model deals with the present-bias key element in different ways. One such way is temporal reframing, which involves presenting environmental costs and benefits in terms of time to provide a sense of near-term future

23 Johnson/Goldstein (2003), p. 1338.
24 Frederick/Loewenstein/O'Donoghue (2002), p. 351.

consequences that are psychologically relevant. For example, carbon tax policies can be presented in terms of daily rather than annual costs, making the financial impact feel more manageable whilst maintaining the same economic incentives.

Immediate feedback mechanisms are yet another way to reduce the effects of present bias. Many conventional environmental policies are based on a lengthy time lag between actions and outcomes, which weakens people's psychological link between their activities and results. The model includes provisions for honest or near-time feedback on environmental impacts, such as smart meter displays and feedback on immediate energy consumption costs, or corporate reporting systems that offer monthly updates rather than annual ones on environmental performance.

Psychological pricing tactics rely upon widely known framing effects to increase the saliency of the sustainable option. Studies have shown that the exact economic cost or benefit can be perceived in quite different ways, depending on how it is framed.[25] Environmental regulation can also be crafted to capitalise on these effects by being sensitive to how costs and benefits are framed. For example, a programme to encourage reusable shopping bags could be framed as either a discount for using reusable bags or a surcharge for using disposable bags. This demonstrates the power of loss-framed messaging over gain-framed approaches, consistent with loss aversion theory which suggests that people experience losses approximately twice as intensely as equivalent gains[26]. The requirement of financial disclosure is a mechanism in the legal regulation of the availability heuristic and other cognitive errors. The availability heuristic is a mental shortcut where people judge the probability of events based on how easily examples come to mind, leading to systematic overestimation of vivid, recent environmental incidents while underestimating gradual, less visible threats.[27] Other relevant biases include present bias, which causes individuals to systematically overweight immediate costs relative to future environmental benefits,[28] confirmation bias, where people selectively seek information that confirms pre-existing environmental beliefs while dismissing contradictory

25 Tversky/Kahneman (1981), p. 453.

26 Kahneman/Tversky (1979), p. 263.

27 Amos Tversky/Daniel Kahneman, 'Availability: A heuristic for judging frequency and probability' (1973), 5(2) Cogn. Psychol., p. 207.

28 Jiaying Zhao/Yu Luo, 'A framework to address cognitive biases of climate change' (2021), 109(22) Neuron, p. 3548.

evidence, and optimism bias, leading individuals to underestimate their personal vulnerability to environmental risks compared to others.[29] The model involves the compulsory reporting of long-term environmental costs and benefits in investment and corporate reports in a manner that is psychologically salient and accessible. For instance, a study demonstrated that environmental impact labels using simple A–F grading systems significantly reduced the environmental impact scores of food purchases across multiple indicators, suggesting that standardised Environmental Impact Scores similar to nutritional labels could enable investors and consumers to easily compare sustainability performance without requiring specialised expertise to interpret complex technical reports.[30]

II. Tier two: social norm integration

The second tier of the model adopts the view that environmental decision-making is essentially social, considering others' actions, social expectations, and how decisions are likely to be perceived by those who matter. This level embeds information about social norms into policy design through tools that render environmental performance visible and that activate social influence processes to promote compliance.

Social comparison mechanisms are an integral part of internalising social norms. It has consistently been found in research that people will change their behaviours when they are informed that they score well or poorly on a comparative basis with similar other people.[31] Inclusion of peer comparison is added, along with compulsory reporting on peer comparison that leads to benchmarking systems, allowing organisations to compare themselves with the industry and ultimately providing public access to information where environmental risk is compared between entities, which again makes relative environmental risk visible to stakeholders.

Public disclosure mechanisms play various roles in the layer of social norm integration. These mechanisms 'make environmental performance

29 John-Oliver Engler/David J. Abson/Henrik von Wehrden, 'Navigating cognition biases in the search of sustainability' (2019), 48(6) Ambio, p. 605.

30 Christina Potter et al., 'Effects of environmental impact labels on the sustainability of food purchases: Two randomised controlled trials in an experimental online supermarket' (2022), 17(11) PLoS One, p. e0272800.

31 Hunt Allcott, 'Social Norms and Energy Conservation' (2011), 95(9–10) J. Public Econ., p. 1082.

more visible to stakeholders, thereby creating reputational incentives for better environmental performance'.[32] They also give the information needed for social comparison processes to operate efficiently and market mechanisms to reward better environmental performance.

Corporate sustainability ratings and indices are an example of the use of public disclosure mechanisms. The model encompasses a need for standardising the reporting of environmental performance for credible comparison among different organisations. The rankings can be designed to mobilise competitive dynamics and reputational concerns to drive environmental improvements beyond what formal regulations alone might accomplish.

Another manifestation of social norm integration is the use of consumer labelling schemes. As environmental performance information on products and services is disseminated, it enables consumers to articulate their environmental preferences through market choices, thereby generating competitive pressures to improve environmental performance.

III. Tier three: default optimisation

The third layer of the model is the salience of default options within choice architecture. Evidence has shown that people are highly likely to opt for the default option, even when another choice would be better for them.[33] This default effect is one of the most robust results in behavioural economics and provides many possibilities to influence sustainable behaviour via the design of the choice architecture.

Default optimisation is a key application of automatic investment flow in environmental policy. The model includes features such as the automatic enrolment of pension funds and others into sustainable investment options, with an opt-out option allowing individuals to make a free choice, while utilising the default effect to achieve environmental aims. Research has shown that auto-enrolment can lead to a huge increase in take-up rates in retirement savings schemes, and the same is likely to be true of sustainable investment options.[34]

32 Thomas P. Lyon/John W. Maxwell, 'Greenwash: Corporate environmental disclosure under threat of audit' (2011), 20(1) JEMS, p. 3.

33 Johnson/Goldstein (2003), p. 1338.

34 Brigitte Madrian/Dennis Shea, 'The Power of Suggestion: Inertia in 401(k) Participation and Savings Behavior' (2001), 116(4) QJE, p. 1149.

The structure of automatic investing systems necessarily needs to reconcile effectiveness with individual autonomy. Opt-out options enable individuals to make alternative investment choices, with the expectation that most will opt for the default distribution. Default options should be evidence-based on what most people would do if they had complete information and ample time to ponder which option they would choose.

Renewable energy defaults represent another application of default optimisation. The model incorporates automatic enrolment in renewable energy programmes for electricity supply, with opt-out provisions that allow individuals to choose conventional energy sources if they prefer. The default effect operates through a combination of psychological mechanisms that make the pre-selected option 'sticky' and resistant to change. Status quo bias leads individuals to maintain existing arrangements due to the cognitive effort required to evaluate alternatives, while loss aversion makes people reluctant to give up what they perceive as already obtained.[35] Additionally, the default option often serves as an implicit endorsement or recommendation from the choice architect, suggesting that this is the preferred or socially appropriate choice.[36] This approach leverages these psychological tendencies to increase renewable energy adoption whilst preserving consumer choice and avoiding the political resistance that might accompany mandatory renewable energy requirements. Field studies in Germany have demonstrated that green energy defaults can achieve adoption rates of approximately 80 % in both household and business sectors, with only 10 % of customers actively choosing to opt out when renewable energy is presented as the standard option.[37]

Banking and financial services can encourage the adoption of low-carbon financial products through default optimisation. The model incorporates financial institutions' obligations to provide low-carbon options as defaults across a range of financial products, from credit cards that automatically offset carbon emissions to bank accounts that redirect a proportion of consumer deposits into sustainable investment funds.

35 Cass R. Sunstein/Lucia A. Reisch, 'Automatically green: Behavioral economics and environmental protection' (2014), 38 Harv. Envtl. L. Rev., p. 127.

36 Ulf Liebe/Jennifer Gewinner/Andreas Diekmann, 'Large and persistent effects of green energy defaults in the household and business sectors' (2021), 5(5) Nat. Hum. Behav., p. 576.

37 Micha Kaiser et al., 'The power of green defaults: The impact of regional variation of opt-out tariffs on green energy demand in Germany' (2020), 174 Ecol. Econ., p. 106685.

E. Policy implications

The utility of a neuro-legal paradigm is applicable in a variety of environmental policy settings, providing tangible approaches to maximise the impact of current policies by lowering the implementation costs and political opposition. The framework's focus on working with, rather than against, psychological instincts provides an opportunity to advance environmental objectives with tactics that feel organic and voluntary to those being regulated.

In the context of a carbon tax, the model suggests a couple of deviations from the classical model that could increase acceptance and adherence. Reframing carbon tax costs (from annual to daily) over time would lower the psychological costs of carbon taxes while maintaining their economic incentives. Inclusion of social comparison information, such as a household's carbon tax payments compared to neighbourhood averages, could potentially capitalise on social proof effects to increase compliance and decrease resistance.

Corporate environmental reporting is another area where the framework makes practical advances. Including peer comparison provisions within mandatory reporting standards may also increase the motivational potential of these regulations by making relative environmental performance more salient to the relevant audience. Such simplified yet psychologically motivated presentation formats may increase the likelihood that environmental information influences stakeholder decision-making.

Financial regulation has been identified as an area with particularly fertile ground for the application of default optimisation techniques. An automatic allocation of people's pensions into sustainable investment options and the right to opt out if you wanted would enable a sea change in investment—a flood of investment to environmentally beneficial projects—without in any way restricting personal choice. Analogous methods might be used for banking products, insurance contracts, and other financial services to support sound and sustainable economic behaviour by designing choice architecture.

F. Economic efficiency considerations

The economic efficiency implications of the neuro-legal framework are typically favourable, as the framework attempts to realise environmental goals by devising mechanisms that lower the costs rather than increase the costs of compliance and monitoring. By integrating regulatory design with underlying psychology, the framework may enhance compliance rates and reduce the need for costly monitoring and enforcement.

Default optimisation rules are especially appealing from an economic efficiency standpoint; they can induce significant changes in behaviour (toward the second-best optimal level) without the need to bear added costs by a regulator or its regulated entities. Compulsory investment of pension funds in sustainable investments would be almost cost-free administratively, potentially channelling billions of pounds into environmentally sound projects.

Cognitive bias mitigation tools are also economically efficient, as they help lower the information processing costs associated with environmental decision-making. By making environmental information accessible as a psychological resource, such approaches may improve the quality of environmental decisions and expedite the processing of complex environmental information by individuals and organisations.

Social norm integration mechanisms could improve economic efficiency by using the market to reward those with better environmental performance. Requirements for public disclosure of response activities and peer comparison-based systems drive competitive pressure for environmental upgrading through market incentives, rather than regulation.

G. Conclusion

This article presents a new neuro-legal paradigm for sustainability law, critically drawing on intersecting lines from neuroscience, behavioural economics, and legal theory to improve environmental regulation. The three-tiered model, which outlines strategies to foster legal compliance through cognitive bias amelioration, social norm incorporation, and default upgrading, has implications for evidence-based policy innovation that align rather than contradict the psychological contours of human decision-making.

The theoretical implications of this article extend well beyond environmental law to encompass broader issues of psychology and legal efficacy. This study is the first to demonstrate how insights from neuroscience and behavioural sciences can be used to inform regulatory design, thereby contributing to the emerging field of neurolaw and providing a foundation for future interdisciplinary collaboration among lawyers, neuroscientists, and behavioural economists.

The policy relevance of this framework is also significant, as it provides policymakers with evidence-based tools to improve their sustainability regulation outcomes and reduce implementation costs and political opposition. The focus on choice architecture and information design makes it possible to achieve environmental goals using methods that respect individual prerogatives, while capturing relevant psychological processes to induce sustainable behaviours.

The policy innovation possibilities of neuro-legal compositionalism are broader than the range of neuro-legal interventions explicitly advanced in this paper; however, they involve a larger shift in how to think about and practice environmental law. This approach, by rooting regulatory design in the science of human psychology, holds the promise of considerably more effective, efficient, and politically durable environmental regulation.

Future advancements in this area will depend on ongoing interdisciplinary engagement among scholars, policymakers, and practitioners. The nature of environmental problems necessitates interdisciplinary approaches that transcend traditional disciplinary boundaries, as encountered in neuroscience, psychology, economics, law, and policy. Only by collaborating in this way can we harness the full potential of neuro-legal approaches to sustainability, which have become an increasingly urgent part of addressing climate change and environmental degradation through better laws.

The framework developed here represents a first step toward a psychologically informed sustainability law. Nevertheless, as empirical work confirms and qualifies these theoretical findings, and as regulators themselves have the chance to test-drive behaviourally informed regulation, the possibilities for achieving environmental policy goals through neuro-legal regimes will necessarily grow, with opportunities for more efficacious responses to the environmental problems that plague modern society.

Sustainable investment treaties: A comparative perspective on balancing investor rights and sustainable development

*Anita Grigoryan**

A. Introduction

At first glance, international investment agreements (IIAs) would appear to inherently promote sustainable development. Investment law is traditionally rooted in a development nexus, as reflected in the opening recital of the Preamble to the Convention on the Settlement of Investment Disputes between States and Nationals of other States (ICSID Convention). Admittedly, foreign investment can contribute to macroeconomic growth, provide a means for financing targeted development projects, and enable the transfer of knowledge and technology.[1] Sustainable development, alongside environmental protection and social progress, fundamentally encompasses economic growth.[2] While IIAs appear to align with the goal of economic development, they often fall short of supporting, or may even hinder, the environmental and social dimensions of sustainability. In particular, certain investment protections may constrain states' regulatory space for imple-

* Anita Grigoryan is a PhD candidate at Saarland University and serves as a Legal Advisor at the Central Bank of Armenia. Her doctoral research examines the resolution of cryptocurrency-related disputes within the framework of international investment arbitration.

1 Stephan W. Schrill/Christian J. Tams/Rainer Hofmann, ‚International investment law and development: Friends or foes?' in: Stephan W. Schrill/Christian J. Tams/Rainer Hofmann (eds.), International Investment Law and Development: Bridging the Gap, Frankfurt Investment and Economic Law Series (2015).

2 Schrill/Tams/Hofmann (2015), p. 18.

menting measures aimed at safeguarding the environment or promoting social welfare. Nevertheless, the architecture of IIAs has gradually evolved to incorporate elements more conducive to sustainable development. New-generation treaties increasingly include sustainability-oriented provisions, reflecting a shift towards a more balanced approach that seeks to align investor protection with broader public policy objectives.

This article provides a comparative analysis of investment treaties through the lens of sustainability. It examines legal mechanisms designed to reconcile investor protection with environmental and social objectives and explores the challenges and prospects for harmonisation across jurisdictions and treaty frameworks.

The first section explores the evolution of IIAs from traditional instruments of investment attraction and protection to frameworks that increasingly embed sustainability provisions and assesses the degree to which these developments resolve the normative tensions between investor rights and public interest regulation. Bearing in mind the evolving balance between international investor rights and sustainable development, the second section identifies legal mechanisms and approaches that may facilitate this balance. Finally, the third section briefly outlines the challenges and prospects of achieving a balance between international investment law and sustainable development.

B. Evolution of investment treaties in terms of sustainability

Primarily designed to encourage foreign investment by mitigating the typical risks associated with long-term investment projects, IIAs create a stable and predictable legal environment that benefits both host states and investors.[3] Accordingly, IIAs are treaties concluded between two or more states with the aim of mutually promoting and safeguarding investments made by investors from one state in the territory of the other.[4]

3 Rudolf Dolzer/Christoph Schreuer, Principles of International Investment Law, 2nd ed. (2012), p. 22; Berfu Beysulen Angin, 'The Right to Regulate vs Investment Protection: Unveiling the Causes of Imbalance and the Limits of Current Reform Efforts in International Investment Law' (2025), ICSID Review – Foreign Investment Law Journal, pp. 16–7.

4 Marius Dotzauer/Lisa Biber-Freudenberger/Thomas Dietz, 'The Rise of Sustainability Provisions in International Investment Agreements' (2024), Global Environmental Politics 24 (4), p. 10, 12.

In parallel, sustainable development can be defined as 'development that meets the needs of the present without compromising the ability of future generations to meet their own needs'[5] and covers nearly all aspects of life, including economic growth, environmental protection, and social advancement.[6] Committed to addressing urgent global challenges, the 193 United Nations member states unanimously adopted the 2030 Agenda for Sustainable Development in 2015. The Agenda outlines 17 ambitious Sustainable Development Goals (SDGs) aimed at promoting equitable and environmentally sustainable progress through unprecedented international cooperation by 2030.[7]

Today, there are over 3,000 IIAs, ranging from bilateral to multilateral treaties, as well as free trade agreements with investment provisions. Nonetheless, it remains contested whether these instruments contribute to the advancement of sustainable development or, conversely, impede its realisation.

I. Traditional IIAs and their sustainability gaps

Traditional IIAs have historically aimed to shield foreign investors from political and regulatory risks by providing a range of substantive protections such as national treatment, most-favoured-nation treatment, protection against unlawful expropriation, guarantees of fair and equitable treatment (FET), and full protection and security, alongside procedural guarantees including access to binding investor–state dispute settlement (ISDS), thereby fostering a favourable climate for foreign direct investment.[8] At the same time, traditional IIAs rarely provided explicit recognition of the contracting states' inherent right to regulate or to introduce new investment-related measures in pursuit of domestic policy objectives, thereby significantly constraining their regulatory autonomy, particularly in areas of public interest such as environmental protection and social policy.

5 United Nations, Report of the World Commission on Environment and Development: Our Common Future, (1987), part 1, chapter 2, para. 1.

6 Schrill/Tams/Hofmann (2015), p. 18.

7 United Nations, General Assembly Resolution 70/1 (21 October 2015) UN Doc A/RES/70/1; Johnson/Sachs/Lobel (2019), p. 60.

8 Dotzauer/Biber-Freudenberger/Dietz (2024), pp. 12; Angin (2025), p. 8.

The constrained regulatory autonomy, coupled with the lack of emphasis on environmental protection in earlier IIAs, has led to investment disputes in which arbitral tribunals were required to determine whether state regulatory measures constituted breaches of the obligations set out in the applicable IIA.[9] In Philip Morris v. Uruguay, a tobacco company challenged Uruguay's anti-smoking regulations, including requirements for graphic health warnings and restrictions on the use of company trademarks, alleging violations of FET and indirect expropriation[10]. Although Uruguay ultimately prevailed,[11] the case exemplified how the exercise of a state's right to regulate in the public interest, particularly in the area of public health, can be challenged by a foreign investor within the framework of ISDS. Similarly, in Vattenfall v. Germany, an energy company commenced arbitration against Germany, arguing that the country's enforcement of more stringent environmental regulations on a coal-fired power plant undermined its investment expectations.[12]

This highlights the fundamental challenge arising from the mismatch between the static, stringent protections in IIAs and the adaptive, forward-looking nature of sustainable development. Whereas sustainable development demands flexible regulatory mechanisms to tackle issues like environmental harm, social disparities, and economic shifts, IIAs frequently constrain states with rigid legal obligations. As Johnson, Sachs and Lobel highlight, numerous IIAs fail to align with the SDGs: these goals call for holistic governance strategies that support, rather than hinder, public interest regulation.[13]

Earlier investment treaties seldom mention sustainable development and even more rarely include provisions to support it, which has, in some cases, discouraged states from adopting new sustainability measures due to the risk of triggering costly ISDS claims – a phenomenon known as 'regulatory

---

9 Angin (2025), p. 8.

10 Philip Morris Brands Sàrl, Philip Morris Products S.A. and Abal Hermanos S.A. v. Oriental Republic of Uruguay, ICSID Case No. ARB/10/7, Award, paras. 9–14.

11 Ibid., para. 590.

12 Vattenfall AB, Vattenfall Europe AG, Vattenfall Europe Generation AG v. Federal Republic of Germany, ICSID Case No. ARB/09/6, Request for Arbitration, paras. 8–12.

13 Lise Johnson/Lisa Sachs/Nathan Lobel, 'Aligning International Investment Agreements with the Sustainable Development Goals' (2019), Columbia Journal of Transnational Law 58, p. 58, 64.

chill'.[14] Moreover, Dotzauer, Biber-Freudenberger, and Dietz empirically show that treaties signed before the early 2000s generally lacked any sustainability provisions, contributing to an overall investment regime that privileged investor rights over environmental and social considerations.[15]

II. Modernisation of investment treaties in pursuit of sustainable development

Notwithstanding, in recent years a growing number of states and international organisations have recognised the need to reform the existing regime and remedy the aforementioned misalignment. Firstly, they do so by revising their existing investment treaties to incorporate sustainability clauses, and by including such clauses in their newly concluded IIAs.[16] A range of sustainability-related provisions can be found in contemporary IIAs, including preambles that link investment to sustainable development, substantive commitments to uphold environmental and labour standards, clauses affirming the state's right to regulate, provisions placing obligations on investors to comply with host state environmental and labour laws, mechanisms that promote sustainable investment, etc.[17] Research has been conducted examining IIAs with the most references to sustainability, identifying the Morocco–Nigeria Bilateral Investment Treaty (BIT) of 2016 as the one containing the highest number with 60 references in total.[18] The Chile–Hong Kong SAR (Hong Kong Special Administrative Region of the People's Republic of China) BIT and the Burkina Faso–Canada BIT, stand out for their frequent references to sustainability.[19] Similarly, the

14 Dotzauer/Biber-Freudenberger/Dietz (2024), p. 13; Vera Korzun, 'The Right to Regulate in Investor-State Arbitration: Slicing and Dicing Regulatory Carve-Outs' (2021), Vanderbilt Journal of Transnational Law 50 (2), p. 355, 360; Angin (2025), p. 24; Kyla Tienhaara, 'Regulatory Chill and the Threat of Arbitration: A View from Political Science' in: Chester Brown/Kate Miles (eds.), EVOLUTION IN INVESTMENT TREATY LAW AND ARBITRATION (2011), p. 606; Bart-Jaap Verbeek, 'The Modernization of the Energy Charter Treaty: Fulfilled or Broken Promises?' (2023), Business and Human Rights Journal 8 (1), p. 97, 99.

15 Dotzauer/Biber-Freudenberger/Dietz (2024), pp. 22–23.

16 Dotzauer/Biber-Freudenberger/Dietz (2024), p. 14; Schrill/Tams/Hofmann (2015), p. 6.

17 Dotzauer/Biber-Freudenberger/Dietz (2024), pp. 23–25.

18 Ibid, pp. 23–24.

19 Ibid.

Comprehensive Economic and Trade Agreement (CETA) between Canada and the European Union (EU) stands out among treaties with investment provisions, with an impressive 950 references and a dedicated chapter to sustainability.[20] These examples reflect a clear shift in the normative framework of international investment law.

This positive trend is visible not only in the treaty texts themselves but also in the drafting recommendations provided by international organisations such as the United Nations Conference on Trade and Development (UNCTAD).[21] UNCTAD's Investment Policy Framework for Sustainable Development (IPFSD) advises treaty negotiators to include provisions that affirm the right to regulate, reference international environmental commitments, and align with sustainable development principles.[22]

Importantly, these clauses go beyond symbolic gestures and establish enforceable standards. As a result, they have the potential to influence treaty interpretation and reduce the risk of arbitral tribunals striking down public interest measures. Moreover, they help reposition investment law as a tool for advancing, rather than obstructing, sustainability objectives.

Eventually, these developments reflect a normative shift, in which sustainability is gradually being repositioned not as an external policy consideration, but as a core element of international investment law itself. This shift is part of a broader trend where investment law is becoming increasingly responsive to public concerns and more closely integrated with global governance norms.

Nevertheless, the degree of innovation varies across regions. While the EU and Canada have been leaders in treaty reform, many agreements signed by or among developing countries continue to focus narrowly on investment protection.[23] Additionally, numerous existing treaties remain unreformed, and the divergent approaches across jurisdictions contribute to fragmentation that may limit the overall systemic impact of these reforms.

Taking these factors into account, the second section analyses the legal mechanisms for balancing investor protection and sustainability, which may further support and positively influence these recent changes.

20 Ibid.

21 Schrill/Tams/Hofmann (2015), p. 6.

22 UNCTAD, Investment Policy Framework for Sustainable Development, https://investmentpolicy.unctad.org/investment-policy-framework (last accessed: 29 June 2025).

23 Dotzauer/Biber-Freudenberger/Dietz (2024), p. 12.

C. Legal mechanisms for balancing investor protection and sustainability

Amidst the shifting priorities and the progressive transformation of treaty practice, the identification of legal mechanisms that can concretely advance the alignment between investor protection and sustainable development becomes increasingly important.

I. Classic treaty-based mechanisms

As already indicated in the preceding section, a key legal mechanism is the explicit recognition in IIAs of a state's right to regulate within its territory and its flexibility to pursue legitimate public policy objectives, such as the protection of public health or the environment, without infringing investors' rights, as exemplified by the CETA.[24] This recognition establishes balance between investor protection and states' regulatory autonomy, providing legal certainty for governments to implement public interest measures without the constant risk of investor-state disputes. In addition to recognising the state's right to regulate, further improvements could be made by incorporating explicit references to sustainable development in the preambles of IIAs.[25]

Additionally, the inclusion of direct investor obligations within investment treaties, as seen in the Netherlands Model BIT (2019), represents another legal mechanism aimed at enhancing the compatibility of IIAs with SDGs and mitigating the inherent tension between international investment law and sustainable development.[26] According to Article 7 (1) of the Netherlands Model BIT (2019) investors and their investments shall comply with domestic laws and regulations of the host state, including laws and regulations on human rights, environmental protection and labour laws. This approach reinforces the accountability of investors, ensuring that their activities align with the host state's development priorities and legal framework, and thus contributes to more responsible and sustainable investment practices. Notably, this mechanism marks a significant departure from traditional IIAs, which largely imposed obligations on states while granting broad rights to investors.

---

24 Shunta Yamaguchi, 'Greening regional trade agreements on investment', OECD Trade and Environment Working Papers 2020/03, (2020), p. 31.

25 Schrill/Tams/Hofmann (2015), p. 29.

26 Yamaguchi (2020), p. 47.

II. Complementary and emerging mechanisms

While the legal mechanisms already embedded in some new-generation IIAs, such as the right to regulate and direct investor obligations, represent the most evident steps towards reconciling investment protection with sustainable development, the question remains whether further mechanisms could help strengthen this balance. In this context, it becomes important to distinguish between more far-reaching mechanisms and softer, complementary approaches that can be implemented without fundamentally altering the existing legal framework.

Among the softer approaches suggested by Schill, Tams, and Hofmann, treaty interpretation represents an important mechanism for integrating sustainable development considerations into international investment law. Arbitral tribunals, even under traditional BITs, increasingly apply interpretative techniques such as proportionality analysis and deferential review,[27] allowing states greater policy space to pursue development objectives and comply with international commitments in areas such as human rights and environmental protection.[28] Ultimately, while traditional treaties may appear rigid, their flexible interpretation by tribunals can support sustainable development, depending largely on the readiness of the arbitrators to adopt such an approach.[29]

Another soft mechanism suggested by the same scholars involves interpreting investment treaty provisions as tools for promoting good governance. This approach views such provisions as requiring states to uphold legal standards that support economic growth, a core component of sustainable development.[30] In particular, arbitral tribunals have concretised the FET standard by aligning it with key principles of the rule of law, including principles such as legal certainty, the protection of legitimate expec-

27 Tecmed v. Mexico (ICSID Case No. ARB(AF)/00/2, 2003), Award (29 May 2003) para. 122; Saluka Investments BV v Czech Republic, UNCITRAL, Partial Award (17 March 2006), para. 306; Total S.A. v. The Argentine Republic, ICSID Case No. ARB/04/01, Decision on Liability (27 December 2010) paras. 123, 197; El Paso Energy International Company v. The Argentine Republic, ICSID Case No. ARB/03/15, Award (31 October 2011) paras. 241–243, 373; Occidental Petroleum Corporation and Occidental Exploration and Production Company v. The Republic of Ecuador, ICSID Case No. ARB/06/11, Award (5 October 2012) paras. 384 ff.

28 Schrill/Tams/Hofmann (2015), p. 30.

29 Ibid.

30 Ibid, p. 31.

tations, due process, and proportionality.[31] When interpreted in this manner, IIAs serve not only to protect investor interests but also to strengthen rule-of-law-based governance frameworks, which contribute to sustainable development in host states.[32]

Among the more far-reaching mechanisms, a noteworthy approach is the strategic encouragement of investments that actively contribute to sustainable development. As Johnson, Sachs and Lobel propose, instead of focusing solely on imposing obligations on host states regarding the treatment of foreign investors, IIAs could adopt a more comprehensive approach to investment governance, one that involves addressing concrete barriers to sustainable investment and incorporating commitments from home states to actively support and encourage investments that align with SDG.[33] Several recent treaties illustrate this shift. The Japan–Mexico Economic Partnership Agreement explicitly commits parties to foster investment in sectors that advance sustainable development and climate action through institutional cooperation, information exchange, and capacity building.[34] Similarly, the Cotonou Agreement between the EU and African, Caribbean and Pacific Group of States includes measures such as capacity building for investment promotion agencies, risk capital provision, and dissemination of business opportunities to encourage investment in underrepresented regions.[35] This mechanism marks an important evolution in treaty practice by aiming not only to protect investments but also to guide them towards outcomes that align with sustainable development objectives.

The second far-reaching mechanism for aligning IIAs with sustainable development, supported by Johnson, Sachs and Lobel, is ensuring that IIAs do not protect harmful investments.[36] Rather than offering broad protections regardless of impact, IIAs should exclude or limit protections for investments that clearly undermine the SDGs, such as those contribut-

31 Saluka Investments BV v Czech Republic, UNCITRAL, Partial Award (17 March 2006), para. 302; Waste Management v. Mexico (ICSID Case No. ARB(AF)/00/3, 2004), Award (30 April 2004), para. 98; Tecmed v. Mexico (ICSID Case No. ARB(AF)/00/2, 2003) Award (29 May 2003), para. 154, CMS Gas Transmission Company v. Argentina (ICSID Case No. ARB/01/8, 2005) Award (12 May 2015), para. 274, Bayindir v. Pakistan (ICSID Case No. ARB/03/29, 2009), Award (27 August 2009), para. 178.

32 Schrill/Tams/Hofmann (2015), p. 32.

33 Johnson/Sachs/Lobel (2019), p. 69.

34 Ibid.

35 Ibid.

36 Ibid, p. 71.

ing to fossil fuel expansion, violating international labour standards, or resulting from corruption. Given that current IIAs often grant foreign investors stronger procedural and substantive rights than those available in domestic legal systems, effectively subsidising harmful activities through ISDS privileges and broad protections, governments should critically assess which types of investments genuinely warrant such regulatory support.[37] IIAs could introduce ex ante and ex post mechanisms to screen, exclude, or condition protection based on environmental, social, and governance criteria.[38] This may include categorical exclusions (e.g. fossil fuel extraction) or requirements that investments meet standards of responsible conduct and legality. Moreover, limiting access to ISDS for investors engaged in harmful or unlawful practices, even if some protections remain, could serve as a disincentive to high-risk, unsustainable activities.[39] Through such tools, IIAs could avoid undermining global sustainability efforts and better align with broader international obligations and policy coherence goals.

In addition to these far-reaching mechanisms, another important mechanism lies in the reform efforts led by international policy-making bodies, particularly the UNCTAD. UNCTAD plays a central role in aligning investment law with sustainable development by addressing key concerns such as the imbalance in treaty focus, lack of transparency and public participation, vague treaty language, and the absence of investor obligations.[40] These challenges have shaped UNCTAD's reform agenda, including the development of the IPFSD, and continue to inform its broader efforts to promote investment that genuinely supports sustainable development.[41]

In conclusion, aligning IIAs with sustainable development requires a multifaceted approach that combines both soft and far-reaching legal mechanisms. Enhancing states' right to regulate, incorporating investor obligations, and leveraging treaty interpretation can create more policy space within existing frameworks. Simultaneously, proactive treaty design, exclusion of harmful investments, and global reform initiatives are essential to promote responsible and development-oriented investment. Notably, the mechanism of not subsidising harmful investments could represent a transformative and potentially radical shift in international investment law, challenging long-standing standards and pushing the regime towards

37 Ibid, p. 72.
38 Ibid, p. 76.
39 Ibid, p. 80.
40 Schrill/Tams/Hofmann (2015), p. 34.
41 Ibid.

greater alignment with global sustainability goals. Together, these strategies contribute to a more balanced and sustainable international investment regime.

D. Challenges and prospects

Despite the growing trend of IIAs and investment law becoming more attuned to public concerns and sustainable development, and the clear identification of legal mechanisms capable of promoting positive change, challenges remain.

As Schrill, Tams, and Hofmann observe, 'international investment law has been gradually built, treaty by treaty (or 'BIT by BIT', as is often said),' resulting in a regime composed of thousands of overlapping and often inconsistent IIAs, each negotiated in distinct contexts and guided by differing objectives.[42] This fragmented structure creates significant challenges, as it undermines the development of common standards and precludes the possibility of reforming the system through a single, comprehensive initiative. The lack of coherence is further exacerbated by the absence of systemic guidance, which has made it difficult to integrate cross-cutting objectives such as the SDGs into the legal framework.

Moreover, the degree of state commitment to integrating sustainability into investment law varies considerably across jurisdictions. While a number of states, most notably EU member states and Canada,[43] have taken proactive steps to incorporate sustainable development clauses into their IIAs, others have remained wedded to a more traditional model. This conventional approach tends to prioritise investor protection, often at the expense of broader public interest considerations such as environmental preservation, human rights, or social welfare. According to research by Dotzauer, Biber-Freudenberger and Dietz, states with higher levels of domestic environmental protection tend to include more and stricter sustainability provisions in international treaties, partly due to lower adaptation costs.[44] Accordingly, developed countries are more likely to incorporate sustainability references in IIAs than developing states, which often priori-

42 Ibid, p. 11.
43 Dotzauer/Biber-Freudenberger/Dietz (2024), pp. 11–12.
44 Ibid, pp. 18–19.

tise economic growth over ambitious sustainability commitments.[45] As a result, the investment regime continues to reflect and perpetuate significant asymmetries between states.

Additionally, the risk of "regulatory chill" poses a barrier to progressive regulation. In particular, states may refrain from adopting stricter environmental or social regulations due to fears that such measures could be challenged under existing treaty obligations and give rise to costly ISDS claims.[46] This chilling effect can undermine governmental willingness to pursue progressive public interest policies, especially in sensitive sectors such as environmental protection, public health, and labour rights. Notably, the governments of Denmark and New Zealand have acknowledged that the mere threat of investor claims has deterred them from implementing more ambitious climate policies.[47] Such instances highlight the broader systemic tension between investment protection and the policy space states require to achieve their sustainable development objectives.

Another key challenge is the inconsistency in arbitral awards, stemming from the decentralised structure of the ISDS system. In the absence of a centralised adjudicatory body or appellate mechanism, different tribunals often interpret similar treaty provisions in divergent ways. Dotzauer, Biber-Freudenberger and Dietz illustrate this with the example of Eco Oro v. Colombia, where the arbitral tribunal held that the general exception clause in the relevant investment treaty did not exempt the state from the obligation to pay compensation.[48] This contributes to fragmented jurisprudence and undermines the legal predictability necessary for both states and investors. Institutional reforms, such as the establishment of a multilateral investment court or appellate body, have been proposed to address this gap, though progress has been slow and politically contested.[49]

While the road ahead is complex, the growing inclusion of sustainability provisions in IIAs offers a foundation upon which a more balanced and coherent investment regime can be built. Provided there is interna-

45 Ibid.

46 Kyla Tienhaara, 'Regulatory Chill in a Warming World: The Threat to Climate Policy Posed by Investor–State Dispute Settlement' (2018), Transnational Environmental Law 7 (2), pp. 229–250, p. 233; Verbeek (2023), p. 99; Angin (2025), p. 24.

47 Dotzauer/Biber-Freudenberger/Dietz (2024), p. 12.

48 Dotzauer/Biber-Freudenberger/Dietz (2024), p. 29; Eco Oro Minerals Corp. v. Republic of Colombia, ICSID Case No. ARB/16/41, Award on Damages (15 July 2024), para. 358.

49 Schrill/Tams/Hofmann (2015), p. 29, Gus Van Harten, Investment Treaty Arbitration and Public Law, Oxford University Press (2007), p. 180 ff.

tional commitment, states can ensure that economic growth aligns with environmental and social objectives, while strengthening international cooperation, enhancing treaty clarity, and aligning with global sustainability commitments will be key to achieving a more balanced investment regime.

Notably, achieving the desired balance between IIAs and sustainable development does not require a radical dismantling of investment law. By recognising specific characteristics of investment law, this balance can still be attained, provided there is genuine political will and commitment from the relevant stakeholders. Moreover, fostering greater cooperation and coordination among investment treaty parties and arbitral institutions is essential to effectively align investment governance with sustainable development objectives.

E. Conclusion

As mentioned in the introduction, IIAs were initially conceived to attract foreign capital and promote development by providing legal certainty and protection for investors. This development-centric rationale aligned, at least in theory, with the economic pillar of sustainable development. However, as the first section demonstrated, traditional IIAs often failed to support the environmental and social dimensions of sustainability and, in many cases, constrained states' regulatory autonomy, contributing to a "regulatory chill."

Today, more IIAs reflect an evolving understanding of investment's role in sustainable development. The inclusion of sustainability clauses in new-generation IIAs signals a normative shift, transforming investment law from a rigid system of investor protection into a more balanced framework that acknowledges states' rights to regulate and promotes sustainable investment. This evolution seeks to bridge the gap between the static nature of traditional IIAs and the dynamic requirements of sustainable development.

Importantly, achieving this balance does not require dismantling investment law. Rather, meaningful reform is possible from within the system, by recognising its structural features, addressing fragmentation, and rethinking how its mechanisms are designed and interpreted. As examined in the second section, legal mechanisms such as the recognition of states' right to regulate, the imposition of direct investor obligations, and provisions encouraging sustainable investment all represent concrete steps towards this goal.

Nonetheless, the challenges discussed in the third section, from fragmented treaty practice to inconsistent arbitral jurisprudence and persistent asymmetries between states, highlight that progress will depend on more than just legal drafting. Political will, institutional coordination, and genuine cooperation will be essential.

Ultimately, the future of international investment law lies not in a binary choice between investor rights and sustainable development, but in integrating the latter into the very fabric of the former. Through legal innovation, thoughtful reform, and political courage, international investment law can be reshaped into a more coherent and sustainability-friendly framework that balances investor protection with the broader public policy objectives.

Climate stress tests in banking: Navigating risk and climate finance

Bahar Ferahköse

A. Introduction

Banking regulators can play an important role for climate change through two primary objectives: safeguarding financial stability by managing climate related risks and through promoting climate finance.[1] This research examines whether climate stress tests can serve this dual purpose: safeguarding financial stability by managing climate-related risks while promoting climate finance. It provides a dual perspective on sustainability law as applied to banking regulation and explores the methodological limits of current approaches and the challenges of extending prudential tools to broader climate policy objectives.

1 European Banking Authority, Report on the Role of Environmental and Social Risks in the Prudential Framework, 12 October 2023, EBA/REP/2023/34.

Traditionally, the primary mandate of banking supervisors has been to ensure the safety and soundness of the banking sector using conventional risk management tools.[2] Consequently, regulators have adopted a risk-based approach to climate change as they acknowledged climate crisis primarily as a financial risk driver. While they recognise the potential role of banking finance in directing financial flows towards climate goals, their capacity to mobilise capital has been mostly limited by purely risk-based strategies.[3] This tension, coupled with the difficulty of quantifying the unprecedented risks pertaining to climate change,[4] has hindered the development of a more proactive regulatory framework. So, even though reaching a common ground has been challenging, one common approach seems to be the adoption of climate stress tests.

Evident in the use of such tests by the supervisors worldwide, climate stress tests have emerged as a key regulatory response.[5] They have been studied in the literature, however their dual role, risk management versus climate finance promotion, and the connection between the two have yet to be critically assessed. They are promising testing frameworks for understanding these dual climate objectives of banking regulations, ensuring the safety and soundness of the banking system while fostering a green transition. Thus, these tests will be analysed below to understand what they can offer and what they cannot solve concerning these two objectives.

To conduct this assessment, the methodology for the research combines a systematic literature review, an analysis of the ECB's 2022 climate stress test, and a doctrinal legal review of the EU regulatory framework and relevant Basel Committee publications.

---

2 Basel Committee on Banking Supervision, Basel III: A global regulatory framework for more resilient banks and banking systems, 1 June 2011.

3 Jerome H. Powell, 'Statement on principles for climate-related financial risk management for large financial institutions' (Speech, Federal Reserve, 24 October 2023), https://www.federalreserve.gov/newsevents/pressreleases/powell-statement-20231024b.htm (last accessed: 8 September 2025).

4 Patrick Bolton/Morgan Després/Luiz Awazu Pereira da Silva/Frédéric Samama/Romain Svartzman, 'The Green Swan: Central Banking and Financial Stability in the Age of Climate Change' (2020), Bank for International Settlements, https://www.bis.org/publ/othp31.htm (last accessed 22 July 2025).

5 See European Central Bank, Climate Stress Test Report, 2022; Bank of England, Results of the 2021 Climate Biennial Exploratory Scenario, 2022.

B. Climate stress tests

Stress testing has been a critical risk management tool and core element in banking supervision especially since the 2008 financial crisis. In these tests, the resilience of individual banks or the whole banking sector is assessed using scenarios involving a variety of adverse exogenous shocks like market volatility, sharp changes in GDP and employment. These shocks usually consist of extremely severe, but quantifiable, parameters. Upon generating such scenarios, banks are tested to see whether they can withstand such tail risks with their present capital. In the event that it is determined that the amount of capital was not enough to survive such shocks, the relevant capital requirement is adjusted upward.[6]

Climate stress tests build on this practice but differ in methodology and focus. The focus of these regulatory tools is to measure the level of exposure of sector participants to climate change related risks. Also, unlike conventional stress tests, the methodology also needs to account for new risk drivers introduced by climate change. These risks materialize through two primary channels: physical risks, arising from the direct impacts of extreme weather events such as sea level rise, wildfires etc. and transition risks, arising due to the policy, technological, legal, and market changes in the transition to low-carbon economy.[7]

In order to assess climate-related shocks, climate stress tests require the development of forward-looking scenarios based on different transition pathways and their impacts on banks and the financial system. These scenarios evaluate exposure to both physical and transition risks capturing the vulnerabilities from sectoral carbon dependencies, asset location such as mortgages, and long-term climate policy trajectories.[8]

The Network for Greening the Financial System (NGFS) has been a front runner in developing the scenarios used in these climate stress tests.[9] Their scenarios provide a common and up-to-date reference point for understanding how climate change and climate policy and technology trends

6 John Armour et al. (2016), p. 636.

7 Bolton et al., Principles of Financial Regulation (2020).

8 Basel Committee on Banking Supervision, The Role of Climate Scenario Analysis in Strengthening the Management and Supervision of Climate-Related Financial Risks, 16 April 2024.

9 Viral V Acharya/Richard Berner Robert Engle/Hyeyoon Jung,/Johannes Stroebel/Xuran Zeng/Yihao Zhao, 'Climate Stress Testing' (2023), 15 Annual Review of Financial Economics, pp. 497 et seqq.

could evolve in different futures. Each scenario offers a distinct perspective on how climate physical risks and transition risks can present themselves in different future contexts. In addition to these risk drivers, further models are used to translate these climate risks into economic and financial variables such as GDP and interest rates which are then used for stress tests.[10]

C. Analysis of climate stress testing from dual perspective

This section is the summary of preliminary findings on the strengths and limitations of climate stress testing for both prudential and climate transition purposes. The analysis is conducted through a systemic review of academic literature, policy documents, and selected supervisory exercises, including the ECB's 2022 climate stress test. Following an initial reading of the main body of work, recurring themes were identified and used to guide a more structured assessment of the sources. These themes formed the basis for the categories used in the analysis. They represent most cited and dominant benefits and limitations, and regulatory implications of climate stress testing as a regulatory tool in light of the initial findings. While the prudential role of climate stress testing can be assessed in terms of its strengths and methodological constraints, its potential role in promoting climate finance is more contested. Building upon the clearer account in Section I of what stress tests currently achieve for prudential purposes, Section II turns to the opportunities and barriers involved in extending these tools to support broader climate policy objectives.

I. Climate stress testing for risk identification and management

Stress testing is already a familiar supervisory instrument, and its application to climate risks has been trialled in practice. These exercises provide valuable insights into risk identification, but also expose the limitations of using risk-based tools to respond to climate crisis. This section reviews the extent to which these tests can succeed in this mission and explore their potential limitations.

10 NGFS, NGFS Climate Scenarios: Technical Documentation (January 2025), https://www.ngfs.net/system/files/2025-01/NGFS%20Climate%20Scenarios%20Technical%20Documentation.pdf (last accessed 21 July 2025).

1. Prudential strengths

a) System wide analysis and closing information gaps

One key objective of climate stress testing is that it allows banks to understand their level of exposure and vulnerability to climate change-related risks. As a risk management tool, stress testing enables a granular assessment of transition and physical risks over a longer time horizon than regular risk assessments.[11]

In the ECB's 2022 stress testing for transition risk, this meant focusing on loan-level data for exposures to 22 carbon-intensive sectors, and for physical risks, mapping exposures at the asset level using location-specific data. Both approaches indicate a granular assessment of climate risks, enabling banks to bridge the gap in understanding how specific assets, sectors, or regions are more exposed. This is essential due to the varying nature of climate risks depending on geography, industry, and time horizon. Stress testing thereby offers significant potential to eliminate the information gap around climate risks in the banking sector.[12]

The lack of data on the risks associated with climate change has been identified as one of the key challenges in sustainable finance. The initiatives and voluntary standards developed to bridge this gap have also created a subsequent problem: inconsistency and incomparability of sustainability data.[13] In contrast, standardised disclosure frameworks, such as those based on regulatory stress testing results, have the potential to meet the demand for consistent and comparable data. In particular, supervisory stress testing

11 Mercy Berman DeMenno, 'Environmental Sustainability and Financial Stability: Can Macroprudential Stress Testing Measure and Mitigate Climate-Related Systemic Financial Risk?' (2023), 24 Journal of Banking Regulation, p. 445.

12 It is worth noting that there is growing discussion in the literature about how the scenarios used in climate stress testing create additional data challenges and are often criticized for their lack of granularity. However, since the goal of regulatory stress testing is the sectoral and geographical quantification of climate risks, this study considers granularity a benefit compared to other regulatory tools.

13 Nathan de Arriba-Sellier, 'The International Regulation and Coordination of Sustainable Finance', in Daniëlla Dam-de Jong/Fabian Amtenbrink (eds), Netherlands Yearbook of International Law 2021: A Greener International Law—International Legal Responses to the Global Environmental Crisis (2023), p. 191.

exercises[14] address the systemic nature of climate-related financial risks and reveal results for all stakeholders, including supervisors and regulators.[15]

Supervisory climate stress tests aggregate firm-level data and present a comprehensive, system-wide analysis of climate change impacts across the financial sector and broader economy by addressing correlated exposures, contagion effect, and risk propagation.[16] As a unique form of systemic risk, climate change has the potential to trigger both exogenous and endogenous sources of systemic instability. The contagion effects captured through climate scenarios show how climate shocks can be magnified within a complex financial system and guide regulators on the true potential impact on the stability of the banking system.[17]

The sophistication of climate stress testing as a risk management tool enables both granular analysis and system-wide assessment of exposures. By breaking down risks by sector and location, these tests reveal climate hotspots.[18] The results provide regulators with a roadmap to introduce targeted regulatory measures.[19] Finally, the disclosure of the data collected and analysed through such exercises enhances market transparency and closes data gaps for market participants to better understand the climate change related financial risks.[20]

---

14 Such as the one prescribed under Directive 2013/36/EU of the European Parliament and of the Council of 26 June 2013 on access to the activity of credit institutions and the prudential supervision of credit institutions and investment firms [2013] OJ L176/338, art 100, as amended by Directive (EU) 2019/878 [2019] OJ L150/253.

15 DeMenno (2023), pp. 449 seqq.

16 Ibid.

17 Although current models still do not capture this accurately, regulators and policy-makers such as the EBA are focusing on this area to incorporate contagion effects into scenario pathways.

18 ECB, Climate Stress Test Report (2022).

19 Matthias Täger/Simon Dikau, 'Purposeful Scenario Analysis: A Framework to Guide Central Banks and Financial Supervisors in the Selection and Design of Climate Scenarios' (2023), Grantham Research Institute on Climate Change and the Environment https://www.lse.ac.uk/granthaminstitute/publication/purposeful-scenario-analysis/ (last accessed: 21 July 2025).

20 As also prescribed by Financial Stability Board, Supervisory and Regulatory Approaches to Climate-Related Risks: Interim Report (29 April 2022) https://www.fsb.org/2022/04/supervisory-and-regulatory-approaches-to-climate-related-risks-interim-report/ (last accessed: 21 July 2025).

b) Forward-looking analysis

Climate-related financial risks present unprecedented, unique, and erratic features that can only be effectively managed through forward-looking methods.[21] Scenario analysis and stress testing relying on scenarios have been highlighted by the Basel Committee[22] and policy makers as one of the most suitable tools for this purpose.[23]

Traditional risk assessment models typically rely on historical data.[24] For example, most risk models banks utilise, calculates the probability of default as the average historical default rate for a given counterparty by analysing 5 to 7 years of historical data on the counterparty and calibrating the rate to the maturity date. This is also prescribed by relevant provisions in the Basel standards.[25] This reliance on historical data within both the Basel and EU regulatory frameworks creates a significant challenge when integrating forward-looking risks, such as climate-related financial risks.[26]

Because no historical precedent exists for physical or transition risk events, traditional models are insufficient for estimating their broader economic effects. The forward-looking nature of scenario analysis and stress testing, gives them a noticeable advantage over other regulatory tools for identifying and managing climate-related risks. This is particularly due to their use of scenario design and economic modelling such as DICE.[27]

c) Scenario development and international cooperation

Process of developing scenarios for climate stress testing leads to improvement in overall climate risk management. This process supports the identification of risks as well as building stronger international cooperation and

21 Bolton et al. (2020).

22 Ebbe Rogge, 'Climate Change Stress Testing for the Banking System', Leiden Law School Research Paper, Hazelhoff Research Paper Series No 14, (2023), https://ssrn.com/abstract=4453047 (last accessed 21 July 2025).

23 Laurent Clerc, 'Managing Climate Change Risks: The Role of Governance and Scenario Analysis' (2021), 15(1) Journal of Risk Management in Financial Institutions, p. 38.

24 Armour et al. (2016), p. 455.

25 Basel Committee on Banking Supervision, Basel III (2011).

26 Basel Committee on Banking Supervision, Climate-Related Financial Risks – Measurement Methodologies, 14 November 2021.

27 Basel Committee on Banking Supervision (2024).

a common language among banking supervisors. NGFS plays a key role in this area and is frequently referenced by both regulators and financial institutions for their own scenario analysis exercises.[28] Although not all supervisors adopt the NGFS scenarios directly, almost all use them as a common baseline and supplement them with additional scenarios relevant to their own economies.[29]

To mitigate climate-related financial risks, the first step is to identify and quantify how climate shocks impact portfolios of banks and, consequently, the financial system. This is an immensely challenging task due to the unprecedented nature of climate change as a financial risk driver, but it remains essential.[30] In this effort, the development of climate scenarios contributes significantly to a deeper understanding of climate-related risks.[31]

The models used in scenario analysis and the translation of these scenarios into economic metrics also enhance understanding of climate risks.[32] The extensive academic literature developed to improve these scenarios supports more accurate estimations. As DeMenno points out, the process of scenario development may also help refine the frameworks for green taxonomies, sustainable accounting methodologies, and climate risk disclosure schemes, thereby advancing climate risk analytics.[33]

Furthermore, the use of common scenarios in climate stress testing promotes international cooperation to identify and mitigate climate-related financial risks.[34] Since climate risks often cross-national borders, regulators must work beyond the limits of their jurisdictions. The use of shared scenarios offers a strong foundation for coordination among jurisdictions. Enhanced collaboration between financial and environmental authorities ensures a more accurate translation of climate models into financial risk scenarios, despite differing assumptions.[35]

28 Rogge (2023).

29 Acharya et al. (2023).

30 Basel Committee on Banking Supervision (2021).

31 Täger/Dikau (2023).

32 Ibid.

33 DeMenno (2023), p. 455.

34 Banque de France, Climate Scenario Analysis to Assess Financial Risks: Some Encouraging First Steps, 8 July 2022.

35 DeMenno (2023).

2. Technical and methodological challenges

a) Radical uncertainty

Stress testing introduces innovative ways to integrate climate change into risk management, but, it still does not resolve the fundamental challenge posed by the radical uncertainty of climate related financial risks.[36] These risks involve immeasurable probabilities due to complex environmental, social, and economic interactions.[37] This complexity also limits the effectiveness of stress testing because these tools rely heavily on assumptions used during scenario design.[38] The climate related financial risks are deeply connected to variables such as environmental tipping points, social transitions, and feedback loops. Because these variables are hard to quantify, climate stress test models often fall insufficient.[39]

There is also uncertainty on the trajectories of transition risks especially considering today's rapidly evolving geopolitical landscape. It is unclear which policies will be adopted to address climate change, and the consequences of those policies for the financial sector are similarly uncertain. While current transition scenarios rely on reasonable assumptions, future developments may follow a different path. As a result, transition risks also remain difficult to assess, even though they are recognised as significant.[40] This applies to all models based on random variation, but it is especially relevant here because of the significant uncertainty that affects every aspect of climate scenario modelling.[41]

---

36 Bolton et al. (2020).

37 María J Nieto/Chryssa Papathanassiou, 'Financing the Orderly Transition to a Low Carbon Economy in the EU: The Regulatory Framework for the Banking Channel' (2022), 24 Journal of Banking Regulation, p. 87.

38 Christine M Albano/Maureen I McCarthy/Michael D Dettinger/Stephanie A McAfee, 'Techniques for Constructing Climate Scenarios for Stress Test Applications' (2021), https://doi.org/10.1007/s10584-021-02983-4 (last accessed: 21 July 2025).

39 Hugues Chenet/Josh Ryan-Collins/Frank van Lerven, 'Finance, Climate-Change and Radical Uncertainty: Towards a Precautionary Approach to Financial Policy' (2021), 183 Ecological Economics 106957.

40 Olaf Weber, 'Climate Stress Testing in the Financial Industry' (2022), 146 Journal of Business Research, p. 463.

41 Basel Committee on Banking Supervision (2021).

b) Other methodological challenges

Preliminary findings of this study reveal substantial number of methodological challenges highlighted in the literature that limit the effectiveness of stress testing in identifying and managing climate related financial risks. The following is a selected subset of these challenges.

One major concern relates to the design of economic scenarios. Models commonly used in these exercises, rely heavily on discretionary assumptions. There remains significant uncertainty about how climate change will influence parameters such as interest rates, inflation and financial volatility which are integral inputs for almost all economic models used in stress testing. Current evidence is mixed, and most scenarios assume that lower economic growth due to climate change will result in declining inflation and interest rates. However, these models often overlook complex interactions between climate dynamics and social or economic systems.[42]

Quantifying contagion effects, which are necessary for system wide analysis also presents a significant challenge. Some researchers have noted that stress tests have not provided reliable early warnings neither for traditional financial risks in the past. As a result, their usefulness as an early warning tool for climate impacts also remains in doubt.[43]

Time horizons present another important limitation. The effects of climate change extend over several decades, while many financial instruments, such as loans, have much shorter maturities. This mismatch between the duration of climate risks and the exposure period of financial contracts makes alignment difficult.[44]

II. Climate stress testing and promotion of climate finance

Stress tests are a traditional prudential policy tool for identifying and quantifying the risks banks are exposed. This is also true of climate stress

42 Luca Bongiorno/Andrew Claringbold/Lisa Eichler/Claire Jones/Bert Kramer/Louise Pryor/Nick Spencer, 'Climate Scenario Analysis: An Illustration of Potential Long-Term Economic and Financial Market Impacts' (2022), 27 British Actuarial Journal, p. 1.

43 Claudio Borio/Mathias Drehmann/Kostas Tsatsaronis, 'Stress-Testing Macro Stress Testing: Does It Live Up to Expectations?' (2014), 12 Journal of Financial Stability, p. 3.

44 Rosella Carè, 'Climate-related Financial Risks: Exploring the Known and Charting the Future' (2023), 65 Current Opinion in Environmental Sustainability 101385.

tests. However, the scale of banking finance in many economies means that banks must redirect financial flows towards pathways that align with climate pledges. Assessing whether stress tests can support this objective and contribute to the mobilisation of climate finance is therefore crucial. Such an assessment goes beyond evaluating the strengths and limitations of the tool in prudential terms. It also raises questions about the legitimacy of using supervisory instruments to pursue broader policy goals that extend beyond the traditional mandate of safeguarding the safety and soundness of the banking system.

For such purposes, this section explores how stress testing may contribute to the mobilisation of climate finance, while also identifying the obstacles to its effectiveness in this more contested role.

1. Potential for supporting climate finance

a) Evidence based regulatory intervention and legal legitimacy

Stress testing is a critical tool for regulators, providing concrete evidence that supports further regulatory action.[45] Climate stress tests offer valuable insights into how climate related financial risks may develop into systemic risks and how they affect particular portfolios. This understanding highlights the need for banking regulators and supervisors to implement targeted microprudential and macroprudential regulations.[46]

Banking regulation and supervision operate under strict mandates that require strong evidence to support any regulatory intervention. Core Principles for Effective Banking Supervision[47] defines the primary objective of banking regulation without leaving any margin for hesitation: *the primary objective of banking supervision is to promote the safety and soundness of banks and the banking system.* Therefore, to leverage banking supervision in combating climate change, the first step is to understand its effects on the safety and soundness of banks. The results from stress tests, showing the impact of the climate change on the banks and banking system, thus can provide the necessary evidence to justify regulatory actions to address climate change.[48]

45 Nieto/Papathanassiou (2022).
46 DeMenno (2023).
47 Basel Committee on Banking Supervision, Core Principles for Effective Banking Supervision, 25 April 2024.

Legal concerns regarding the scope of supervisory authority are frequently raised in discussions about the role of banking regulators in promoting climate finance. This is particularly evident in the United States, where prudential tools and supervisory actions often undergo more legal scrutiny.[49] As a result, new initiatives aimed at addressing climate risks may face significant delays. However, stress testing stands out as a tool that falls within the core mandate of banking regulators, the safety and soundness of the banking system, and thus satisfies legal and institutional legitimacy.

b) Incentives for banks and investors

As a market-based solution, climate stress testing has the potential to incentivise banks and investors to shift away from investments and institutions that are more exposed to climate change risks and therefore carry higher financial risk. To explore this potential, several studies have examined whether climate stress tests influence investor decisions specifically, whether test results prompt investors to divest from banks with weak climate risk management practices, such as those heavily engaged with carbon intensive and less climate aligned sectors.[50]

While the findings are not unanimous, there is a growing body of evidence supporting the conclusion that climate stress tests can guide financial institutions towards low carbon lending by exposing the risks associated with misalignment with climate goals. For example, one empirical study on the stock reactions to the ECB climate stress testing concludes:

> We find that the worst effect was caused by the publication of results (i.e., 08 July 2022), with a sharp decline in both raw and abnormal cumulative returns around the announcement. This is consistent with the main results of the ECB stress test: the exercise revealed many deficiencies, data gaps and inconsistencies across institutions, still at a very early stage in the measurement and management of climate risks.[51]

---

48 Nieto/Papathanassiou (2022), p. 120.

49 Rory Van Loo, 'Stress Testing Governance' (2022), 75 Vanderbilt Law Review, p. 553.

50 Romain Hubert/Alexandre Hilke, 'Connecting the Dots Between Climate Risk Management and Transition Finance' (2024), https://www.i4ce.org/wp-content/uploads/2024/02/Connecting-the-dots-between-climate-risk-management-and-transition-finance.pdf (last accessed: 22 July 2025).

This finding also suggests a financial incentive for banks to reduce exposure to carbon intensive assets and counterparties in order to maintain investor confidence.

2. Why potential remains limited?

a) Environmental impacts vs. financial risk and return

Although climate change is an established source of financial risk,[52] the carbon intensity of an asset or a loan does not necessarily reflect its exposure to climate related physical risks. This mismatch between environmental harm and financial risk-return results is a significant shortfall for the use of stress testing.[53] For this reason, even the stress tests that succeed in accurately identifying and quantifying climate risks, may not result in increased financing of green projects.

Additionally, climate related opportunities ie a greener portfolio is generally not included in these exercises. For example, while the risk of stranded assets is typically included, the potential upside of low carbon or green investments is rarely considered.[54]

b) Lack of regulatory action

As explained in findings of ECB 2022 climate stress test, climate stress tests are currently conducted for exploratory purposes. Unlike regular stress tests, which have capital implications, the exploratory nature of climate stress tests means they have not yet led to any regulatory changes.[55] This lack of actionable outcomes means, without further development and commitment, climate stress tests may remain ineffective in mitigating climate-related financial risks.

---

51 Franco Fiordelisi/Ornella Ricci/Gianluca Santilli, 'Spotlight on Physical Risk: Assessing the Banks' Stock Reaction to the ECB Climate Stress Test' (2025), 98 International Review of Financial Analysis, 103882.

52 Kern Alexander, Stability and Sustainability in Banking Reform: Are Environmental Risks Missing in Basel III? (CISL and UNEP 2014).

53 Weber (2022).

54 Ibid.

55 Rogge (2023).

In conventional stress testing, if it is assessed that the amount of capital is insufficient to survive such shocks, the relevant capital requirement is adjusted upward. This is not yet the case for climate stress tests. It is also argued by some[56] that, although more innovative than other tools, stress testing still qualifies as a quantitative risk management method and therefore poses a danger by creating the illusion that banks have successfully identified and controlled the risks related to climate change. In reality, the assumptions used in a limited number of scenarios may reinforce blind spots in the risk management process and harm overall resilience.

c) Gaming the methodologies

The other side of international cooperation and harmonisation achieved through scenario development presents a challenge for the effective use of stress testing in mobilising capital. NGFS developing and making the climate scenarios accessible is a step forward for a more holistic and harmonised analytical framework.[57] However, the same transparency around the underlying methods and assumptions may lead to banks arranging their portfolios in line with the methodology of the stress tests so that there are no problems identified in their risk management, without actually increasing investment in climate friendly businesses and projects.[58]

D. Conclusion

The preliminary results on the study reveal that climate stress tests can support both climate risk management and the climate transition as it provides a consensus of benefits. However, relying on them alone risks falling short, even of its core prudential objectives evident in the limitations discussed above. Banking regulators and supervisors thus can fulfil both objectives as complementary parts of a broader supervisory strategy, using stress tests as one tool among many.

56 James Fanto, 'Anticipating the Unthinkable: The Adequacy of Risk Management in Finance and Environmental Studies' (2009), 44 Wake Forest Law Review, pp. 731, 752.

57 Täger/Dikau (2023), p. 5.

58 DeMenno (2023); Ben S Bernanke, 'Stress Testing Banks: What Have We Learned?' (Maintaining Financial Stability: Holding a Tiger by the Tail Conference, Federal Reserve Bank of Atlanta, Stone Mountain, 8 April 2013).

Bridging the natural disaster insurance gap: Between market failure and legal obligation. A comparative approach

Dr. Aneta Paleczna-Zgonina, Oskar Zgonina

A. Introduction

As climate change increases, the frequency and severity of natural catastrophes, the financial burden on individuals, businesses and governments are growing. There is still a significant protection gap in the natural disaster insurance market. The main purpose of this paper is to provide a comprehensive analysis of the effectiveness of currently existing legal frameworks and to identify universal principles that would allow to develop an insurance coverage model in the field of natural risks. First, it is necessary to consider whether the natural disaster insurance policies currently on offer provide adequate insurance coverage. This is important in the context of the distribution rules under the Insurance Distribution Directive. Residential property/household insurance plays a key role in this area nowadays.

The next question is whether to introduce compulsory natural disaster insurance. This raises not only legal questions, including the constitutionality of such solution, but also social and economic ones.

By adopting a comparative approach, this study examines how different jurisdictions address the natural disaster insurance gap. Additionally, this paper integrates an interdisciplinary perspective, drawing insights from law and economics, behavioural science and environmental policy to evaluate whether legal provisions incentivise risk mitigation or lead to moral hazard. In this way, the paper explores the role of sustainability in different legal systems. The presented topic shows an interplay between public and private enforcement.

Against this background, among others, the following research questions should be posed: 1) What are the legal, economic and social implications of a gap in natural disaster insurance? 2) How do the different insurance models (voluntary or compulsory) affect the availability of insurance for all? (idea of sustainable finance) 3) Does compulsory natural disaster insurance create a moral hazard or can it be an effective way of managing natural disaster risks? The study is based on case law analysis, doctrinal and regulatory interpretation of EU, Polish and German law. The analysis also includes solutions adopted in Switzerland, Spain and France.

B. Insurance gap and its consequences

Insurance gap is defined as any financial losses suffered as a result of particular events that have not been covered by insurance, either under the private or public model.[1] For a couple of years, a worldwide increase has been noted in the number of extreme weather phenomena that are a consequence of global warming. As a result of climatic changes, also natural

1 * This research was funded in whole by the National Science Centre, Poland, project number: 2021/41/N/ HS5/02285. For the purpose of Open Access, the author has applied a CC-BY public copyright licence to any Author Accepted Manuscript (AAM) version arising from this submission. Article financed from funds available under a project of the National Science Centre, Poland, project number: 2021/41/N/HS5/02285.

Polska Izba Ubezpieczeń, 'Polacy i ryzyko – jak się ubezpieczamy? Luka ubezpieczeniowa w Polsce' (2024), https://piu.org.pl/wp-content/uploads/2024/05/PIU_luka-ubezpieczeniowa_low_21_05_24.pdf (last accessed: 31 August 2025), p. 6.

disasters strike with growing intensity, especially in the form of floods, flash floods, torrential rains or fires.[2]

I. A growing insurance gap

Between 1980 and 2023, weather- and climate-related events caused total economic losses of more than EUR 790 billion across the 38 European Environment Agency member and partner countries. During this period, the gap in insurance coverage was significant. In most countries, more than half of the losses were not insured, and in many instances the share of uninsured losses was above 90 %.[3] In Germany, in 2020, only about 46 % residential buildings were insured against damages caused by natural forces.[4] This means that more than a half of all residential buildings in Germany are not insured against floods, torrential rains or landslides. According to data from the Polish Insurance Chamber, 73 % of single-family residential buildings are insured, while 63 % are covered against the risk of flooding. The figures are lower for multi-family buildings and dwellings, with only 41 % and 36 %, respectively, insured against flooding.[5]

2 European Insurance and Occupational Pensions Authority, 'Dashboard on insurance protection gap for natural catastrophes in a nutshell', EIOPA-24/473, https://www.eiopa.europa.eu/document/download/bbdc653b-e335-41f0-8293-0d8280a09855_en?filename=EIOPA-BoS-24-473_Dashboard%20on%20insurance%20protection%20gap%20for%20natural%20catastrophes%20in%20a%20nutshell%20-%202024%20version.pdf (last accessed: 31 August 2025), p. 3.

3 'Economic losses and fatalities from weather- and climate-related extremes' (2025), https://www.eea.europa.eu/en/analysis/publications/economic-losses-from-climate-extremes (last accessed: 31 August 2025).

4 Gesamtverband der Versicherungswirtschaft ‚Serviceteil zum Naturgefahrenreport 2021' (2021), https://www.gdv.de/resource/blob/71296/4682dd50c4ffdedb048e56020213f35e/download-serviceteil-naturgefahren-report-data.pdf (last accessed: 31 August 2025), p. 45.

5 Polska Izba Ubezpieczeń, 'Klimat rosnących strat. Rola ubezpieczeń w ochronie klimatu i w transformacji energetycznej' (2023), https://piu.org.pl/wp-content/uploads/2023/07/PIU-raport-klimatyczny-2023_27-lipca_premiera.pdf (last accessed: 31 August 2025), pp. 58–59.

II. Consequences of the insurance gap

Residential building insurance plays a key role, especially in the face of the growing number of serious natural disasters. Events such as storms, heavy floods or hailstorms can give rise to severe damages to buildings and pose a significant financial burden to their owners. In the face of natural disasters, the injured parties are often left alone with considerable financial burdens. The insurance gap has a massive impact on the development of national insurance resilience and leads to a situation in which the economic risk of climatic disasters is shifted to the society as a whole, due to *ad hoc* public aid granted from the state budget. This may lead to higher costs for taxpayers and foster the phenomenon of 'charity hazard'.[6]

C. Regulation models of natural disaster insurance

In literature, four basic natural disaster insurance models are distinguished: public, private, mixed and international.[7] However, attention should be drawn to the fact that there are countries in which there are not only no legal solutions that could be assigned to the above models but also insurers, as such, do not offer products affording protection against the consequences of natural disasters. Such system can be referred to as a 'zero' model.[8]

I. The public model

The public model is based on the assumption that the state – carrying out its welfare function – takes up responsibility for the risk of occurrence

---

6 Markus Roth, 'Verpflichtende Elementarschadenversicherung – Ausländische Vorbilder und Zulässigkeit einer deutschen Regelung' (2021), 41 NJW, p. 3000.

7 The presented division of models has been adopted after: Monika Wałachowska/Michał P. Ziemiak, 'Ubezpieczenia od ryzyk katastroficznych w Polsce i na świecie', in Eugeniusz Kowalewski (ed.), Ubezpieczenie budynków od ryzyk katastroficznych: aspekty prawno-ekonomiczne (2013), pp. 75 et seq.

8 Michał P. Ziemiak, 'Ubezpieczenia od skutków ryzyk katastroficznych. Kilka uwag na tle raportu Polskiej Izby Ubezpieczeń Klimat Ryzyka oraz ubezpieczeń na wypadek suszy' [Catastrophic risks insurance. Some comments on the Polish Chamber od Insurance report Climate of Risk and drought insurance], in Katarzyna Malinowska/Dorota Maśniak/Anna Tarsiuk (eds.), Environmental risk and insurance (2021), p. 199.

of natural disasters. In practice, this means that a state institution is established to pay out compensations within the framework of public aid. This model covers also solutions under which a state insurance institution offers, in the market, a coverage against climate risks – both on voluntary and compulsory basis. However, a disadvantage of the public model is its vulnerability to political changes, limited competitiveness and the risk of financial inefficiency.[9]

II. The private model

On the other hand, the private model assumes that insurance coverage is afforded only by private insurance companies. Under this approach, customers are free to conclude contracts covering risks relating to natural disasters. However, in practice, this is the model that most frequently gives rise to an insurance gap. It is often the case that insurers do not have insurance products on offer that meet the needs of customers located in natural disasters risk zones. On the other hand, even if these products are available, it also does not mean that customers are interested in concluding contracts covering this risks. It may also happen that the offered solutions do not correspond to actual needs, and the amount of premium makes them inaccessible to an average customer. In addition, situations cannot be excluded in which insurance companies refuse to conclude an insurance contract on account of a high risk of occurrence of the insured event or the cost of this insurance is too expensive (e.g., location of the property in a floodplain or an area threatened by flooding).[10]

III. The mixed model

The mixed model, adopted among others in France or Spain, offers a mix of public law and private law solutions, and combines the elements of both systems discussed above. It can be based on a distribution of risk between

9 Ziemiak (2021), p. 198.

10 Schwarze, 'Institutionenökonomischer Vergleich der Risikotransfersysteme bezüglich Elementarschäden in Europa. Studien und Gutachten im Auftrag des Sachverständigenrats für Verbraucherfragen' (2019), p. 5.

private insurers and the state.[11] In practice, this could mean that the private insurance sector is supported by a public reinsurer. It enables protection costs to be spread out and insurance gaps to be eliminated. In the event of major catastrophes, reinsurance funds support claims payments, which can otherwise overwhelm insurers and threaten their solvency.

IV. The international model

Finally, in practice there are also international systems, based on cooperation of more than one country. They are adopted especially in locations where a common source of risk is at play – e.g., a border river – and requires supranational solutions in the area of insurance protection.[12]

D. An overview of selected national jurisdictions

I. Germany and Poland

At the time being, both in Poland and in Germany, it is not required to conclude an insurance contract against natural risks. The scope of every insurance contract covering a building can be individually negotiated with the insurer. The model applicable in the discussed jurisdictions – according to the classification presented above – corresponds to the private model, in which the market itself caters to the needs of the parties seeking insurance protection.

The requirement of compulsory insurance used to apply in Germany at the regional level of federal states (Lands), for example in Baden-Württemberg until 1994, however, it was lifted as a consequence of adopting so called "Third non-life insurance Directive".[13] In this context, since the disastrous flood in July 2021, there has been a discussion about instruments that could reduce the insurance gap.[14] This includes also introduction of compulsory insurance against damages caused by natural forces. Most of-

11 Ziemiak (2021), p. 199.

12 Ibid, p. 199.

13 See: Directive 92/49/EEG; Thorsten Kingreen, 'Verfassungsfragen einer Versicherungspflicht gegen Elementarschäden an Wohngebäuden' (2022), 9 NVwZ, p. 599.

14 Martin Notthoff, 'Gebäude- und Elementarversicherungen' (2024), 3 r+s, pp. 108.

ten, risks such as storm or hailstorm are covered by the standard insurance scope applicable to residential buildings. However, damages caused by other natural phenomena, such as flood, earthquake, landslide or avalanche – generally have to be covered by a separate natural disaster insurance.[15] Once natural disasters occur, legislators frequently decide to introduce *ad hoc* legislation and aid programmes, which in fact serve to compensate the losses suffered by the parties affected by the consequences of natural forces. By way of example, it can be pointed out that in Poland the Act of 16 September 2011 on special solutions relating to the removal of the effects of flood was adopted.[16] This referred to a specific natural disaster, that is flood. The injured parties were offered public aid, such as financial support assuming the form of targeted benefits, support for entrepreneurs, or support for employees in the form of additional leave, as well as other measures.

II. Switzerland

In Switzerland, in the private insurance sector, there is a requirement of compulsory insurance against damages caused by natural forces, which has been attached to fire insurance. It has been provided for under Art. 33 VAG[17] and Art. 171–181 AVO[18]. The scope of insurance and premium rates in the insurance against natural disasters are uniform and binding on all insurance companies. The statutory requirements need to be followed by insurance companies irrespective of the type of products offered.[19] Under

---

15 Reimund Schwarze, 'Institutionenökonomischer Vergleich der Risikotransfersysteme bezüglich Elementarschäden in Europa. Studien und Gutachten im Auftrag des Sachverständigenrats für Verbraucherfragen' (2019), https://www.svr-verbraucherfragen.de/wp-content/uploads/2024/11/Schwarze_Institutionenoekonomischer_Vergleich.pdf (last accessed: 31 August 2025), pp. 8, 21–22.

16 Ustawa o szczególnych rozwiązaniach związanych z usuwaniem skutków powodzi [Act of 16 September 2011 on special solutions relating to the removal of the effects of flood], Journal of Laws 2024, item 654, as amended.

17 Bundesgesetz betreffend die Aufsicht über Versicherungsunternehmen (Versicherungsaufsichtsgesetz, VAG) of 17. December 2004, https://www.fedlex.admin.ch/eli/cc/2005/734/de (last accessed: 31 August 2025).

18 Verordnung über die Beaufsichtigung von privaten Versicherungsunternehmen (Aufsichtsverordnung, AVO) of 9. November 2005, https://www.fedlex.admin.ch/eli/cc/2005/735/de, (last accessed: 31 August 2025).

19 Roth (2021), p. 3001.

Art. 33 VAG, insurance against damages caused by natural forces must be included in a fire insurance contract.

The reason for introducing compulsory insurance against damages caused by natural forces in the legal system is called double solidarity. This refers to, in the first place, solidarity among the insured parties demonstrated by paying a uniform premium. The purpose of such solidarity is to make insurance, for an affordable premium, available in all regions of Switzerland. Second, one can speak about solidarity among the insurers: because of a diversified burden depending on the region and a uniform premium, which is neutral in term of risk. Practically all insurers have associated in a special fund for the purposes of mutual risk compensation – reinsurance.[20]

III. Spain

The Spanish system of natural disaster insurance is an example of the public model, in which an essential role is played by Consorcio de Compensación de Seguros (CCS).[21] This is a public institution in the form of an insurance company, operating in parallel to the private sector. The CCS's function is complementary in relation to the market. It guarantees insurance protection in the event of materialisation of extraordinary risks.[22] The system is financed through a mechanism of a compulsory surcharge added to insurance premiums. Particular insurance contracts concluded in the private sector must provide for an additional payment dedicated to the CCS fund.[23] In practice, this means that every insured person automatically obtains protection against extraordinary risks, regardless of the contents of the contract concluded with the insurance company. Compensations are

20 Eidgenössische Finanzmarktaufsicht FINMA, ‚Elementarschadenversicherung in der Schweiz (ES-Versicherung). Historie und Anwendungsbereich' (2022), https://www.finma.ch/de/~/media/finma/dokumente/dokumentencenter/myfinma/2ueberwachung/versicherungen/spartenspezifische-instrumente/elementarschaden-historie-anwendungsbereich.pdf?sc_lang=de&hash=5A4B383D38AEF29C2A43153D42CF6C33, (last accessed: 31 August 2025), p. 9.

21 Sonia García/Joaquin Sempere, 'Two-Level System for Optimal Flood Risk Coverage in Spain' (2025), 17(13) Water, pp. 1–2.

22 Ibid, p. 2.

23 Consorcio de Compensación de Seguros, 'Insurance Cover for Extraordinary Risks in Spain', https://www.consorseguros.es/documents/10184/48069/RREE_ING_2016.pdf/f4fd891a-770c-494a-b8da-9f5e18cbb43e (last accessed: 31 August 2025), pp. 12–13.

paid directly by CCS, which is liable only for the liquidation of damages caused as a consequence of extraordinary events.

The Spanish solution allowed to reduce the insurance gap, which is hard to eliminate in systems based only on voluntary insurance. The construction of CCS ensures universal and equal access to insurance coverage, and spreads the burden of risk. At the same time, the model is based on the principle of social solidarity. This means that the insured parties participate in the insurance protection costs, which allows to compensate damages also in regions particularly vulnerable to natural disasters. The average insured residential property in Spain is 74 %, so the insurance protection gap for catastrophic hazards is significantly smaller in Spain than in similar countries.[24] With regard to the floods that occurred in Spain in 2024, the CCS, in a note published on 30 October 2024, confirmed that it would cover damage to properties and vehicles resulting from the flood, as this cause is included in the list of what are legally termed "extraordinary risks."[25]

IV. France

The French system of natural disaster insurance does not provide for compulsory insurance. However, the legislator limits the freedom to determine the scope of insurance coverage by requiring that contracts covering residential buildings include provisions ensuring protection against the consequences of natural disasters.[26] Due to the above, as many as 98 % of French households are insured against losses caused by natural forces, which in practice reduces the insurance gap to a minimum.[27]

The CatNat system combines private property insurance with a reinsurance mechanism supervised by the state. Insurers can take advantage of reinsurance by Caisse Centrale de Réassurance (CCR) – a private company

24 Francisco Espejo Gil, 'Growing risks: the role of insurance' (2024), 21 Consor Seguros Revista Digital, p. 3.

25 Consorcio de Compensación de Seguros, Note published on 30 October 2024, https://webserver-ccsweb-prd.lfr.cloud/ (last accessed: 30 September 2025).

26 Roth (2021), pp. 3001–3002.

27 Deutscher Bundestag, ‚Einführung einer Pflichtversicherung gegen Elementarschäden. Unionsrechtliche Vorgaben' (2024), EU 6 – 3000 – 029/24, https://www.bundestag.de/resource/blob/1033378/EU-6-029-24-pdf.pdf (last accessed: 31 August 2025), p. 18.

fully owned by the state.[28] In practice, insurance protection against consequences of natural disasters is afforded by the private insurance sector. Insurance companies are required to include appropriate clauses in all contracts having as subject residential buildings. Although there is no universal, statutory requirement imposed on citizens to take out insurance, in practice, insurance of a residential building is usually a necessary condition for concluding a tenancy contract or a contract for the sale of the property.[29] The system of determining the amount of insurance premium is based on the principle of solidarity: each and every household – irrespective of the extent of its exposure to risk – must pay a surcharge calculated in proportion to the total of the premium determined by the insurance company. The amount of such surcharge is specified by statutory law, under Art. A 125–2 Code des assurances.[30]

E. Voluntary insurance and compulsory insurance

Another criterion according to which the existing models can be additionally subdivided is whether a given jurisdiction allows for voluntariness in the conclusion of natural disaster insurance contracts. Accordingly, one can distinguish between models in which the conclusion of an insurance contract covering the discussed risks is voluntary and models in which the legislator has introduced a universal requirement to take out an insurance contract.

28 Schwarze, 'Institutionenökonomischer Vergleich der Risikotransfersysteme bezüglich Elementarschäden in Europa. Studien und Gutachten im Auftrag des Sachverständigenrats für Verbraucherfragen' (2019), pp. 20–21.

29 Zentrum für Europäischen Verbraucherschutz e.V., ‚Studie: Das französische System der Elementarschadenversicherung – eine Kooperation von öffentlicher Hand und privater Wirtschaft' (2023), https://www.cec-zev.eu/fileadmin/Media/PDF/publications/Etudes-Rapports_DE/Studie_Elementarschadenversicherung_Frankreich_ZEV.pdf, p. 6.

30 Code des assurances, https://www.legifrance.gouv.fr/codes/texte_lc/LEGITEXT000006073984/ (last accessed: 31 August 2025).

I. The voluntary model

Voluntary insurance is based on the principle of the freedom of contract. Such model does not impose a requirement to take out insurance, neither does it specify the scope of insurance coverage. It is that voluntary nature – especially with regard to the insurance of buildings – that often does not bring satisfactory results and leads to the emergence of an insurance gap, which can be clearly seen in the context of insurance against climate risks.[31]

However, one can also distinguish intermediary solutions in which insurance contracts are formally concluded on voluntary basis but their dissemination is promoted by specific economic stimuli. As an example, one can point to tax incentives or making the payment of public benefits of compensatory nature conditional on prior holding of an insurance policy. In practice, this can mean a reduction or even elimination of state aid in case of damages that could have been covered by insurance available on the market.

II. The compulsory model

On the other hand, compulsory insurance is based on a statutory requirement to conclude an insurance contract, and strictly speaking, on the requirement to hold insurance coverage at a specific time and place. In such situations, the legislator should precisely specify the subjective scope of the requirement, its form, as well as review mechanisms and sanctions for con-compliance.[32]

However, this model should be distinguished from a situation in which the legislator inserts certain compulsory clauses in the contracts extending the scope of coverage – as is the case in Switzerland or in France. In such situations, we do not have to do with classical compulsory insurance but with a standardisation of the products available in the market. An introduction of the requirement to take out insurance, however, is not limited to legal aspects only. To an equal, or even greater extent, it is dependent on political decisions and economic conditions.

---

31 Schwarze, 'Institutionenökonomischer Vergleich der Risikotransfersysteme bezüglich Elementarschäden in Europa. Studien und Gutachten im Auftrag des Sachverständigenrats für Verbraucherfragen' (2019), pp. 5.

32 Ibid., pp. 3–5.

III. Arguments for and against introducing a requirement to take out insurance

In the first place, it must be noted that the introduction of a requirement to take out insurance could significantly reduce the insurance gap. This is particularly important in the context of climate change and the growing risk of catastrophic damages. In the same way, such solution is supported predominantly by economic factors.

From the social perspective, a requirement to take out insurance would contribute to equal distribution of burdens among the owners of buildings, by affording protection to both properties situated in high-risk and low-risk areas.[33] Another argument deployed in the discussion is that we are jointly responsible for the climate change caused by human activities and, therefore, one should accept the fact that, as a society, we will jointly suffer the consequences of damages following from extreme weather phenomena.[34] Accordingly, the risk would shift to a wider range of persons, due to which the risk of extreme weather phenomena could be proportionately distributed. It is also argued that compulsory insurance against natural risks would provide an incentive to take many preventive measures. Certain role in that regard could be played by insurers themselves. They could play a significant role by seeking, in the case of buildings located in high-risk areas, to employ all available protective measures against extreme weather events (e.g., risk-mitigation clauses).[35] Investing in hydrological infrastructure and improving land use planning could significantly reduce the impact of future events. Introduction of compulsory insurance would also lead to a situation in which insurers react properly to a risk of serious weather disasters. This would include development of minimum standards for the insurance protection, corresponding to the needs of the customers, that is to needs of the entire society. Moreover, this solution would promote transparency and integrity in the context of insurance contracts, and policyholders would become more and more conscious of their rights.[36]

---

33 Notthoff (2024), p. 109.

34 Hans-Peter Schwintowski, 'Pflichtversicherung für Elementarschäden – Pro und Contra' (2024), 9 VuR, p. 322.

35 Franziska Arnold-Dwyer, 'Using insurance for natural hazard loss prevention', in Douglas Kysar/Ernest Lim (eds.), The Oxford Handbook of Climate Change and Private Law (2025) [Preprint], https://papers.ssrn.com/sol3/papers.cfm?abstract_id=5250978 (last accessed: 31 August 2025), p.

36 Ibid., p. 8–9.

Finally, the requirement to take out insurance could also increase resilience of the society to serious weather disasters. Appropriate insurance protection and state regulations can reduce the impact of damages caused by natural forces and facilitate recovery after such events. Adoption of a model of compensating the sustained damages by insurers would also relieve the state budget and reduce to a minimum the need to grant *ad hoc* public aid. However, there are also arguments against introducing a requirement of compulsory insurance against catastrophe risks. First of all, one should point to potential public opposition following from the perception of an insurance premium as a specific quasi-tax. Another danger is the possibility of the phenomenon of moral hazard, consisting in the reduction of motivation to prevent damages in a situation of guaranteed insurance protection.[37]

An additional challenge before the insurance industry would be to develop appropriate methods of risk assessment and premium calculation so that the financial stability of the system could be maintained.[38] The state would also have to establish a system of review and sanctions for non-complying with the requirement. Critics of compulsory insurance also argue that the risk of natural disasters is not evenly distributed. Such solution would be unfavourable to those whose property is not located in an increased risk area, e.g., exposed to the danger of a flood.[39] In the same way, a uniform premium amount, in the opinion of such property owners, could be viewed as unfair.

F. Constitutional challenges and the EU perspective

I. The constitutional aspects

Introduction of a requirement to take out insurance always interferes with fundamental rights and freedoms of the individual. As a result, that solution inevitably gives rise to questions of constitutional nature, concerning its compatibility with higher-rank legislative acts, including especially constitutional norms. This problem is not solely theoretical – it poses a real challenge to the legislator who, aspiring to cut down the insurance gap,

37 Michał Romanowski, 'Umowa ubezpieczenia w Kodeksie cywilnym fasadą umowy nazwanej' (2025), 1 Wiadomości Ubezpieczeniowe, pp. 11–16 and ref. therein.

38 Roth (2021), p. 3003.

39 Notthoff (2024), p. 109.

must at the same time take into account constitutional guarantees of protecting the rights of the individual.

This question was discussed, among others, in German academic literature, where it attracted much attention when it came to the admissible limits of state intervention.[40] It is worth noting that the Federal Constitutional Court in Germany has already addressed the issue of compulsory insurance against natural hazards and upheld it.[41]

II. The EU law perspective

Legal solutions introducing an appropriate model of natural disaster insurance must be compatible with the system of UE law, both primary and secondary. Based on the case law of the CJEU, no fundamental objections under EU law can be identified with regard to the introduction of compulsory insurance[42]. It must be concluded that it is incorrect to assume that EU law stands in the way of introducing compulsory insurance.[43] In this context, one can only recall the Green Paper on the insurance against natural and man-made disasters of 2013.[44] The purpose of the Green Paper was to expand the knowledge of persons working in the insurance industry when it came to advantages of insurance against natural disasters and catastrophes. Its authors highlighted how the culture of safety measures and knowledge about market management should develop. Most importantly, the Green Paper contained recommendations concerning, among others, the introduction of compulsory natural disaster insurance.[45]

---

40 Thorsten Kingreen, 'Verfassungsfragen einer Versicherungspflicht gegen Elementarschäden an Wohngebäuden' (2022), 9 NVwZ, p. 598 et seqq.

41 BVerfG, 14 January 1976 – 1 BvL 4 u. 5/72.

42 Deutscher Bundestag, ‚Einführung einer Pflichtversicherung gegen Elementarschäden. Unionsrechtliche Vorgaben' (2024), p. 17.

43 Thorsten Kingreen, 'Vereinbarkeit einer Versicherungspflicht gegen Elementarschäden an Wohngebäuden mit europäischem Unionsrecht und deutschem Verfassungsrecht. Studien und Gutachten im Auftrag des Sachverständigenrats für Verbraucherfragen' (2022), https://fragdenstaat.de/dokumente/238805-kingreen-studie-vereinbarkeit-versicherungspflicht-verfassungsrecht/ (last accessed: 31 August 2025), pp. 6 et seqq.

44 European Commission, 'GREEN PAPER on the insurance of natural and man-made disasters' (2013), COM(2013) 213 final, https://eur-lex.europa.eu/LexUriServ/LexUriServ.do?uri=COM:2013:0213:FIN:EN:PDF (last accessed: 31 August 2025).

45 Ibid., p. 8.

Notably, however, even without introducing compulsory insurance or standardising natural disaster insurance contracts, already at the time being all insurance distributors are obliged, under IDD[46] and national provisions, to assess the customer's demands and needs. The demands and needs test requires determining if the risk of natural disasters is considerable – and if so, verifying if the offered insurance contract covers such risk. In case of a negative answer to that question, the distributor must notify that fact to the customer and recommend the customer an additional or extended insurance. Disclosure obligations and the requirement of the demands and needs test are intended to ensure appropriate protection to customers in the light of the growing climate risks.[47]

Nevertheless, the EU legislator should aspire to establish a harmonised natural disaster insurance model. Introduction of a legal framework on the level of the European Union would contribute to the elimination of a gap in insurance coverage and ensure a consistent protection level in all member states.

III. The hybrid model conception

Along with the increase of climate risks, the boundary between public liability and private law insurance is becoming less and less clear. Neither a fully market-based model (private model) nor full control of the state over the system of compensating natural disasters can guarantee the desired results. Therefore, one should consider developing a hybrid model, offering an approach that combines public law regulation and private law insurance instruments.

46 Directive (EU) 2016/97 of the European Parliament and of the Council of 20 January 2016 on insurance distribution, Official Journal of the European Union L 26/19.

47 Oskar Zgonina/Aneta Paleczna, 'The idea of sustainable insurance as a trust-building tool in the insurance contract – comparative law analysis' (2024), in Margarida Lima Rego/Maria del Val Bolivar Oñoro/Maria Elisabete Ramos (eds.), 2nd International Conference of the Jean Monnet Module on EU Insurance Law: Challenges in the SDG Era. SDG 8: Decent Work and Economic Growth, pp. 128–133.

IV. The role of prevention and education

Traditionally, insurers are regarded as security providers – parties acting only once the insured loss arises. On the contrary, such an approach is insufficient in the face of intensification of natural disasters and the impact of climate change. It is necessary to put emphasis on action even prior to the event. This means a shift of the weight of responsibility in the insurance sector from damage liquidation to prevention.[48]

This conception expands the role of an insurer to preventive measures. One can point to the support of investments in infrastructure limiting the consequences of natural disasters (e.g., flood infrastructure), support of effective early warning systems, use of weather forecasts, promotion of public awareness or spatial planning.[49] The presented approach brings benefits not only to insurers, by actually cutting down losses, but also supports the availability and accessibility of protection to the society. In addition, it forces a change in the style of action: instead of focusing on indemnification, the insurer becomes an active player in the process of building social resilience.[50]

V. The significance of insurance in mitigating the consequences of natural disasters

The presented conception of a hybrid model assumes supplementation of the existing forms of protection against the consequences of natural forces by elements enhancing preventive action and by strict cooperation between the public and private sector.

In such model, insurers, apart from performing the traditional compensatory function, should actively participate in undertakings of preventive and educational nature, raising public awareness when it comes to catastrophe risks. Such an approach would also entail a reduction of the phenomenon of moral hazard, which arises in a situation when the missing

48 Katarzyna Malinowska, 'Prevention in Environmental Insurance', in Katarzyna Malinowska/Dorota Maśniak (eds.), Managing Environmental Risks through Insurance. Legal and Economic Aspects (2024), pp. 284–287.

49 Zentrum für Europäischen Verbraucherschutz e.V., ‚Studie: Das französische System der Elementarschadenversicherung – eine Kooperation von öffentlicher Hand und privater Wirtschaft' (2023), pp. 17–19.

50 Arnold-Dwyer (2025), p. 13.

liability of market operators leads to excessive reliance on financial aid after the damage.[51] The role of the state in this model should concentrate on establishing a stable legal framework, setting the standards of insurance coverage and – with regard to especially exposed areas -guaranteeing reinsurance mechanisms or instruments supporting financial robustness of the entire system.[52] The model so designed would enable fair distribution of costs between the society, insurers and the public sector. The centre of gravity would shift from simple financing of losses to a change of behaviours, systemic market management and development of long-term resilience to the consequences of climate change and appropriate social trust. In consequence, insurers would become not only security providers but an integral part of the infrastructure for climate risk management.

The EU legislator puts an increasing emphasis on questions relating to climate change, including sustainable development aspects. This is reflected through multiple legislative acts that affect the financial services sector, including the insurance services sector. The idea of "sustainable insurance" is becoming more and more popular, meaning insurance implementing so called sustainable development objectives, i.e. SDG.[53]

G. Conclusions and recommendations

At present, there is no obligation to take out natural catastrophe insurance in Poland and Germany. The situation is different in Spain, France and Swiss cantons. On the one hand, compulsory insurance against natural disasters would lead to the implementation of many preventive measures that are currently not implemented or are only discussed in the event of a natural disaster. However, it could lead to "moral hazard."

The adoption of appropriate legal regulation can ensure that insurers respond appropriately to the risk of natural disasters. This will establish minimum standards of insurance coverage that will compensate property owners for damages at an appropriate level. This approach promotes trans-

51 Kati Kraehnert/Daniel Osberghaus et al., 'Insurance Against Extreme Weather Events: An Overview' (2021), 72(2) Review of Economics, p.76.

52 Kraehnert/Osberghaus (2021), p. 76.

53 Piotr Wrzesiński, 'Uwzględnienie preferencji klienta w zakresie zrównoważonego rozwoju przy dystrybucji umów ubezpieczenia na życie o charakterze inwestycyjny' (2022), 4(113) Prawo Asekuracyjne, pp. 24 et seqq.

parency and fairness in insurance contracts. In turn, policyholders will become aware of their rights and the insurance products available to them. In addition to damage caused to households and buildings, there is also damage to the supply chain (business interruption) and damage related to the death of relatives, which justifies the payment of compensation for the harm suffered. Insurers should also take indirect damage into account. This, in turn, is important for the creation of new insurance products and the amount of the insurance contribution.[54]

The publicization of private law and state intervention makes it possible to standardise the scope of insurance (model adopted in France and Spain) or to introduce a compulsory insurance system. At the same time, private law instruments such as the concept of protecting the weaker party, transparency of contracts and liability for breach of trust can be effective mechanisms in themselves. Combining private and public law may result in a hybrid model of protection. The examined issues require evaluation from the point of view of private and public insurance law, insurance distribution principles, civil liability and constitutional law. Taking into account European integration and the attempt to create a universal protection model, it is also necessary to analyse Union law and the available unification options.

54 Aneta Paleczna, 'The concept of rationalising damage and the scope of insurer's liability' (2024), 1 Wiadomości Ubezpieczeniowe, pp. 33–44.

Serious environmental crimes as crimes against future generations: a legal good theory problem

*Vítor de Souza Ishikawa**

A. Introduction

The traditional model of wrongdoing in criminal law in German and Brazilian doctrine centres on acts or omissions that violate the legal goods of others with whom the perpetrator coexists. This framework applies to a wide range of offences, including homicide, theft, tax evasion, corruption, and participation in or association with armed criminal organisations.

In recent decades, however, criminal law scholarship has increasingly recognised that certain forms of conduct may give rise to harmful consequences that extend beyond the immediate present, affecting both current and future interests or legal goods.[1] Such conducts are often linked to industrial activity, technological development, or climate change and create risks or produce harms within a temporally distorted framework. Serious offences that result in long-term environmental damage, for example, violate legal goods of future generations.

---

* Doctoral student in criminal law at the University of São Paulo, Brazil and criminal lawyer. This paper is a summarized version of a Master's thesis that was funded by a CAPES scholarship for two consecutive years.

1 Future interests of present generations refer to long-term interests of those currently alive in a particular moment, such as an interest in living in a future environment free from pollutants, and future interests of future generations, to all interests of those who will come to exist in the future. This difference will be further addressed.

This paper addresses two central questions: (i) Is it justifiable to criminalise conduct that harms future generations? And (ii) is it justifiable to aggravate criminal sanctions for conduct that affects both present and future generations? The first question pertains primarily to the role of the legislature and elected policymakers, while the second is directed toward the judiciary and the interpretation and application of criminal penalties.

The protection of future generations through criminal law challenges the traditionally present or near-future-oriented core of the legal good doctrine. In order to adequately address the two questions outlined above, it is necessary to clarify (B) the aim and criteria presented by the legal good theory, (C) the three different positions adopted by the proponents of the legal good doctrine and their corresponding reasons, (D) how the concept of 'future generations' can be defined as an analytical category. Finally (E, F), this paper will argue that criminalising and/or punishing conduct violating legal goods of future generations is legitimate when its consequences affect present generations whose members (at least in part) will continue to exist in the future, taking into account the feature of succession, as in serious environmental crimes.

B. The legal good theory (Rechtsgutslehre) as a limit to the state's power to criminalise conduct

As a theory of criminalisation, the legal good theory seeks to establish substantive criteria for the legitimate use of criminal law.[2] Its central premise is that democratic legitimacy is insufficient to justify criminalisation: Even when a criminal provision is enacted through a procedurally

2 Due to space constraints, this paper will not examine two fundamental aspects of the contemporary debate surrounding the legal good theory, which may be described as its external and internal crises, nor the predominance of the harm principle doctrine in the United States and United Kingdom. Externally, the legal good theory has experienced a significant decline in influence, even in countries where it was dominant, such as Germany and Brazil. This decline is especially evident in Germany, where the Federal Constitutional Court (*Bundesverfassungsgericht*) has explicitly rejected its constitutionality. Internally, the theory suffers from a marked lack of consensus among its proponents, with ongoing disagreements regarding the definition of 'legal goods', the theory's liberal roots, and its capacity to fulfil its promises as a critical or limiting framework within criminal law. For further discussion, see Ivo Appel, Verfassung und Strafe, 1998, pp. 199–203; Carl-Friedrich Stuckenberg, 'The Constitutional Deficiencies of the German *Rechtsgutslehre*' (2013), 3(1) OSLS, p. 31, pp. 31 et seqq.

valid and democratically legitimate process, the resulting offence may still be acknowledged as substantively unjustified.

In response to the central question of under what material conditions the state may legitimately punish behaviours through criminal law, the legal good theory provides the following answer: only if that specific conduct (act or omission) creates a risk to, or causes a harm to, a legal good (ie when the conduct violates a legal good). However, this initial formulation still lacks clarity, as one must clarify what constitutes a 'legal good' and explain the reason for subjecting democratic decisions to this normative and critical device.

Claus Roxin and Luís Greco define 'legal goods' (*Rechtsgüter*) as 'those essential to the individual's free development, the exercise of one's fundamental rights, and the proper functioning of a constitutional state designed to uphold these objectives'[3]. At the core of this definition lies the idea that criminal law must ensure conditions for peaceful and free coexistence while protecting individual rights.[4] Accordingly, punishing mere moral transgressions is not legitimate because it does not protect legal goods nor contribute to guarantee the peaceful and free coexistence of citizens.

The legal good framework thus operates as a substantive limitation on the state's punitive authority in favour of personal freedom. It asserts that an offence is only substantially legitimate when it is grounded in the protection of the person, adopting a human-oriented perspective: as Winfried Hassemer states, its fundamental idea is that punishment is restricted by 'the existence of a legitimate interest on the part of one citizen (that is, of a legal good), and the violation of that interest by another citizen'[5].

Individuals, however, are not merely independent and self-sufficient agents, but rather social beings embedded in collective life. Life, property, and physical integrity are legal goods as legitimate as collective legal goods. Their indivisibility defines the latter: A collective good cannot be partitioned or allocated among individuals, as it is shared and experienced collectively, eg the environment.[6]

---

3 Claus Roxin/Luís Greco, Strafrecht Allgemeiner Teil, Band I, 5th ed. (2020), p. 26 [own translation].

4 Ibid.

5 Winfried Hassemer, 'The Harm Principle and the Protection of "Legal Goods" (*Rechtsgüterschutz*): a German Perspective', in AP Simester/Antje Du Bois-Pendain/ Ulfrid Neumann (eds.), Liberal criminal theory: essays for Andreas von Hirsch (2014), p. 187, 193.

6 Roxin/Greco (2020), pp. 27–28.

The legitimacy of collective legal goods depends on their personal dimension: violations must ultimately have repercussions on individual interests at least indirectly.[7] For example, a punishable conduct against the environment doesn't need to affect specific individuals A, B, or C; it suffices that the offence impacts conditions essential for personal development.[8] In this sense, acts such as air or water pollution may threaten individual well-being, and their criminalisation is justifiable even in the absence of a concrete harm, as these behaviours restrict or undermine the integrity and usability of shared natural resources and degrade the general conditions necessary for a healthy and balanced environment, essential for human life.

Ultimately, the main challenge in extending criminal protection to future generations lies in justifying the punishment of violating legal goods that will occur in the future, after the conduct itself has already ceased. In such cases, criminal sanctions would be imposed even before the consequences–normatively, the violation of legal goods–fully materialise. This raises a critical question: Can such forms of criminalisation and/or punishment be justifiable within the legal good theory framework?

C. Future generations in the legal good theory discourse

Scholars who follow a legal goods theory framework offer three different responses to the future generations problem in criminal law: (i) a negative answer, (ii) a positive answer, and (iii) an out-of-the-theory answer.

Cornelius Prittwitz and Philipp-Alexander Hirsch represent the negative answer (i). Prittwitz argues that there is no place for future generations within a (personal) legal good theory, whose framework is centred on live and real people.[9] More broadly, Prittwitz adopts a sceptical stance regarding the capacity of Criminal Law to address 'mega social problems of today and tomorrow', particularly given that many of the behaviours most harmful to future generations remain legally permissible.[10]

---

7 Winfried Hassemer, 'Lineamentos de uma teoria pessoal de bem jurídicos', in Luís Greco/Fernanda Lara Tórtima (eds.), O bem jurídico como limitação do pdoer estatal de incriminar?, 2th ed. (2016), p. 9, 18 et seq.

8 Helena Regina Lobo da Costa, Proteção penal ambiental (2010), pp. 26 et seq.

9 Cornelius Prittwitz, 'Teoria pessoal do bem jurídico e as "vítimas de amanhã"', in Raphael Boldt (ed.), Teoria crítica e Direito Penal (2020), p. 123, 128.

10 Ibid, pp. 131–135.

Hirsch, in turn, bases his position on the grounds of reciprocity. A liberal model of criminal law requires that the perpetrator and the victim(s) must be capable of interacting with each other in a relationship of mutual acknowledgement and equal freedom.[11] Since future generations do not yet exist, they are not entitled to rights, and their identity is inherently indeterminate, dependent on the contingent actions of present individuals.[12] A justice-based approach must take into account the autonomy and concrete interests of existing persons and resist defining individual interests in abstract terms imposed by the state, as this would contravene the normative core of a liberal model.[13]

In contrast, the positive answer (ii) encompasses two distinct lines of reasoning.

Bernd Schünemann and Luis Gracia Martín advocate for a 'dualistic' concept of legal goods, according autonomy to collective legal goods and dismissing the requirement of individual referentiality.[14] From a social contract perspective, future generations must be regarded as participants whose interests merit protection and consideration.[15] The very legitimacy of the state presupposes its ability to guarantee the minimal conditions necessary for the self-development of future persons as a foundational norm.[16] On this view, intergenerational equity and the preservation of a healthy, balanced natural environment are elevated to the status of supreme values.

---

11 Philipp-Alexander Hirsch, 'Klimastrafrecht und materieller Unrechtsbegriff. Probleme einer liberalen Strafrechtsbegründung angesichts der Herausforderungen des Klimawandels', in Helmut Satzger/Nicolai von Maltitz, Klimastrafrecht (2020), p. 111, 115 et seq.

12 Ibid, p. 118.

13 Ibid, pp. 119–121.

14 Bernd Schünemann, 'O princípio da proteção de bens jurídicos como ponta de fuga dos limites constitucionais e da interpretação dos tipos', in Luís Greco (ed.), Estudos de direito penal, direito processual penal e filosofia do direito (2013), p. 39, 50; Luis Gracia Martín, 'Contribución al esclarecimento de los fundamentos de legitimidad de la protección penal de bienes jurídicos colectivos por el Estado social y democrático de derecho' (2012), 12(1) RPCP, p. 263, 379.

15 Bernd Schünemann, 'Consideraciones críticas sobre la situación espiritual de la ciência jurídico-penal alemana', in Manuel Cancio Meliá (ed.), Cuestiones básicas del Derecho Penal em los umbrales del tercer milênio (2006), p. 187, 193; Luis Gracia Martín, 'A modernização do Direito Penal como exigência da realização do postulado do Estado de Direito (Social e Democrático)' (2011), 88 (1) RBCCrim, p. 95, 130.

16 Bernd Schünemann, 'Principles of Criminal Legislation in Postmodern Society: The Case of Environmental Law' (1997), 1 (1) BCLR, p. 175, 191–192.

Departing from a social contract reasoning, Ulfried Neumann and Helena Regina Lobo da Costa argue that it is sufficient, in an initial analysis, to establish whether the affected legal good could be qualified as personal.[17] The interests of those who will exist in the future remain fundamentally human interests. The indeterminacy of future individuals' identities does not disqualify them from protection under the legal good doctrine, just as it does not disqualify collective legal goods.[18] Future generations' interest in a healthy and balanced natural environment is a valid one, and its justification rests on personal grounds.

Finally, the position advanced by Claus Roxin and Luís Greco could be characterised as an out-of-the-theory answer (iii). Behaviours that violate legal goods of future generations do not interfere with the peaceful and free coexistence of humans, and therefore cannot be justified within the legal good theory approach.[19] Nonetheless, both authors recognise the legitimacy of protecting future generations through criminal law as an exception to the theory for two reasons: (i) present generations deprive future generations of means of subsistence through exploitation and environmental degradation; and (ii) the responsibility of present generations towards future ones is rooted in the principle of solidarity between generations, which is enshrined as a constitutional duty in Art. 20a of the German constitution.[20]

Accordingly, Roxin and Greco propose a relativisation of the traditional legal good framework, asserting that it is legitimate to criminalise and punish conduct based on the violation of legal goods of future generations by invoking additional criteria, such as the principle of solidarity and constitutional duties.[21] In this expanded view, the legal good no longer functions as the sole substantive criterion for the legitimacy of criminalisation, thereby creating space for a broader normative justification.

D. Two definitions of 'future generations'

Before analysing the three positions outlined above, it should be noted that Criminal Law scholarship often lacks a clear and consistent definition of

17 Ulfrid Neumann, 'Ergänzung "extensive Interpretation" oder Erweiterung der personalen Rechtsgutslehre?', in Beatrice Brunhöber et al. (eds.), Strafrecht als Risiko (2023), p. 157, 170 et seq.; Costa (2010), pp. 27 et seq.

18 Neumann (2024), pp. 170 et seq.

19 Roxin/Greco (2020), p. 64.

20 Ibid, pp. 63 et seq.

21 Ibid, p. 64.

'future generations'. The term is typically used to refer to those who do not yet exist at the time of the harmful conduct. However, conceptualizing 'future generations' exclusively as individuals who will only exist in the future and whose interests or legal goods are absent in the present fails to account for those who are already alive and will continue to exist in the future.

The notion of 'human generation' as a snapshot that freezes time and attributes the status of members of the present generation only to its participants is, at best, arbitrary and artificial. Human life and generations are marked by continuity: births and deaths occur in a non-stop succession. That raises questions as 'Are new-borns members of the present or future generations?' and 'Do individuals who have just passed away still belong, in some sense, to the present generation or already to the past?'. Even if one takes the moment a particular offence is committed as a temporal reference point, its consequences may extend far beyond that moment and affect successive generations. These considerations suggest that the meaning of 'future generations' is neither self-evident nor static, and requires conceptual refinement in order to serve as an effective analytical tool.

The feature of intergenerational continuity appears to be the key to delineating the boundaries between past, present, and future generations and how they overlap.[22] By intergenerational continuity, one refers to the unbroken succession of human generations and the persistence of specific fundamental interests or legal goods, such as those related to environmental protection.

A *lato sensu* or broad definition of future generations includes those who are currently alive and those who will exist in the near future, reflecting an overlapping relationship between generations. Consider, for example, an individual named A, who is 27 years old, who coexists with their 80-year-old grandmother and 3-year-old nephew. All three share a common and present interest in a healthy and balanced natural environment, a collective legal good. Even if environmental harm resulting from present conduct will affect the youngest member of this group in the future, that legal good already exists and is violated in the present. This is especially evident in the case of children's legal goods, due to the inherently future-oriented nature

22 Andre Santos Campos, 'Long-term urgent interests and human rights practice: a challenge to the political conception' (2020), CRISPP, https://doi.org/10.1080/13698230.2020.1737478 (last accessed: 22 July 2025), p. 13.

of some of their rights. As Campos notes, 'they have special interests in the future that are subject to present truth conditions'[23].

By contrast, a *stricto sensu* or strict definition of future generations, usually adopted by criminal law scholars, refers exclusively to non-overlapping generations, focusing primarily on individuals who will exist only in the future and do not exist at the moment that the offence is committed. In these cases, there is no present interest or legal good. That would be the case of human germline genetic engineering, which is criminalised in Germany under the Law of Embryo Protection (*Embryonenschutzgesetz*) and in Brazil under the Biosafety Law (*Lei de Biossegurança*). It also applies to recent proposals of climate crimes – those examples will be addressed further.

Distinguishing between a *lato sensu* and a *stricto sensu* definition of future generations contributes to developing a present-rights-of-future-generations view, grounded 'on the succession and continuous overlap between members of different generations'[24]. Only by recognising the succeeding intervals can one avoid non-reciprocity and non-identity problems as detailed before.

E. Protecting future generations through protecting present generations

Taking into account a present-rights-of-future-generations approach, one can adequately engage with the arguments raised by the negative, the positive, and the out-of-the-theory answers.

Duties to protect future generations are grounded in two fundamental aspects that may be summarised by the idea of the domain held by present generations against future generations. People currently in existence possess the power to shape the living conditions of those who are yet to exist: the availability of resources, the natural foundations for personal and collective self-development, and even the political framework necessary for the exercise of fundamental rights. This capacity to influence and effectively determine how future generations will live correlates with their vulnerability, since they are unable to reciprocate (*stricto sensu* definition), or only in a limited manner (*lato sensu* concept). In criminal law, this domain becomes relevant when assessing the danger or harm posed to their legal goods.

23 Ibid, p. 14.
24 Ibid, p. 13.

This introductory assessment provides a more concrete and less theoretical approach than that proposed by social contract theories, as adopted by Schünemann and Gracia Martín. This new approach also confirms the personal aspect involved in protecting future generations' legal goods, as stated by Neumann and Lobo da Costa. Still, the challenges posed by the objections of non-identity, non-reciprocity, and the lack of impact on free and peaceful coexistence remain the primary liberal arguments against the legitimacy of criminalising conduct that exclusively harms the legal goods of future persons.

One alternative, as previously noted, is to renounce the exclusivity of the legal good theory as the sole substantive criterion for assessing the legitimacy of criminal provisions, thereby opening space for other criteria. However, the answer proposed by Roxin and Greco should not be accepted, as it would entail a substantial weakening of the legal good theory: Incorporating extraneous criteria not derived from the concept of legal goods would severely diminish its liberal and critical function. Vague principles, such as the solidarity principle, could then be arbitrarily invoked to justify questionable criminal provisions. The appropriate answer must remain within the theoretical boundaries of the legal good doctrine, whether through a negative (critical or transcendental) or a positive formulation (teleological or intrinsic).[25]

The core challenge in Criminal Law concerning future generations lies in determining how the legal goods of persons who do not yet exist at the time of the crime are violated, particularly in a non-overlapping or *stricto sensu* definition of future generations. Against this backdrop, it must be acknowledged that while such concerns arise in cases like human germline genetic editing, they do not apply to all forms of conduct that affect future generations, for example, environmentally harmful behaviours.

Germline gene editing may produce long-term effects that span generations; still, at the time of the act, those who would suffer these consequences do not yet exist, including the individual directly subjected to genetic manipulation, as germ cells and embryos are not considered holders of fundamental rights under current frameworks. Criminalising such

25 A critical or negative formulation of the legal good theory provides an analytical tool to challenge the legitimacy of criminal provisions: It seeks to answer whether the reasons for criminalising a behaviour are justified by a violation of legal goods. Otherwise, a teleological or positive formulation of the legal good theory serves as an interpretation reference, establishing what is intended to be protected through a particular criminal provision.

conduct would therefore be illegitimate from the standpoint of the legal good theory, as there is no existing person whose legal good is violated. Justifying such criminalisation would require recourse to other robust reasons within the legal good theory, which lies beyond the scope of this paper.

Environmental crimes, in turn, have the capacity to harm legal goods of present people at the moment of the conduct. These harms can not only be 'extended' over a continuous period, but their consequences, such as the deprivation of natural resources, can be interpreted as including harm to future generations. Under a *stricto sensu* definition of future generations, aggravating criminal sanctions solely on that basis would still be illegitimate, due to the three aforementioned objections.

However, adopting a present-rights-of-future-persons view and embracing a *lato sensu* definition of future generations mitigate those objections. Environmental harm affects legal goods of present individuals and communities within the continuity and succession of generations: Those who existed at the time of the conduct will continue to exist as new generations are born, resulting in overlapping coexistence. The conditions of a determined identity, the ability to reciprocate and engage of the victim(s), and the impact on the free and peaceful coexistence are fulfilled and maintained over time, justifying the criminalisation or aggravation of sanctions.

As a general rule, then, it must be concluded that it is only legitimate to criminalise and/or punish based on protecting future generations when the conduct in question violates legal goods of individuals who exist at the moment and will continue to exist thereafter. One must, still, pursue efforts of concreteness and identify the specific cases in which this proposition may be appropriately applied.

F. Serious environmental crimes as crimes against future generations: human-made natural disasters, ecocide, and climate crimes

Depending on how the notion of 'affecting future generations' is interpreted, numerous criminal offences could potentially be classified as crimes against future generations, insofar as their consequences negatively impact the legal goods of persons living in the future. For example, offences such as corruption and tax evasion deprive future generations of public resources that could be allocated to essential services, including healthcare, education, and infrastructure.

Given the *ultima ratio* character of criminal law, a restrictive perspective must be adopted, following the constitution as the primary normative reference. This leads to the conclusion that mainly environmental crimes whose consequences transcend generation boundaries, affecting legal goods of future generations while simultaneously violating legal goods of the present one, should qualify as crimes against future generations. Notably, the constitutions of Brazil and Germany expressly link the duty to protect future generations to the obligation to safeguard the environment.

Article 225 of the Brazilian Constitution (*Constituição Federal*) recognises a 'right to an ecologically balanced environment, which is an asset of common use and essential to a healthy quality of life', establishing the duty of the government and the community 'to defend and preserve it for present and future generations' and submitting environmentally harmful behaviours to criminal and administrative sanctions. Similarly, Article 20a of Germany's Basic Law (*Grundgesetz*) asserts that the state bears responsibility towards future generations by mandating the protection of the natural foundations of life and animals.

On the basis of this constitutional foundation and through a restrictive perspective, the main conclusion of this paper is that only serious environmental degradation may be legitimately criminalised and/or punished with the express aim of protecting future generations, as those crimes would have to violate legal goods of present persons and simultaneously of future persons that are correspondent with them, understood within a framework of intergenerational continuity.

To test the validity of this normative claim, it is helpful to examine two prominent criminalisation demands in environmental criminal law that explicitly aim to protect future generations: ecocide and climate crimes.

Ecocide is conceptualised as 'the extensive damage to, destruction of or loss of ecosystem(s) of a given territory, whether by human agency or by other causes, to such an extent that peaceful enjoyment by the inhabitants of that territory has been severely diminished'[26]. Other terms frequently employed to describe ecocide are 'severe', 'widespread', 'long-term', 'sub-

26 Polly Higgins/Damien Short/Nigel South, 'Protecting the planet: a proposal for a law of ecocide' (2013), 59(1) CLSC, p. 1, 10.

stantial', 'irreversible' and 'damage to the natural environment'[27], all of which emphasise the gravity and longevity of the harm inflicted.

In this sense, human-made disasters or anthropocentric hazards may fall within the category of ecocide. In the Brazilian context, notable examples include the Mariana dam disaster (2015) and the Brumadinho dam disaster (2019), both of which occurred in the state of Minas Gerais. In each case, mining companies responsible for tailing dams released massive quantities of toxic waste following structural failure, resulting in catastrophic loss of life and severe, lasting environmental degradation. In the aftermath of these events, two legislative proposals were introduced in the Brazilian Congress seeking to criminalise ecocide as a direct political response.[28]

By definition, ecocide involves the infliction of long-term negative consequences on the environment, in a continuous violation of legal goods of present and future generations regarding the relationship between human beings and their environment, as well as their resources. The aforementioned dam disasters exemplify this: they cause immediate, large-scale destruction while simultaneously degrading the conditions necessary for future generations in a broad sense to enjoy and rely upon those natural resources.

In turn, climate crimes refer to criminalisation demands to protect the atmosphere or the climate as legal goods, framed as part of broader state policies to meet net-zero emissions targets, such as those required by the Paris Agreement.[29] Helmut Satzger and Nicolai von Maltitz claim that, in order to avoid excessive and illegitimate criminalisation, climate crimes must be subject to a 'relevance clause' that excludes punishment of 'neutral conduct', ie, necessary and/or common daily actions.[30] Paul Krell further argues that climate crimes would essentially punish two types of behaviours: illegally and substantially increasing the concentration of

27 Helmut Satzger/ Nicolai von Maltitz, 'Der "Ökozid" – ein Tatbestand des "Klimavölkerstrafrechts"?', in Helmut Satzger/Nicolai von Maltitz (eds.), Klimastrafrecht (2020), p. 437, 441 et seq.

28 As of September 2025, neither of the proposals has been approved by the Brazilian Congress (Congresso Nacional).

29 Helmut Satzger/Nicolai von Maltitz, 'Das Klimastrafrecht – Ein Rechtsbegriff der Zukunft' (2021), https://doi.org/10.1515/zstw-2021-0001 (last accessed: 22 July 2025), pp. 2–5.

30 Ibid, pp. 16–18.

greenhouse gases in the atmosphere, and operating a company that does not satisfy the requirements of emission certificates.[31]

In criminal law, however, one can only be punished for one's own conduct and not be responsible for others' actions. It is highly questionable whether a single conduct, no matter how serious, is capable of harming the atmosphere as a whole or altering the global climate in a manner consistent with the principle of personal responsibility, even in a cumulative danger structure that is generally accepted in criminal law doctrine.

Although the atmosphere and climate affect personal interests, they cannot be considered legitimate legal goods as they are not capable of being put in danger or harmed by a single or by cumulative conduct.[32] Instead, their degradation arises from the long-term functioning of complex economic systems over decades.[33] Moreover, the effects of any given conduct on these global anthropocentric phenomena tend to materialise only in the distant future, raising additional difficulties regarding the temporal connection between the behaviour and the harm, which would take place in a far-off future perspective.

While the criminalisation of ecocide satisfies the criteria for legitimate protection of future generations under criminal law, the case for climate crimes proposals initially remains questionable. This, however, represents only a preliminary assessment. For any criminal provision, further evaluation is required in light of other foundational principles such as the legal certainty principle and the *ultima ratio* of criminal law.

G. Conclusive remarks

Criminalising or aggravating sanctions on the basis of protecting future generations is justifiable when the conduct in question causes serious environmental harm, thereby violating legal goods of people who are alive at the time of the act and will continue to exist and have personal legal goods in the future, be it individual (such as life, well-being, health) or collective (such as environment). An exception to this thesis concerns hu-

31 Paul Krell, 'Zur Legitimität von Kumulationsdelikten', in Helmut Satzger/Nicolai von Maltitz (eds.), Klimastrafrecht (2020), p. 139, 146.

32 See Maria Kaiafa-Gbandi, 'Strafrecht und Klimawandel', in Helmut Satzger/Nicolai von Maltitz (eds.), Klimastrafrecht (2020), p. 41, 45 et seq.

33 Christoph Burchard/Finn-Lauritz Schmidt, 'Kritik des Klimastrafrechts', in Helmut Satzger/Nicolai von Maltitz (eds.), Klimastrafrecht (2020), p. 83, 95 et seq.

man germline engineering, whose criminalisation must satisfy additional normative conditions to be deemed legitimate. Accordingly, the answers to the two questions posed in the introduction are affirmative.

Future generations, as a normative concept, must be understood not only as persons who will only come into existence in the future (*stricto sensu*), but also as those who already exist and are entitled to legal goods that can be adversely affected by the future negative consequences of present conducts (*lato sensu*). This *lato sensu* approach provides a coherent and rational foundation for imposing or increasing criminal sanctions for environmentally harmful behaviours whose consequences transcend generations, without relying solely on indeterminate principles such as the solidarity or the sustainability principle, or a rights-of-future-persons framework.

In conclusion, (i) aggravating criminal sanctions for anthropocentric hazards and (ii) criminalising ecocide pass the legitimacy test and satisfy the conditions to protect future generations through criminal law justifiably. In contrast, (iii) existing proposals for climate crimes do not meet the legitimacy threshold, due to the impossibility of a single conduct, even in a cumulative sense, to violate the legal goods 'atmosphere' or 'climate balance' attributed to present or near-future individuals.

Bridging legal gaps in ecocide prosecution: A hybrid enforcement model

Jamal Hajiyev[*]

A. Introduction

Rapid degradation of ecosystems, collapse in biodiversity, and irreversible environmental damage have unveiled the legal weaknesses of current systems to deal with ecological crimes at large. Ecocide is defined by the Stop Ecocide Foundation's panel of experts as unlawful or wanton acts, committed with knowledge that there is a substantial likelihood of severe and either widespread or long-term damage to the environment being caused by those acts.[1]

The International Criminal Court (ICC) has offered limited protection for environmental harm, confined to instances that arise in armed conflict involving the intentional, disproportionate damage to the environment. It does not cover destruction of the environment on a large scale in

* Master of Laws Candidate, Vilnius University, jamal.hajiyevv@gmail.com.
1 Independent Expert Panel, 'Legal Definition of Ecocide' (2021), https://www.stopecocide.earth/legal-definition (last accessed: 30 June 2025).

peacetime, nor does it provide for liability on corporations or corporate executives.

On the domestic level, the legislative reaction to environmental damage reflects defragmentation, symbolism, and political capture or a deficient legal framework. Most common courts use civil or administrative procedures and lack a deterring effect, and do not reflect the actual severity of the environmental disaster. The outcome is an international responsibility gap for structural and interstate ecological damage.

The paper aims to offer a novel enforcement system resting on a three-tier system: domestic courts, Regional Environmental Tribunals (RETs), and an International Tribunal on Ecocide (ITE). It is built in the framework of a treaty based on a complementarity/subsidiarity-based approach and integrates interdisciplinary science, e.g., satellite evidence and forensic ecology, to gain legitimacy and efficacy.

The paper proceeds as follows: Section 2 analyzes the statutory weaknesses of the present international and domestic practice in regard to ecocide. Section 3 forms the concepts of the three-tier enforcement model. In Section 4, the institutional, evidentiary, and political design for implementing the system is discussed. The conclusion reflects on the proposal's feasibility and urgency in light of the global evolution of law.

B. The lack of a binding legal framework for ecocide

I. Under the Rome Statute

Although the damage to the environment is increasingly seen as a worldwide calamity, ecocide has not yet been identified by international criminal law as an independent crime. The Rome Statute, establishing the International Criminal Court, was adopted in 1998, and establishes the Court's jurisprudence over the issues of genocide, crimes against humanity, war crimes, and the crime of aggression. It contains only a few references to the environment, being covered only in Article 8(2)(b)(iv) in cases of warfare resulting in the widespread, long-term, and severe damage to the natural environment. Nevertheless, this is restricted to wartime acts and also contains a high standard of evidence, which renders it inapplicable to peacetime ecocide.[2]

As discussed in the introduction, the Stop Ecocide Foundation has put together a panel of experts who have proposed a legal definition of ecocide. Although the definition is symbolically significant, it is not legally binding because states have not formally supported it, nor has the amendment procedure under Articles 121 and 123 of the Rome Statute, which govern how amendments to the Statute are proposed and adopted by States Parties, been invoked. Structural capacity is also poor at ICC in terms of the lack of prosecution of legal entities, such as multinational corporations, that perpetrate environmental destruction on a large scale.[3]

One of the main shortcomings of the Rome Statute is that it concerns the criminal responsibility of natural persons only. Article 25(1) specifically does not apply to corporations and other legal entities of the Court.[4] It is a considerable loophole because transnational corporations, especially in extractive sectors, the agribusiness sector on a massive scale, and power generation, cause or intensify most of the worst environmental harms. Whereas some domestic frameworks, including France under the Loi Climat et Résilience (2021), have implemented a corporate liability system in relation to environmental offences, international law has not established this mechanism.[5] Without corporate criminal responsibility in the ICC system, systemic ecocide is virtually beyond the scope of international criminal law.

The ICC cannot enforce the law and thus depends solely on state cooperation, arrest, collection of evidence, and execution of sentences.[6] The absence of major powers, such as the United States, which has not ratified the Rome Statute, undermines the universality of the ICC and weakens its international ability to deal with environmental crimes.[7]

---

2 Rome Statute of the International Criminal Court, 2187 UNTS 90, Art. 8(2)(b)(iv).

3 Armina Savanovic, Corporate Criminal Liability in International Criminal Law "ex nihilo nihil fit" (Master's thesis, Lund University 2017), p. 58.

4 Rome Statute of the International Criminal Court, 17 July 1998, 2187, UNTS 90, Art. 25(1).

5 Code de l'environnement, Loi n° 2021–1104 du 22 août 2021 portant lutte contre le dérèglement climatique et renforcement de la résilience face à ses effets [Climate and Resilience Law], Art. L.231 – 3.

6 Rome Statute, Art. 103.

7 David Bosco, Rough Justice, (2014), pp.108–12.

These weaknesses, absence of jurisdiction, the lack of rules addressing corporate accountability, and dependency on state enforcement, amount to a legal vacuum in the international arena. According to the legal theorist McDonnell-Elmetri, this shows a defect in its structural design: international criminal law was ideally suited to crimes against humanity and war crimes, not ecologically generated crimes.[8] The current ICC is inappropriate, without some serious systemic adjustment, to combat the nature, magnitude, and cause of ecocide.

II. Fragmented domestic approaches

The national responses toward ecocide have usually been dissimilar and largely symbolic. In 2021, France introduced the offence of ecocide by the Loi Climat et Résilience [Climate and Resilience Law], which integrated Article L.231-3 into the Environment Code, stipulating that ecocide is defined as the intentional execution of certain grave environmental offences which cause "serious and irreversible damage" to health, flora, fauna, and natural resources.[9] The provision was criticized as having imprecise thresholds, being administration-oriented, and being ambiguous to prosecutors.[10] Similar measures can also be found elsewhere: in 2001, Ukraine added a criminalisation of ecocide to its Criminal Code under Article 441[11], and Bolivia also adopted legislation discussing ecocide[12], but in both instances, the implementation, especially of corporations and state organs, is uneven.[13]

8 Zahra McDonnell-Elmetri, The Crime of Ecocide: The Answer to Our Environmental Emergency? (LLB (Hons) thesis, University of Otago, 2020), p. 45.

9 Code de l'environnement, Art. L.231 – 3 (introduced by Loi n° 2021–1104 du 22 août 2021 portant lutte contre le dérèglement climatique et renforcement de la résilience face à ses effets [Climate and Resilience Law].

10 Clifford Chance, 'The Environmental Crime Directive' (8 June 2024). https://www.cliffordchance.com/content/dam/cliffordchance/briefings/2024/06/the-environmental-crime-directive-a-game-changer-for-ecosystem-protection.pdf (last accessed: 1 July 2025).

11 Кримінальний кодекс України [Criminal Code of Ukraine], Law No. 2341-III of 5 April 2001, Art. 441.

12 Ley de Derechos de la Madre Tierra [Law of the Rights of Mother Earth], Law No. 071 of 21 December 2010, Art. 7.

13 Li Wei/Mariana Oliveira/Camila Rodríguez, Prosecuting Ecological Destruction: Comparative Legal Perspectives on the Crime of Ecocide (2025), 4 Interdisciplinary Studies in Society, Law, and Politics, pp. 281–282.

Institutional barriers are experienced in national systems as well. Where legal systems are highly politicised and vulnerable to executive interference, ecocide laws are at risk of political capture and non-prosecution. Many resource-dependent low- and middle-income countries (LMICs) have legal systems constrained by their extractive sector's economic dependency. It has also been noted that courts are influenced to balance economic investment over environmental liability, especially when jurisdictions have no dedicated environmental benches. Conversely, where independent environmental courts are present, litigation risk is greater for companies, which may make them comply rather than have unfettered development.[14]

This situation is aggravated by the fact that there is no standard legislation or implementation procedures. Although some jurisdictions, such as Ecuador, constitutionally recognise 'Rights of Nature' under Articles 71–74 of the 2008 Constitution, ecosystems in most countries are still regarded as property, rather than legal subjects.[15] This leads to a legal patchwork where regulatory arbitrage and forum shopping by polluters are possible.

Proximity enforcement needs national laws, but cannot be achieved through them alone. Domestic jurisdictions are still fragmented, with inconsistent definitions of environmental offences, varying penalties, and a variable degree of judicial independence. Further, many states lack the technical capacity, money, or political will to bring powerful corporate or state-linked polluters to justice. Enforcement is particularly constrained in the case of transboundary harm, whether it is deforestation, cross-border river pollution, or atmospheric damage, which cannot be effectively regulated by any state. This set of limitations makes it clear that reliance on national systems alone is insufficient and that a wider coordinated approach is required.

C. A three-tiered model for ecocide enforcement

This article suggests a three-tiered approach to filling this enforcement gap in the face of significant environmental harm. At the lowest level of adjudication, domestic courts would continue to be the principal fora for

14 Lianchao Yu/Haobin Sha/Qiang Liu/Guowan Yan 'Environmental Judicial Independence and Corporate Investment Efficiency: Evidence from a Quasi-Natural Experiment in China' (2024), 96 International Review of Economics & Finance, pp. 12–15.

15 Constitución de la República del Ecuador [Constitution of the Republic of Ecuador], 2008, Arts. 71–74.

the prosecution of environmental crimes. Above these, Regional Environmental Tribunals (RETs) would be available to adjudicate cases having a regional element, where ecosystems and harms are transboundary. Finally, in those cases of greatest transboundary and large-scale ecological devastation, an International Tribunal on Ecocide (ITE) would be the final arbiter of accountability.

Although the aspects of this model have been addressed individually, this particular article embarks on creating a combined, manageable structure of enforcement. The framework envisages a future Ecocide Treaty that would bring definitions, jurisdiction, and standards of proof into alignment. Cases would be distributed in accordance with the principle of subsidiarity and the proximity rule, in view of institutional capacity and the magnitude of the environmental harm.

I. Domestic jurisdiction and legal reform

The first venue for prosecuting an ecocide-type of environmental crime is national courts.[16] They have, however, a number of structural and systemic obstacles to their effectiveness.

In most jurisdictions, environmental damage is managed via civil or administrative proceedings or through fragmented criminal provisions. In the United States, to illustrate, large-scale pollution is frequently prosecuted under the Clean Water Act[17] or Clean Air Act[18] using administrative penalties instead of criminal penalties. In India, environmental crimes are usually pursued through the National Green Tribunal, which may impose civil penalties under the National Green Tribunal Act, but cannot impose criminal penalties.[19] In the cases of criminal laws, these are frequently constrained, applied inconsistently, or subordinated to financial interests.[20]

16 E. Roberts/J. Dobbins, ´The Role of the Citizen in Environmental Enforcement´(ELI 2016), p. 2, https://www.eli.org/sites/default/files/eli-pubs/57aa3700d853b-themetheroleofcitizensinenvironmental-full.pdf (last accessed: 3 February 2026); see also Rakova and Winter, 'Leveraging Traditional Ecological Knowledge' (2020) https://arxiv.org/abs/2006.12387 (last accessed: 1 July 2025), p. 4.

17 Clean Water Act, 33 U.S.C. § 1251 et seq. (1972).

18 Clean Air Act, 42 U.S.C. § 7401 et seq. (1970).

19 National Green Tribunal Act, 2010, No. 19 of 2010 (India).

20 Michael Faure, 'Revolution in Environmental Criminal Law' (2017), 35 Virginia Environmental Law Journal, p. 327, 330.

As the European Law Institute (ELI) has noted, in most jurisdictions, penalties are available against individual acts of ecocide, such as pollution or destroying a habitat, but these partial measures do not reflect the holistic and systemic nature of ecocide.[21]

In addition, political or economic influence is experienced in some states and the courts. The governments rich in resources or development-centric might coerce them to commit more towards investments and less towards environmental responsibility.[22] Prosecutors can be afraid of retribution, lack judicial independence, or lack technical capacity.[23] This risk, in my opinion, is especially acute in jurisdictions that have limited independence of the judiciary or in which environmental law is under-enforced because of the lack of technical capacity.

I present a series of reforms to enhance the legal response to ecocide. First, the terms 'widespread', 'long-term', and 'severe harm' should be defined more precisely, and ecocide should be the subject of a discrete crime. Second, the procedural role of the affected communities and NGOs should be acknowledged, and they should be afforded legal personality and access to remedy. Third, prosecutions should be systematically informed by scientific knowledge, based on ecological assessment and environmental forensics. Finally, special ombudspersons and international support networks need to be established in order to help investigators and prosecutors in sensitive prosecutions.

There are legal developments that provide guidance. In 2008, the Constitution of Ecuador gave nature a status of rights, which means that citizens can bring legal actions on behalf of ecosystems, with mixed success.[24] In Europe, the Aarhus Convention enhanced the public's access to environmental justice, the most prominent of them being Article 9, which asserts

---

21 ELI, Manual for a National Criminalisation of Ecocide (2025), pp. 10–12.

22 Yu et al. (2024), p. 13.

23 David M. Uhlmann, 'Prosecutorial Discretion and Environmental Crime' (2014), 38 Harvard Environmental Law Review 159, pp. 162–164. https://journals.law.harvard.edu/elr/wp-content/uploads/sites/79/2014/04/Uhlmann_Print1.pdf (last accessed:1 July 2025).

24 Craig. M. Kauffman/Pamela L. Martin, 'How Ecuador's courts are giving form and force to rights of nature norms' (2023), Transnational Environmental Law 12(2), pp. 366–395.

that Parties should provide access to judicial and administrative remedies in environmental law.[25]

Finally, the concept of ecological justice cannot be imagined without national enforcement as its basis. National courts are the first line of accountability, as they are closest to the harm, the victims, and the evidence. However, as pointed out, many national systems lack the institutional design, resources, or independence necessary to effectively prosecute ecocide. They then need to restructure themselves internally, for instance, by boosting the powers of environmental courts, clarifying substantive offences, or enhancing prosecutorial capacity. At the same time, they also need external strengthening, in the form of integration into a wider hybrid structure. International and regional mechanisms can serve as overseers, harmonizers of definitions, and as backstops when states neither want nor can prosecute. Ecological justice is therefore built on a foundation: strong national implementation within a coordinated regional and global framework.

II. Regional Environmental Tribunals (RETs)

This article proposes Regional Environmental Tribunals (RETs) as a geographical enforcement institution, capable of holding the potential of covering persistent gaps in the international legal repression of ecological damages and implications on a large scale. Being modelled after regional human rights courts like the European Court of Human Rights (ECtHR), the African Commission on Human and Peoples' Rights (ACHPR), and the Inter-American Court of Human Rights (IACtHR), the RETs would be special to environmental justice in that they would trade in transboundary or systemic ecological damage.[26] RETs aspire to provide a judicial, policy-sensitive means of responding to ecocide where the state or corporate immunity exists. Both the local and international mechanisms of enforcement have been inadequately reactive. As discussed above, the ICC has limited jurisdiction, depends on the cooperation of states, and lacks the liability of corporations, while national courts are often not independent, experienced,

25 Convention on Access to Information, Public Participation in Decision-Making and Access to Justice in Environmental Matters (Aarhus Convention), 25 June 1998, 2161, UNTS 447, Art. 9.

26 Don McCrimmon, Regional Human Rights Regimes and Environmental Protection (PhD Diss, Dalhousie Univ 2017).

or equipped with procedural capacity to do justice to complex transnational environmental damage.[27] In such a vacuum, the RETs may be an option on a credible regional instrument with specific legal capacity to respond to the destruction of the environment that lies between sovereign and global legal regimes.

An important precedent is the Advisory Opinion No. OC-23/17 of the IACtHR, which states that the violation of human rights can be caused by environmental damage, and such violations can bind even countries that are far away.[28] RETs have the capability of taking this rights-based approach to enforce ecocide liability. Their proximity to affected ecosystems and communities helps them to collect evidence better and be sensitive to their local context. Further, their exposure to common ecological systems provides them with greater legitimacy to deal with transboundary harms. Drawing on pluralism within the law, RETs may bring together regional treaties and domestic legal traditions, and thus offer a more accessible and contextualised forum for enforcement than distant international courts.

Further, indigenous and traditional ecological knowledge is an important asset for the conservation of biodiversity. Grounded in long-term stewardship and place-based management, it provides context-specific knowledge about sustainable land use, species conservation, and ecosystem resilience. Regional courts are better suited to include such knowledge than global institutions, not least because they sit closer to the communities involved, and because they can identify local ecological practices within their adjudication.[29] For instance, the Inter-American Court of Human Rights in *Saramaka People v Suriname* (2007)[30] and the African Commission on Human and Peoples' Rights in *Endorois Welfare Council v Kenya* (2010)[31] both recognised the value of indigenous ecological knowledge and land-based identities for ecosystem protection. RETs could also use such jurisprudence to articulate ecologically based norms of ecological injustice and harms based on the areas in which they operate.

---

27 Francisco Durand, Extractive Industries and Political Capture (Oxfam 2018), pp. 22–25.

28 IACtHR, Advisory Opinion OC-23/17, paras. 49–60.

29 Fikret Berkes, Sacred Ecology (3rd edn, Routledge 2018), pp. 223–26.

30 IACtHR, 28 November 2007 – Series C No. 172 – *Saramaka People v Suriname.*

31 Centre for Minority Rights Development (Kenya) and Minority Rights Group International on behalf of Endorois Welfare Council v. Kenya, Communication No. 276/2003, 4 February 2010.

Furthermore, standing is one of the most problematic issues in environmental litigation. RETs could be designed to include standing for local communities, NGOs, activists, and affected individuals, thus overcoming the restrictive rules of admissibility, which often work against environmental defenders.[32] They ought to be enabled to award diverse solutions, including injunctive relief and damages through ecosystem restoration orders, as well as criminal sanctions. Ecocide cases should be adjudged in time and meaningfully, with such flexibility of processes, more so when traditional courts can be resource-constrained, protracted in their procedures, or even compromised by political influence.[33]

Last but not least, RETs may be incorporated in current regional legal-political institutions that are legitimized, like the African Union (AU), Association of Southeast Asian Nations (ASEAN), or Southern Common Market (Mercosur).[34] For instance, in Commission v France (C-239/03, 2004), the CJEU held that France had violated EU environmental law on bathing water quality, and showed that regional courts can assert their authority over the states in environmental regulation. This precedent helps reinforce that RETs are a viable model.[35] RETs may also be used as permanent adjudicatory bodies and future models of developing jurisprudence and the liability of international environmental crimes.

In conclusion, RETs can help to bridge enforcement gaps in ecocide law by working closer to the affected community, relying on regional and indigenous knowledge, and providing flexible remedies. Their integration into local institutions would also enable them to develop coherent jurisprudence while enhancing accountability for environmental crimes.

III. International Tribunal for Ecocide (ITE)

Finally, a permanent, treaty-based international tribunal, the International Tribunal for Ecocide (ITE), can be established to try major transboundary environmental criminals. Although the idea of an ecocide court has been

32 Lisa Vanhala, 'Legal Opportunity Structures and Environmental Mobilization in the UK' (2012), 46 Law and Society Review, pp. 530–31.

33 Alan Boyle/Catherine Redgwell, Birnie, Boyle, and Redgwell's International Law and the Environment (3rd edn, OUP 2009) pp. 267–68.

34 Geert van Calster, EU Environmental Law (2nd edn, Edward Elgar 2017), pp. 202–04.

35 CJEU, 7 October 2004 – C-239/03, ECLI:EU:C:2004:598, para. 30 – *Commission v France.*

discussed in scholarly and activist circles, it remains outside of enforcement networks.[36] Therefore, the paper proposes a novel contribution to the current analysis by incorporating the ITE into the top of a three-tier accountability framework, in addition to the domestic systems and the Regional Environmental Tribunals (RETs). This approach transforms the one-sided enforcement into a de facto multi-level system.

Building on earlier scholarly discussions about establishing an ecocide treaty,[37] this paper proposes this treaty as the legal basis for a permanent ITE within a three-tier enforcement system. Inspired by the Rome Statute, which established the ICC, this model is intended to address the institutional and jurisdictional limitations of the ICC's treaty-based design.[38] As discussed above, the ITE would extend to individuals and corporations, eliminating the gap that has existed between international crimes and corporations.[39]

This tribunal would operate based on the principle of complementarity, meaning it would not exercise jurisdiction where national or regional bodies have effective remedies, but rather where states are reluctant or unable to act.[40] This avoids sovereignty issues and addresses inaction, regulatory capture, and politicisation. It could allow communities, indigenous peoples, and non-governmental organisations to submit evidence, amicus briefs, and requests for inquiries.[41]

Nonetheless, the establishment of such a tribunal assumes the acceptance of ecocide as a global criminal offense. Currently, no universally binding norm criminalises ecocide for all actors. The suggested ecocide treaty would then offer the requisite normative basis by establishing ecocide as a crime under international law. Enforcement by an International Tribunal

---

36 See, for example, Alexandria M. Hanna, 'Killing Our Home: The Case for Creating an International Crime of Ecocide' (2023), 6 Willamette Law Review Online, p. 1, discussing the need for ecocide courts.

37 Richard Falk, 'Environmental Warfare and Ecocide' (1973), 9(1) RBDI 1 annex, pp. 21–24.

38 Matthew Gillett, 'Ecocide and Framework Integration at the ICC' (2024) 29(6) International Journal of Human Rights pp. 1009–1045.

39 Joanna Kyriakakis, Corporations and the International Criminal Court: The Complementarity Objection Stripped Bare (June 1, 2007), Criminal Law Forum, 2008, Vol 19, Issue 1, pp. 115–151., available at SSRN: https://ssrn.com/abstract=2309162 (last accessed: 3 February 2026).

40 Willliam A. Schabas, An Introduction to the ICC (5th edn, CUP 2017), pp. 91–93.

41 Dinah Shelton, 'NGO Participation in International Judicial Proceedings' (1994), 88(4) American Journal of International Law pp. 611–42.

for Ecocide (ITE) can only be both legally and politically possible once this norm is established.

Last but not least, the legitimacy of the tribunal should not depend on universal ratification. Based on the successful models of the Extraordinary Chambers in the Courts of Cambodia (ECCC) and the Special Tribunal for Lebanon, the ITE could be established through a plurilateral mechanism provided by like-minded states, even when global consensus is absent.[42] Both tribunals were established in cooperation between governments and the United Nations, and despite their limited jurisdiction, their jurisprudence evolved into the creation of international criminal law. Analogously, an ITE supported by a coalition of willing states could begin to generate normative standards through its decisions, much as regional human rights courts have shaped international norms, despite lacking universal ratification. Even when the ratification rate is not high, its decisions have the potential to become a global norm, as with regional human rights courts.

In balancing normative ambition with legal feasibility, the ITE is an important element of the three-tier model proposed in this paper as a comprehensive solution to the problem of ecocide. It will be based on both domestic and regional initiatives and reinforce ecocide as an international criminal offence.

D. Ecocide enforcement: institutions, evidence, and integration

I. Treaty-based institutionalization

Several academic, civil society, and other expert organisations, including the Stop Ecocide Foundation and the 2021 Independent Expert Panel, have suggested an ecocide treaty.[43] This treaty could form the normative and institutional basis for the three-level implementation model proposed in this article. The treaty would establish the legal framework for a permanent International Tribunal on Ecocide, operating alongside Regional Environmental Tribunals (RETs) and national jurisdictions.

42 Sarah Williams, Hybrid and Internationalised Criminal Tribunals (Hart 2012), pp. 54–63.

43 Philippe Sands/Dior Fall Sow, Legal Definition of Ecocide (Stop Ecocide Foundation 2021), https://www.stopecocide.earth/legal-definition (last accessed: 1 July 2025).

The treaty would expand the already given definition of ecocide by the Independent Expert Panel.[44] It is a realistic formula in legal identification and ecological lucidity. In order to provide a multilateral enforcement basis, it should be perfected in more profound conversations with industry experts, states, Indigenous peoples, and researchers. Certainty on the levels of harm required and the mental element will be of vital essence in operationalizing the definition in the court practice.[45]

The treaty must establish judicial and prosecutorial agencies, and also feature an interdisciplinary advisory body of experts in environmental science, forensic ecology, climate risk and socioecological injury. The treaty needs to have such agencies take binding decisions and coordinate across the levels. It should involve a complementarity clause to grant ITE jurisdiction where states or regional courts have neither the means nor the willingness to act.

As discussed above, one of the key innovations of the proposed treaty would be the incorporation of corporate criminal liability, closing a major gap left by the Rome Statute. In regard to the political instability, the agreement must have steps of cooperation, namely, binding evidence/arrest implementation, and rewards such as technical assistance and green financing.[46] Procedural accessibility can positively improve trust and legitimacy for the amici curiae, victims, and groups who are impacted.

II. Evidence and Adjudication for Ecocide

The main distinction between my proposed model and existing criminal systems would be the scope of evidence. Existing criminal tribunals rely on witness testimony, victim statements, and physical evidence to detect gradual or cumulative ecological damage. The solution is for the ITE and RETs to embrace a wide range of evidence, including scientific, interdisciplinary, and digital elements.

44 Ibid.

45 Oscar van den Heede, 'Ecocide and the Rome Statute' (2023), 55 NYU Journal of International Law and Politics, pp. 436–41.

46 Adil Najam/Mihaela Papa/Nadaa Taiyab, Global Environmental Governance: A Reform Agenda (International Institute for Sustainable Development, 2006), pp. 29 et seqq., https://www.iisd.org/system/files?file=publications/geg.pdf (last accessed: 3 February 2026).

This article particularly suggests the use of forensic ecology, satellite imaging, environmental modelling, and AI as the main tools for building cases and adjudicating.[47] These tools would help identify any ecological damage in terms of time and space, even in areas that are inaccessible or politically unstable. These methods have been proven to be useful in climate attribution studies and environmental monitoring by agencies such as the European Space Agency.[48]

The ITE would comprise Trial and Appeals Chambers, a Prosecutor, and a Scientific-Ecological Adviser, who would contribute expertise in interdisciplinary areas such as forensic ecology, satellite tracking, and conservation biology. A 2012 study by the London Institute of Space Policy and Law, commissioned by the European Space Agency, illustrates that the use of data on satellite-derived earth-observation (EO) can be an admissible piece of evidence in court and administrative cases, especially where such evidence may be the sole or most cost-effective source of evidence available.[49] I suggest these approaches might be modified to allow EO-based evidence of ecological harm to be presented and considered in the ITE. The ITE would also receive evidence of ecological damage, such as cumulative or gradual damage, which tends to be excluded from atrocity paradigms. This would be particularly important for measuring the widespread destruction of ecosystems, the loss of biodiversity, and the irreversible tipping points of the climate.

Complicated data should be interpreted by panels comprising ecologists, hydrologists, climatologists, Indigenous experts, and digital forensics experts. These panels should operate at both the pre-trial and trial stages to ensure that technical evidence is robust, relevant, and clear.[50]

Furthermore, the notion of admissibility should be less strict and based on criminal standards. A hybrid type of evidence would enable tribunals to consider environmental indicators, ecosystem baselines, and longitudinal

---

47 Nabil Ahmed, 'Proof of Ecocide: A Forensic Practice' (2019), 5 Forensic Approaches to Ecocide Studies, pp. 144–45.

48 Heinz Ginzky, 'Satellite Images as Evidence in Legal Proceedings relating to the Environment – A US Perspective' (2000), 25(3) Air and Space Law, pp. 129–138.

49 Clore Centre/IALS, Evidence from Space (2012), pp. 9–10, https://www.space-institute.org/app/uploads/1342722048_Evidence_from_Space_25_June_2012_-_No_Cover_zip.pdf, (last accessed: 24 September 2025).

50 UNEP, Environmental Courts and Tribunals: Guide for Policy Makers (2016), pp. III–IV and 40–42.

information alongside the facts of a case. This would allow for a broader, temporally just approach to systemic ecocide.

III. Integration of the proposed model into existing legal and political systems

The ecocide enforcement scheme is required to complement the current legal and political systems. ITEs and RETs should conform to the jurisdictional and procedural frameworks of the pre-existing bodies such as the ICC, the UN Human Rights Council, and regional human rights courts, for example, the European Court of Human Rights (ECtHR) or the Inter-American Court of Human Rights (IACtHR), rather than operating in isolation.[51] At the domestic level, the framework should not replace national systems. This is especially relevant where environmental law is poorly enforced or the judiciary has reduced independence, as international or regional supervision may offer requisite protection.

This requires referral, subsidiarity, and complementary mechanisms, in the same way international jurisdiction is created in the Rome Statute of the International Criminal Court, where national jurisdiction is applied only when domestic courts are unwilling or unable to act.[52] RETs can be politically supported by regional organizations (e.g., African Union (AU), Association of Southeast Asian Nations (ASEAN), Organization of American States (OAS)), which would assist in embedding them into the frameworks of existing institutions. Such localized structures might be used to coordinate the enforcement of ecocide with development objectives, including the Sustainable Development Goals (SDGs)[53], climate strategies under the Paris Agreement[54], and present-day international environmental agreements such as the Convention on Biological Diversity (CBD)[55] and the United Nations Framework Convention on Climate Change.[56]

Furthermore, the integration cannot be based solely on top-down legal harmonization. Significant implementation and oversight stakeholders

51 Carsten Stahn, The Law and Practice of the ICC (OUP 2015), pp. 303–305.

52 ICC, Policy on Environmental Crimes under the Rome Statute (Dec 2024), pp. 12–13.

53 United Nations General Assembly, Transforming our World: the 2030 Agenda for Sustainable Development, UN Doc A/RES/70/1 (21 October 2015).

54 Paris Agreement, 12 December 2015, 3156 UNTS 177, Arts. 2–4.

55 Convention on Biological Diversity, 5 June 1992, 1760, UNTS 79, Arts. 1 and 8.

56 United Nations Framework Convention on Climate Change, 9 May 1992, 1771, UNTS 107, Arts. 2–4.

must comprise native peoples, civil society, and government at the local levels. They are needed to collect evidence and contextualize harm, guarantee locally oriented justice, and rebuild processes. The framework acquires political and economic momentum by launching the enforcement of ecocide into trade agreements, environmental investments, and green finance. Such a multi-scaled integration provides a guarantee that the implementation of ecocide is not only juridically sound but politically founded and universally appealing.

IV. Roadmap for implementation and next steps

In order to turn the proposed enforcement architecture into reality, it must be implemented in phases and in a politically realistic manner. A coalition of willing states with strong environmental and human rights records could launch treaty negotiations under a UN or plurilateral regime to establish a legal basis for the International Tribunal for Ecocide (ITE) and Regional Environmental Tribunals (RETs). Drafting model laws that countries could adopt and incorporate at the domestic level could also enhance normative harmonisation and make the subsidiarity of enforcement feasible.

Pilot RETs could be integrated into existing regional courts or treaty systems (e.g., the Inter-American Court of Human Rights or the African Commission on Human and Peoples' Rights) to evolve such institutions. These tribunals could subsequently evolve into independent bodies with environmental competencies and procedural innovations.

E. Conclusion

This paper has suggested that international and national systems are structurally inadequate for prosecuting ecocide. The Rome Statute is limited to the destruction of the environment in wartime, does not hold corporate responsibility, and is largely dependent on the cooperation of states. Domestic strategies are fragmented and unequal, and thresholds of liability differ, with poor judicial independence and a low level of enforcement against transnational actors.

To address this enforcement gap, the paper has offered a three-tiered complementary model comprising national courts as the initial point of responsibility, Regional Environmental Tribunals (RETs) to adjudicate transboundary harms with reference to regional knowledge and jurisprudence, and a permanent International Tribunal for Ecocide (ITE) to adjudicate the most serious cases of global concern. This system is based on a treaty that recognises ecocide as an international crime and supplies the normative basis that seals the loophole left by the Rome Statute, and extends the risk to both individuals and corporations.

The model also incorporates new evidence-based practices, such as forensic ecology, satellite tracking, and interdisciplinary panels of experts to ensure capture of cumulative and systemic environmental damage. It also enhances access to justice by allowing local communities, Indigenous Peoples, and NGOs to have a role in proceedings.

Although ambitious, the proposal is legally and politically feasible. Based on the experience of hybrid tribunals and regional courts, it provides a viable way of institutionalizing ecocide in the international law of crime. By doing so, it shifts the argumentative mode of rhetorical advocacy into the actual institutional framework, which is a timely but urgently needed response to the growing ecological crisis of the twenty-first century.

Which direction to take? On (in)direct obligations to climate proof buildings in dutch public and private law

Nora Bouzoraa[*]*, Yassine Hasnaoui*[**]

A. Introduction

The built environment contributes significantly to the emission of greenhouse gases and reducing these emissions is essential for the preservation of the environment. To accelerate the renovation of the built environment, the Dutch government has introduced various measures in both public and private law that directly or indirectly compel the owners of buildings to sustainably retrofit[1] those buildings. Public law measures either impose an obligation directly or provide authorities with the competence to impose an obligation to renovate, while private law measures impose these obligations indirectly by empowering private citizens to compel other private citizens to perform sustainable retrofitting.

Public law obligations to renovate can be found in the *Omgevingswet* [Environmental and Planning Act (EPA)], as well as the *Besluit bouwwerken leefomgeving* [Environment Buildings Decree (EBD)]. For instance, Article 3.87 EBD demands all owners of office buildings to refrain from use

* Mr. N.L. (Nora) Bouzoraa is PhD Candidate at the University of Groningen.
** Mr. Y. (Yassine) Hasnaoui is PhD Candidate at the University of Groningen.

1 In this contribution we use the terms "sustainably retrofitting" and "climate-proofing buildings" synonymously. These terms are used to address all measures that can be taken to improve the environmental sustainability of a building, i.e. energy-saving measures, insulation etc.

of their building if it does not meet a certain minimum energy performance standard (MEPS). De facto this means that the owners of such buildings are forced to renovate, since they will not be allowed to use their property if they do not take measures to meet the MEPS. As we have specified, indirect private law measures can also be found in Dutch law. An example of this is Article 7:243 of the Dutch Civil Code (DCC), which grants tenants of residential buildings the right to force their landlord to perform certain kinds of sustainable retrofitting.

While these regulations aim to reduce emissions, they interfere with property rights by limiting the owner's freedom to manage their property as they see fit. Additionally, compliance with renovation obligations requires substantial investments which causes further interference, since it creates financial burdens for property owners. This raises important questions about how these obligations, and the public (environmental) interests they serve, relate to the protection of these property rights and whether the extent of this protection differs when the obligations are imposed by public law as opposed to private law.

In this paper, we will explore the relationship between the aforementioned two ways of implementing sustainability obligations and the protection of private property under article 1 of the First Protocol to the European Convention on Human Rights (A1P1) as well as the degree to which national legal norms protect the interests of those affected by these measures. Firstly, we will give some examples of public law obligations to climate proof buildings, as well as the safeguards that are in place to ensure protection of those who need it (B). Then, we will discuss a legislative proposal which proposes lowering the voting threshold in the association of owners of apartment buildings to a simple majority for all decisions relating sustainability. This will grant the majority to compel a minority to tolerate and contribute to the costs of the renovation works, and thus forms what we define as a private law obligation to climate proof buildings (C). In the final section (D), we will provide an analysis of the safeguards that are in place to protect vulnerable persons when public law obligations apply, as opposed to safeguards that are in place to protect vulnerable persons when private law obligations are utilized.

B. Public law obligations and safeguards

Dutch public law imposes sustainability obligations on the owners of buildings in two ways, either through a general obligation that specifies a minimum level of sustainability for specific categories of buildings, or by providing authorities with the competence to impose a renovation obligation in a specific case. Since these obligations can be found in public law, public law determines which public body has the competence to impose renovation obligations, as well as which safeguards guards apply to ensure that an imposed or enforced obligation is lawful.[2]

I. General obligations

An example of a general obligation to sustainably retrofit a building is the above-mentioned Article 3.87 EBD. This article requires owners of office buildings to have their office building meet a minimum energy performance standard (MEPS). According to this regulation, office buildings should have an Energy Performance Certificate of 'C.' All measures of which the investment can be recovered within ten years should be taken to reach this rating. If all measures of which the investment can be recovered within ten years lead to a lower standard than the 'C' certificate, that is also acceptable.[3] If the owner of an office building does not comply with the obligation, they risk closure of their building.[4] Article 3.84 of the same decree requires owners of non-residential buildings that use more than 50.000 kWh of electricity and 25.000 m^3 natural gas a year to take all energy-measures of which the investment can be recovered within five years. In short, owners of buildings that fall under either article 3.84 or article 3.87 are obliged to take energy saving measures of which the investment can be recovered within a certain timeframe. There is a list of recognized measures that can be taken to comply.[5] Implementing all applicable measures on

2 Jacco Karens/Björn Hoops, 'Obligations for Owners to Climate-Proof Buildings in the Netherlands' (2024), 13(1) ELPJ, p. 161, 163.

3 Article 3.87(5) EBD.

4 Karens/Hoops (2024), p. 162.

5 Rijksdienst voor Ondernemend Nederland, 'Erkende maatregelenlijst (EML) [List of recognized measures]' (2023), https://www.rvo.nl/sites/default/files/2023-11/erkende-maatregelenlijst-eml-2023-v-1-3.pdf (last accessed: 21 July 2025).

the list ensures fulfilment of the obligation.[6] If an owner would rather take alternative measures not included in the list, the *Omgevingsregeling* [Environmental and Spatial Planning Regulation] provides a method to calculate the time needed to recover an investment.[7]

If authorities enforce these general energy-saving measures by, for instance, ordering the closure of the building or imposing a fine, the owner can file a notice of objection if he feels this is disproportionate or an infringement of A1P1.[8] The enforcing authorities (most often the municipality) are then required to re-assess this decision, and motivate whether it was or was not proportionate. If they decide the closure was proportionate, the owner of the building can lodge an appeal with the Administrative Court. Then, an independent judge will rule whether the closure was in line with legal principles such as proportionality as well as the right to peaceful enjoyment of possessions.

II. Situation specific obligations

As specified above, public law provides general obligations to climate proof buildings but also grants authorities competences to impose obligations in specific situations. For instance, article 3.7 provides the municipal executive with the competence to lay down *maatwerkvoorschriften* [situation-specific regulations] regarding the technical condition of a building.[9] Through such a regulation, the owner may be required to improve the condition of the building. However, the required level of improvement should not exceed the standard that the EBD prescribes for new construction.[10] This provision can be used to obligate owners to climate proof buildings, by for instance requiring the owner to install double-glazed windows or take measures

6 Ministerie van Binnenlandse Zaken en Koninkrijksrelaties, Besluit van 10 juli 2023 tot wijziging van het Besluit bouwwerken leefomgeving in verband met de actualisatie van de energiebesparingsplicht voor utiliteitsgebouwen en enkele andere wijzigingen, 10 July 2023, Stb. 2023, 272, p. 6.

7 Appendix XV to the *Omgevingsregeling* [Environmental and Spatial Planning Regulation].

8 Article 7:1 & 8:1 Dutch Administrative Code (DAC).

9 Arjan Bregman, 'De mogelijkheden van gemeentelijke sturing op duurzaamheid en klimaatadaptatie op grond van de Omgevingswet [The possibilities of municipal steering for sustainability and climate adaptation in the Environmental and Planning Act]' (2024), 97 *TBR*, p. 723.

10 Karens/Hoops (2024), p. 169.

regarding the insulation of the building.[11] If this competence is used, the owner of the building that should be renovated can file a notice of objection.[12] Similarly to the notice of objection discussed earlier, the municipal executive will then reassess their decision, and motivate whether it was or was not proportionate, with the possibility for the owner to lodge an appeal with the Administrative Court.[13]

A legislative proposal, the *Wet gemeentelijke instrumenten warmtetransitie* [Act on Municipal Instruments for the Heat transition] will grant the municipal executive the power to designate certain areas in which the buildings will have to convert from the use of natural gas to the use of alternative sustainable resources, starting January 2026.[14] The municipal executive will be able to lay down these designations in the so-called *omgevingsplan* [environmental plan]. To ensure foreseeability, the environmental plan must indicate the point in time from which the use of natural gas is prohibited.[15] Since it takes time to (prepare to) convert to a sustainable alternative, a reasonable timeframe must be provided between the designation and the actual transition from natural gas to an alternative.[16] A timeframe of eight years can be regarded as a guideline, but a shorter or longer timeframe is also possible. Regardless of the length, the municipal executive is always obliged to motivate and justify the length of the transition period.[17] When the municipal executive lays down a designation in the environmental plan, the owners of buildings in this area can appeal directly before the *Afdeling Bestuursrechtspraak van de Raad van State* [Administrative Jurisdiction Division of the Council of State], which is the highest administrative law court of the Netherlands.[18] The judge will then decide whether the designation was in line with legal principles such as proportionality.

---

11 Karens/Hoops (2024), p. 162.
12 Article 6:4 DAC.
13 Article 7:1 & 8:1 DAC.
14 *Kamerstukken II* 2022/23, 36387, nr. 3, p. 30.
15 Ibid p. 17.
16 Ibid p. 17.
17 Ibid p. 17.
18 Appendix 2 article 2 to the DAC.

III. Protection of property rights

As illustrated above, when a general obligation to climate proof is enforced or the competence to lay down an obligation is used, the owner of the building it applies to can ask a court for a ruling on the lawfulness and proportionality of the obligation or enforcement. The court can then decide whether the obligation or enforcement is in line with the right to peaceful enjoyment of possessions, as laid down in article 1 protocol 1 of the European Convention on Human Rights (A1P1) and in line with Dutch law principles such as proportionality.

Climate proofing obligations can be classed as a 'control of use' of property rights in the sense of A1P1.[19] That means that it is an interference in the right of peaceful protection of possessions and should thus be justified in order to be lawful and not deemed in breach of A1P1. A1P1 requires any interference to be lawful, serve a legitimate public interest and strike a fair balance between the general interest and the protection of the individual's fundamental rights.[20] When an owner of a building subject to an obligation to climate proof appeals before a court, the court should thus determine whether the enforcement or imposing of the obligation is lawful. This means that the applicable laws and rules should be sufficiently clear, precise, and foreseeable in their applicability.[21] Moreover these laws should provide some sort of protection against arbitrariness. As briefly mentioned, the court should also answer the question of whether the interference serves a legitimate public interest. This should however, not be much of a problem, since the European Court of Human Rights recognizes protection of the environment to be a legitimate public interest.[22] Lastly, when exploring whether a fair balance was struck, the court has to assess whether the owner has to carry a disproportionate and excessive burden.[23] To discern this, the court should examine all interests in issue.

19 An example of an obligation imposed on a landowner, which the Commission considered 'control of use' can be found in ECtHR, 18 January 1989 – 12570/86 – Denev v Sweden.

20 e.g. ECtHR, 5 January 2000 – 33202/96, para. 108–114 – Beyeler v Italy.

21 e.g. ECtHR, 25 October 2012 – 71243/01, para. 96 Vistins and Perepjolkins v. Latvia and ECtHR, 23 January 2014 – 19336/04, para. 167 – East/West Alliance Limited v. Ukraine.

22 ECtHR, 27 November 2007 – 21861/03, para. 79–80 – Hamer v. Belgium.

23 e.g. ECtHR, 5 January 2000 – 33202/96, para. 114 – Beyeler v Italy; ECtHR, 23 September 1982- 7151/75, para. 73 – Sporrong and Lonnroth v Sweden.

While there is no complete list of aspects the court has to consider when conducting a fair balance test, there are some aspects that seem to be relevant in most cases. For instance, the owner of an affected building should be able to put their case to the enforcing or obligating authorities, being able to effectively challenge the measures taken. Furthermore, when less intrusive measures could be used to achieve the same goal, those measures should be taken. And of course, the enforcing or obligating authorities should assess the personal circumstances of each case. If these have not been taken into account, it could result in a violation of A1P1.[24]

As specified, these obligations are not just subject to A1P1, but also to the principle of proportionality, which can be found in the Dutch Administrative Code.[25] When assessing a case regarding a public law obligation to climate proof, a judge should also take these principles into account. This means that the use of the competence to impose or enforce an obligation to climate proof should be suitable, necessary and proportionate in the narrow sense.[26] The application of this principle overlaps to an extent with A1P1, since it requires the court to assess whether a measure that is taken was suitable and necessary.[27] Thus, whether it is suitable to reach a certain goal in the public interest, as well as whether there are less intrusive means available to reach the same goal. As well as requiring a balancing of interests.

When the court deems (the enforcement of) an obligation in line with A1P1 as well as the principle of proportionality, the owner can still ask for compensation for loss resulting from administrative acts.[28] Whether this compensation is awarded, depends on the situation. The general rule is that there is no compensation for lawful administrative acts, but those affected disproportionately in relation to others, can under some circumstances be awarded compensation.[29]

---

24 E.g. ECtHR, 5 May 1995 – 18465/91, para. 46 – Air Canada v the United Kingdom; ECtHR, 21 February 1986 – 8793/79, para. 51 – James and others v the United Kingdom.

25 Article 3:4(2) DAC.

26 ABRvS, 2 February 2022 – ECLI:NL:RVS:2022:285, para. 7.4 – 7.8 – Harderwijk.

27 Tom Barkhuysen/Michiel van Emmerik, 'De eigendomsbescherming van artikel 1 van het Eerste Protocol bij het EVRM en het Nederlandse bestuursrecht [Protection of private property under Article 1 of the First Protocol to the European Convention on Human Rights and Dutch administrative law]' (2003), JBPlus, p. 2, 13.

28 Article 4:126 DAC & section 15.1 ESA.

29 Michiel Tjepkema, Nadeelcompensatie op basis van het égalitébeginsel: een onderzoek naar nationaal, Frans en Europees Recht [Compensation for loss based on the

It is clear that there are several safeguards and procedures available for those affected by (the enforcement of) obligations to climate proof buildings. While these obligations do require owners' investments and willingness to renovate, and thus form an interference with their property rights, they are subject to judicial review.

C. Private law obligations and (the lack of) safeguards

Public law is not the only avenue through which the Dutch legislator tries to stimulate the sustainable upgrading of buildings. Two private law measures have been implemented, or are going to be implemented, that enable private citizens to force each other to sustainably retrofit their buildings. Both measures are aimed at situations where multiple people have an interest in the same immovable property, specifically within rental law and condominium law.

I. Sustainable retrofitting in Dutch rental law

The first is a rental law measure, implemented in article 7:243 of the Dutch Civil Code (hereafter: DCC). This measure grants tenants of residential property the power to request a judge to issue an order compelling their landlord, who owns the property in question, to improve the thermal isolation of the external walls, the floor that separates the building from the ground or replace the central heating installation with a more sustainable alternative.

If a tenant wants a judge to grant their request, they must be prepared to pay an increased rental fee. This increase must be reasonably proportionate to the costs the landlord has to make to implement the requested measures. An increased rental fee is proportionate when it allows the landlord to recover the costs of the investment within a reasonable timeframe.[30] Additionally, judges are granted a significant amount of discretion in determin-

---

principle of equality: an investigation into national Dutch, French, and European Law] (2010), p. 2 et seqq.

30 Justine van Lochem/Elmer van der Kamp, in Bart Krans/Carel Stolker/Lodewijk Valk (eds.), Tekst & Commentaar Burgerlijk Wetboek [Text and Commentary Dutch Civil Code], art. 7:243 DCC.

ing whether or not to compel the landlord to apply the requested measures. They can take all relevant interests and arguments into account as a part of their assessment, such as the current state of the building and the practical and financial obstacles to implementing the measures.[31]

This measure strikes a balance between the interests of the tenant and the interests of their landlord. There is a fundamental tension in the relationship between two parties when it comes to the sustainable retrofitting of the rented residential property. The tenant is most benefited by the retrofitting, as they will see a decrease in energy consumption as a result thereof. The landlord is, in principle, the one who decides whether or not to retrofit the building, and the one who has to pay for those costs, while not directly benefiting from the retrofitting.

Article 7:243 DCC resolves this tension by giving the tenant limited room to make decisions regarding the retrofitting of the rental property that would normally belong to the owner. The interests of the landlord are protected in two ways: firstly through the requirement of a proportionate rental fee increase, sufficient to cover the investment the landlord is required to make, and secondly through judicial oversight, through which a judge will examine whether the interests of the landlord are sufficiently protected.

This combination of factors results in a measure that promotes the sustainable retrofitting of buildings in a legal dynamic that would otherwise prevent such retrofitting, while sufficiently protecting the interests of the landlord.

II. Condominium law and indirect sustainability obligations

A defining characteristic of condominium law is that multiple owners have an equal right to (parts of) a condominium building and have to govern it together. Under Dutch law, the whole of the building is jointly owned by the condominium owners, with each owner having a fractional share in the property right of the building, and attached to that fractional share the right to exclusively use a part of that building, hereafter referred to as the condominium units.[32]

31 Marcel van Wezel, in Jan Heikens et al. (eds.), Groene Serie Huurrecht [Green Series Rental Law], art. 7:243, para. 2.1.

32 Article 5:106 para. 4 DCC.

Dividing a building into condominium rights requires the founding of a special kind of legal person, called the Association of Owners (hereafter: AoO). Article 5:125 par. 2 DCC states that all condominium owners automatically become members of the AoO, and that only condominium owners can be members.

The AoO is tasked with the maintenance and management of the jointly owned building, with the exception of the condominium units.[33] The condominium owners must take decisions relating to the maintenance and management in the general assembly of the AoO. This decision making process is democratic by nature: each owner has a certain amount of votes as described in the notarial deed of division, and decisions can in principle be taken with a simple majority, with the possibility to choose a greater minimum amount of votes for specific decisions in the deed of division.[34] In practice, impactful decisions typically require a 3/4ths or 2/3rds majority vote.

A crucial detail is that decisions, once taken, bind all condominium owners, including those who voted against the decision. They will have to pay their share of the costs involved in executing the decision, even if they do not benefit directly from the decision.[35]

The Dutch Minister of Housing and Spatial Planning (hereinafter: the Minister) has proposed an amendment to the current system of condominium law. This amendment would lower the required number of votes from 3/4ths or 2/3rds of the total votes to a simple majority, to promote the sustainable retrofitting of condominium buildings.[36]

The logical consequence of this amendment would indeed be that it becomes easier to take decisions relating to sustainability. At the same time, this would also mean that a smaller majority of owners can take decisions that bind a larger minority of owners than is currently possible, which can lead to undesirable consequences.

To provide a brief example which illustrates this: Imagine a condominium complex with five owners, of which two owners have trouble making

33 Article 5:126 para. 1 DCC.

34 Article 5:127 para. 1 DCC.

35 Article 5:113 DCC.

36 Ministry of Interior and Kingdom Affairs of the Netherlands, Versnellingsagenda verduurzaming
gebouwen in beheer van Verenigingen van Eigenaars (VvE's) [Acceleration agenda or the sustainable retrofitting of buildings maintained by an Association of Owners] 15 June 2023, p. 2 et seqq.

ends meet. They actively reduce their energy consumption to lower their costs, for example by not heating their houses but wearing warmer clothes instead. The other three owners have sufficient money and are not concerned about their energy consumption.

In this case, sustainably retrofitting the condominium building might be appealing to the three owners. It would lower their energy consumption, reducing their monthly costs as well, without having to sacrifice their quality of life, and they have the means to pay for it. For the two owners with less money, such a proposal is less attractive. Their monthly savings would be minimal as they already use very little energy, and they do not have the means to pay their share for the required works. In other words: the majority of owners would benefit from the decision, while the minority would be harmed.

If the required number of votes is two-thirds of the total amount of votes, the majority of three could not take the decision without the approval of one of the two minority owners. If the required number of votes is lowered to a simple majority however, three votes would be sufficient, and the majority could force the minority to tolerate and pay for the retrofitting of their shared building.

The process of democratic decision making could lead to unjust outcomes that harm the justified interests of the minority that voted against the decision. In order to protect the justified minority interests, Dutch condominium law contains several safeguards. Firstly, as is the case for most areas of Dutch private law, the relationship between the condominium owners is governed by the standards of reasonableness and fairness.[37] Even though the democratic decision-making process itself contains no inherent limitations to the scope and impact of the decisions taken by the AoO, owners are in general required to behave *ex aequo et bono* in relation to each other, including in the ways they use their votes.[38]

Article 5:130 DCC opens the possibility for an owner to request the avoidance of a decision of the AoO by a Cantonal judge, within one month after the day on which the owner became aware of the decision. The grounds for avoidance are those listed in article 2:15 DCC, a provision applicable to all legal persons. There are three distinct grounds for avoidance: if the decision was taken in conflict with procedural rules originating from

37 Harriët Schelhaas, Redelijkheid en billijkheid [Reasonableness and fairness] (2017), para. 1.

38 HR 30 October 1998 – ECLI:NL:HR:1998:ZC2759, para. 3.8.

the law or the articles of incorporation of the legal person, if the decision conflicts with the standards of reasonableness and fairness or if the decision was taken in conflict with internal regulations of the legal person.

The standards of reasonableness and fairness can also entail that refusing to take a decision is unreasonable. For that reason, article 5:121 DCC allows a condominium owner to request authorisation from the Cantonal court to perform certain acts that affect the common parts of the condominium building, in cases where such acts require the approval or cooperation of the AoO or other condominium owners. The court will grant authorization if, after weighing the interests involved in the decision, it comes to the conclusion that there are no reasonable grounds on which the other parties refuse their approval or cooperation.[39]

Articles 5:130 and 5:121 DCC taken together make it possible to invoke judicial protection both in cases where an unreasonable decision is taken and where a reasonable decision is taken on unreasonable grounds. In both cases the potentially unfair results of the democratic decision-making process are tempered by the possibility of judicial review.

The proposal of the Minister to lower the required number of votes for measures related to sustainability can therefore be seen as a shifting of the burden of invoking judicial protection. By lowering the required number of votes, it becomes easier to take a decision and as a result, the minority of owners against the decision will have to seek judicial protection more often, while the majority in favour of the decision can take the decision without having to seek judicial authorisation.

One major advantage of this shift is that it acts as a filter for owners voting against a decision on illegitimate grounds. A recurring issue in Dutch condominium law is the tendency of owners to abuse their votes by blocking decisions for reasons not related to that decision, such as a conflict with their neighbours. A lower required number of votes makes it more difficult for owners to block a decision on these grounds, and it is unlikely a judge will void the decision if there are no legitimate reasons for their vote against the decision.

There are, however, two disadvantages as well. Firstly, requiring owners who voted against a decision to invoke judicial protection puts an additional burden on those with a legitimate interest against the decision. This is especially problematic when it concerns condominium owners with little money: they will have to pay the costs for the trial, with the risk of having

39 Hof Amsterdam 11 December 2012 – ECLI:NL:GHAMS:2012:4274, para. 3.7 et seq.

paid for nothing if the court does not void the decision, on top of having to pay the costs for the execution of the decision. Additionally, there is the mental and time burden of having to go to court. Finally, they must decide whether to invoke judicial protection within the unusually short timeframe of one month. These factors combined create a barrier to seeking judicial protection.

Secondly, the shift from those in favour of a decision having to seek authorization to those against a decision having to seek avoidance of that decision also entails a shift in the scope of judicial review. Judicial review under the authorization procedure of article 5:121 DCC is a full review, with room for a careful weighing of the different interests involved in the decision, while judicial review under article 5:130 and 2:15 DCC is limited: judges can only evaluate whether the AoO could reasonably take the decision in question.[40]

Dutch case law on the scope of judicial review under article 5:130 and 2:15 DCC shows there are two aspects that are important in this review. The first of these aspects is the way the decision was taken. A decision conflicts with the standards of reasonableness and fairness when there was no weighing of interests by the AoO at all.[41] The second aspect is the consequences of the decision. When the consequences are patently unreasonable, such as an owner facing significant financial difficulties as a result of the decision, the decision can also be unreasonable.[42]

Judicial review under article 5:130 and 2:15 DCC is significantly more limited than the full review of article 5:121 DCC. Avoidance under article 5:130 and 2:15 DCC is only possible when the AoO could not reasonably have taken this decision, which leaves room for decisions that are unreasonable towards some owners, as long as the interests of those owners were in some way acknowledged and the consequences are not so unreasonable that they cause significant difficulties for the owners.

The question is whether the positive aspects of the proposed change to the voting requirements for sustainability decisions weigh up against the negative aspects, specifically the increased burden on the minority of owners against the measure and the decreased scope of judicial review, thus creating more room for decisions that negatively impact some owners.

40 HR 12 Juli 2013 – ECLI:NL:HR:2023:BZ9145, para. 3.4.3.
41 Rechtbank Oost–Brabant 8 February 2024 – ECLI:NL:RBOBR:2024:829, para. 5.10.
42 Hof Arnhem–Leeuwarden 29 September 2024 – ECLI:NL:GHARL:2024:6655, para. 3.6.

III. Is private law regulation the way forward?

This paragraph focused on two examples of private law regulation that aim to promote sustainability. In both examples one or more private persons are empowered to compel one or more other private persons to perform or tolerate and pay for sustainability measures, even when it goes against their own interests.

The degree of protection of those interests differs massively, however. The rental law measure discussed in paragraph 3.1. requires *ex ante* judicial review, which includes an evaluation of the burden placed on the landlord and the degree to which the proposed rental fee increase covers his costs. By requiring judicial review, the reasonability of the proposed measure is guaranteed.

The proposed condominium law measure discussed in paragraph 3.2. is fundamentally different. It does not directly grant anyone the ability to compel another condominium owner to tolerate and pay for the sustainable retrofitting of the shared building. Instead, it lowers the voting threshold to take decisions regarding sustainability within the AoO, indirectly increasing the amount of situations in which a minority of condominium owners opposes a certain decision, and creating more room to take decisions that negatively impact one or multiple owners. There is room for *ex post* judicial review, but a combination of the short timeframe during which an owner can invoke judicial protection, the limited scope of judicial review and the uncertainty of outcome lead to a situation where a condominium owner can be negatively affected by a decision of the AoO without successfully seeking judicial protection.

D. Conclusion

The Dutch legislator has opened several avenues through which the owners of buildings can be compelled to make their buildings more sustainable, both in public law and in private law. There are, however, major differences in the ways the legitimate interests of the owners of the buildings are protected in these two fields of law.

For the public law measures, the interests of the owners have to be taken into account based on national legal principles and the article 1 of Protocol 1 to the European Convention on Human Rights. Administrative bodies have to weigh the interests of those affected by the measure before taking a decision and potentially provide compensation for the damage suffered by them, either because the measure would otherwise not be proportionate to the public interest it serves, or because an owner is disproportionately affected by the measure.

The private law measures function without interference by a public body. Both measures are aimed at promoting a public interest, the prevention of climate change, by granting individuals the power to compel others. By implementing these measures in private law, the measures are placed outside of the public law framework designed specifically for situations in which a private person has to make a sacrifice in the public interest.

Instead, private law balances interests through a general reasonableness and fairness test, either administered *ex ante* or *ex post* by a judge. In either case, seeking judicial protection raises barriers to the effective use of those measures or to the effective protection of the legitimate interests of those compelled to perform or pay for the sustainable retrofitting.

A fundamental but still unanswered question is whether private law is the most suitable place for interventions in the public interest, in light of the lack of public involvement in the protection of the justified interests of private individuals.

Sustainable Urban Mobility Plans (SUMPs): A German and Spanish comparative legal overview

*Vincent-Carlos Barduhn**

A. *Introduction*

Cities play a major role in achieving Europe's sustainability goals. 'The battle for sustainable development will almost certainly be decided in cities (...)'.[1] Accordingly, urban mobility must become sustainable. Sustainable Urban Mobility Plans (SUMPs) can be a powerful tool for achieving urban sustainability. A SUMP is a strategic plan designed to meet the mobility needs of individuals and businesses in urban areas and their surroundings,

---

* Doctoral candidate and research associate at the Research Center for European Environmental Law of Prof. Dr. Claudio Franzius (University of Bremen) as well as member of 'KomUR', a Network of Competence on Future Challenges of Environmental Law funded by the German Federal Ministry of Education and Research. The author extends his gratitude to Jannik Laß for his valuable support with the formalities. Contact information: barduhn@uni-bremen.de.

1 Quoting former EU Regional Policy Commissioner, Danuta Hübner, addressing the Informal Ministerial Meeting on Urban Development on the 24th May 2007 in Leipzig.

with the aim of improving their quality of life.[2] It contains a series of measures aimed at implementing more sustainable transport options within a city.[3]

This article gives an overview of SUMPs in Germany and Spain. First, it will determine why a comparative approach between these two countries is particularly interesting on this matter (B). After laying out the concept of (sustainable urban) mobility planning (C.I), the situations of SUMPs in Germany (C.II) and Spain (C.III) will be analysed. The article concludes with an outlook (D).

B. Why Germany and Spain

Comparative law does not require justification.[4] A comparative approach is not obliged to have a specific "sense" of self-understanding or justification.[5] The added value results from the scientific findings ('*Erkenntnisse*')[6] themselves, regardless of their actual benefits[7]. Thus, the selected legal systems for a legal comparison do not inevitably require a rationale. However, especially when applying the "functional method"[8] in the context of comparative law, the so-called "comparable baseline" ('*Parallelität der Ausgangslage*') plays an important role.[9] Incomparable matters cannot be reasonably com-

2 Rupprecht Consult (ed.), Guidelines for Developing and Implementing a Sustainable Urban Mobility Plan, 2nd ed. (2019), p. 9.

3 See Phase 3 of the SUMP-cycle, Rupprecht Consult (ed.) (2019), p. 103 et seqq.

4 Uwe Kischel, Rechtsvergleichung [Comparative law] (2019), § 2.

5 Cf. Kischel (2019), § 2 Rn. 4.

6 Kischel (2019), § 2 Rn. 4; Till Markus, 'Zur Rechtsvergleichung im nationalen und internationalen Umweltrecht [Comparative law in national and international environmental law]' (2020), 80(3) ZaöRV 80, p. 649, 666.

7 Markus (2020), p. 666: '(...) weitgehend unabhängig von ihrem konkreten Nutzen [(...) mostly independent of their specific purpose]'; Kischel (2019), § 2 Rn. 4: '(...) keinerlei spezifischer "Sinn" für Selbstverständnis oder Rechtfertigung erforderlich [(...) no specific "sense" of self-understanding or justification required]'.

8 For a broad overview, see Ralf Michaels, 'The Functional Method of Comparative Law', in: Mathias Reimann/Reinhard Zimmermann (eds.), The Oxford handbook of comparative law, 2nd ed. (2019), p. 345, 346 et seqq. *Michaels* highlights on p. 347 that '(...) there is not one ('the') functional method, but many' types of functional methods.

9 Guy Beaucamp, 'Umweltrechtsvergleichung – Hoffnungen, Probleme und Ausschnitte aus der Realität [Comparative environmental law – hopes, problems, and excerpts from reality]' (2001), UPR, p. 134, 137: 'Parallelität der sachlichen Ausgangssituation [parallelity of the factual starting situation]'; Markus (2020), p. 698.

pared.[10] The point of origin of a comparative approach should lie in a similar (factual) issue (‘*nachvollziehbare Sach- und Problemlage*’)[11] which concerns the selected countries.[12] The comparison is therefore in need of a similar context.[13] This context has a factual and a legal dimension.

I. Factual terms

To start with, both countries manifest a similar distribution of their population. The majority of Germany’s and Spain’s inhabitants lives in densely populated areas. More than 90 % of Spain’s population is located in approximately 30 % of its territory.[14] Spaniards, especially young people, tend to leave rural areas and immigrate to bigger cities in order to improve their quality of live.[15] In Germany, the population is concentrated in agglomerated areas (‘*Ballungsräume*’).[16] More than 70 % of Germans live in large cities

---

10 Hein Kötz/Konrad Zweigert, Einführung in die Rechtsvergleichung [Introduction to comparative law], 3rd ed. (1996), p. 33; cf. Markus (2020), p. 698.

11 Cf. Till Markus, Rechtsvergleichung im Völkerrecht [Comparative law in international law], (2021), p. 70.

12 Cf. Markus (2021), p. 64: ‘funktional vergleichbare Sachprobleme [functionally comparable factual problems]’, p. 70: ‘(...) nachvollziehbare(r) Vergleich von Sach- und Problemlagen [(...) comprehensible comparison of factual situations and problems]”; Markus (2020), p. 663 et seqq.: ‘(Die Gegenüberstellung der Sach- und Problemlagen) bestimmt nicht unwesentlich darüber, ob und inwieweit ein Rechtsvergleich überhaupt sinnvoll ist [(The comparison of the factual and problematic situations) plays a significant role in determining whether and to what extent a legal comparison is meaningful at all]’; Beaucamp (2001), p. 137. A broader approach can be found in Van Hoecke, ‘Methodology of Comparative Legal Research’ (2015), Law and Method, p. 1, 5.

13 Cf. Markus (2020), p. 698; Beaucamp (2001), p. 137. For example: Germany and Spain both deal with bad air quality in their cities due to excessive pollution originating from motorized vehicles.

14 Laenderdaten.info, Bevölkerungswachstum in Spanien [Population growth in Spain], https://www.laenderdaten.info/Europa/Spanien/bevoelkerungswachstum.php (last accessed: 8 June 2025).

15 EFE, ‘El éxodo de los jóvenes rurales a las grandes ciudades españolas [The exodus of rural youth to the major spanish cities]’ (2017), https://www.abc.es/sociedad/abci-exodo-jovenes-rurales-grandes-ciudades-espanolas-201704141320_noticia.html (last accessed: 8 June 2025). This phenomenom is called *españa vaciada* (empty Spain).

16 Sachverständigenrat für Umweltfragen (ed.), Umweltgutachten 2012: Verantwortung in einer begrenzten Welt [Environmental Report 2012: Responsibility in a limited world], (2012), para 342.

and their surroundings.[17] This context contributes to the fact that in both cases, cities deal with several mobility-related issues. The high density of motorized vehicles[18] severely impacts the environment, quality of live as well as overall health of the city's population.

Moreover, Germany and Spain share a similar economic structure regarding its influential automotive sector. Germany is known as an *Autonation* worldwide. The automotive industry is a key part of Germany's economy[19] and has a national impact on gross value added, investment volumes, and employment figures.[20] Spain's automotive industry also represents a substantial part of the country's economy. Spain is, right after Germany, the biggest car manufacturer in Europe.[21] More than 9 automobile brands produce automotives in over 17 Spanish automotive plants, promoting the automotive sector to the countries third biggest economic sector.[22]

---

17 Destatis, 'Bevölkerung: Großstadtregionen im Wandel [Population: Metropolitan regions in transition]', https://www.destatis.de/DE/Themen/Querschnitt/Demografischer-Wandel/Aspekte/demografie-grossstadtregionen.html (last accessed: 8 June 2025). See the map on the website.

18 Four out of five cities have more vehicles than inhabitants: Europa Press, 'Cuatro de cada cinco ciudades españolas tienen más vehículos que habitantes, según DriiveMe [Four of five Spanish cities have more vehicles than inhabitants, according to DriiveMe]' (2018), https://www.eleconomista.es/ecomotor/motor/noticias/8867764/01/18/Economia-Motor-Cuatro-de-cada-cinco-ciudades-espanolas-tienen-mas-vehiculos-que-habitantes-segun-DriiveMe.html (last accessed: 8 June 2025). Germans tend nowadays to own at least three cars, Robert Klatt, 'Immer mehr Drittwagen: Zahl der Autos pro Einwohner in Deutschland auf Rekordhoch [More and more tertiary vehicles: Number of cars per inhabitant in Germany at record high]' (2022), https://www.forschung-und-wissen.de/nachrichten/oekonomie/zahl-der-autos-pro-einwohner-in-deutschland-auf-rekordhoch-13376652 (last accessed: 8 June 2025).

19 Thomas Puls/Manuel Fritsch, Eine Branche unter Druck: Die Bedeutung der Autoindustrie für Deutschland [An industry under pressure: The importance of the automotive industry for Germany], (2020), p. 13: 'Schwergewicht [heavyweight]'.

20 Puls/Fritsch, (2020), p. 3, 12 et seq., 16.

21 Victor Méndez-Barreira, ´Car Makers Pour Money Into Spain: Country has emerged as Europe's second-biggest production hub, with flexible labor laws and a vast network of local suppliers` (2016), https://www.wsj.com/articles/car-makers-pour-money-into-spain-1470613487 (last accessed: 8 June 2025).

22 Ana Elena Heras, 'España es el 2º mayor fabricante de vehículos europeo y se situó 9º a nivel mundial en 2021 [Spain is the second-largest vehicle manufacturer in Europe and ranked 9th wordwilde in 2021]', https://www.investinspain.org/content/icex-invest/es/sectors/automotive.html (last accessed: 8 June 2025).

II. Legal terms

From a legal point of view, there is a similar legal framework. Not only are Germany and Spain Member States of the EU and therefore underly Union law. There are also several national parallels. Due to historical reasons, the *Constitución Española* (Spanish constitution) was inspired by the *Grundgesetz* (German constitution).[23] The Spanish constitution assumed the fundamental structure of the German constitution, which explains their close interrelation.[24] Both countries therefore also share a similar state organisation. While Spain does not have a federal system (*Föderalismus*), their state division follows a territorial model which has a lot of resemblance to the German model. Spain has 'semi-federalistic'[25] elements, has established over the years, in practical terms, a federal entity[26] and is one of Europe's most decentralised countries[27]. The constitutional resemblance also influenced the Spanish administrative law.[28] Spanish public law is

23 Pedro Cruz Villalón, 'Landesbericht Spanien [Country report Spain]', in Christian Starck (ed.), Grundgesetz und deutsche Verfassungsrechtsprechung im Spiegel ausländischer Verfassungsentwicklung [The Basic Law and German Constitutional Jurisprudence in the light of foreign constitutional developments] (1990), p. 194, 194; Dirk Kurbjuweit, 'Nach der Franco-Diktatur: Warum die Spanier das deutsche Grundgesetz kopierten [After the Franco dictatorship: Why the Spanish copied the German Basic Law]' (2019), https://www.spiegel.de/politik/70-jahre-verfassung-warum-die-spanier-das-deutsche-grundgesetz-kopierten-a-3db45a46-1530-45b4-a632-07076997c551 (last accessed: 8 June 2025); Dominik Rabe, Der 'Verwaltungsakt' nach deutschem und nach spanischem Recht [The 'Administrative Act' under German and Spanish Law], (2012), p. 46.

24 Mariano Bacigalupo/Francisco Velasco, 'Wirkungen der deutschen Verwaltungsrechtslehre nach außen – am Beispiel Spaniens [External effects of German administrative law doctrine – using Spain as an example]' (2003), 36(3) Die Verwaltung, p. 333, 343.

25 Ole Brühl, Immissionsschutzrechtliche Vorhabengenehmigung in Deutschland und Spanien [Project approval under immission control law in Germany and Spain], (2002), p. 14: 'quasiföderal [semi-federal]'. See as well Alexander Tacer, Die territoriale Struktur Spaniens [The territorial structure of Spain] (2010), p. 2.

26 Juan José Solozábal Echavarría, 'A ruling on the federalization of the state', in Alberto López Basaguren/Leire Escajedo San Epifanio (eds.), The Ways of Federalism (2013), p. 467, 468.

27 Dieter Nohlen/Andreas Hildenbrand, 'Regionalismus und politische Dezentralisierung in Spanien [Regionalism and political decentralisation in Spain]', in Dieter Nohlen/José Jian Gonzáles Encinar (eds.), Der Staat der Autonomen Gemeinschaften in Spanien [The State of the autonmous communities in Spain] (1992), p. 9, 9.

28 Bacigalupo/Velasco (2003), p. 343 et seq.; Rabe (2012), p. 46 et seq.

known to be receptive to the influence of foreign public law.[29] Nevertheless, German administrative law has stood out with its very distinct impact on Spanish administrative law.[30] Although it was not always consistent in its approach, Spain systematically adopted Germany's administrative law in several phases.[31] German administrative law served for Spain's administrative law as 'main inspiration source'.[32]

C. (Sustainable Urban) Mobility Planning

Before turning to Germany (C.II) and Spain (C.III), the concept of sustainable urban mobility planning must first be defined (C.I).

I. Defining the concept

1. Mobility

Mobility is a very ambivalent term: defining it is tricky. Not only does its definition depend on the specific context or perspective[33], but the term is

29 Bacigalupo/Velasco (2003), p. 333; Velasco (2003), p. 391; Oriol Mir Puigpelat, 'Spanien [Spain]' in Armin von Bogdandy/Sabino Cassese/Michael Huber (eds.), Handbuch Ius Publicum Europaeum: Band V [Handbook of Ius Publicum Europaeum: Volume V] (2014), § 84 para. 3.

30 Francisco Velasco, 'Die Rezeption des deutschen Verwaltungsrechts in der spanischen Rechtsordnung: Zugleich eine theoretische Darstellung der Gründe, Etappen und Probleme des unidirektionalen Rechtsvergleichs [The reception of German administrative law in the Spanish legal system: At the same time a theoretical presentation of the reasons, stages, and problems of unidirectional legal comparison]' (2015), 48(3) Die Verwaltung, p. 383, 388 et seq.

31 Bacigalupo/Velasco (2003), p. 343; Velasco (2015), p. 394; Alfredo Gallego Anabitarte, 'La influencia en al Derecho Administravio español desde 1950 a hoy [The influence on Spanish administrative law from 1950 to the present]' (1999), 150 RAP, p. 75, 108.

32 Velasco (2015), p. 383, 402.

33 Carsten Gertz, 'Planungsgrundlagen [planing principles]', in Dirk Vallée/Barbara Engel/Walter Vogt (eds.), Stadtverkehrsplanung: Band 1 [Urban transport planning: Volume 1] (2021), p. 1, 6. See the image on page 7 as well.

also confronted with regional discrepancies[34] and constantly in motion[35]. As a result, it is not uncommon to encounter the term of (sustainable) mobility in an undefined manner.[36] Nevertheless, most of us have a general idea of the concept of mobility, even if it is hard to put in words. Mobility is normally equated, at least in Germany, with transport (*'Verkehr'*). Even though these terms are used similarly on a daily routine, their meanings differ.[37] In the context of SUMPs, mobility is the possibility for people to change their location[38] or, at least, their desire to do so[39]. The actual tool for commuting is transport.[40] Transport represents the entirety of all physically realised journeys per time unit in an area or a location.[41] Therefore, it can be said that transport is the tool that enables the (desire to) change location, which is mobility. Consequently, a large amount of transport may exceed a roadway's capacity and therefore result in traffic (congestion).

---

34 For example, VCD e.V., `Entwurf für die Regelungsinhalte eines Bundesmobilitätsgesetzes [Draft for the regulatory content of a federal mobility law]`, in Georg Hermes/Urs Kramer/Holger Weiß (eds.), Das Recht der Verkehrswende [The law of the transport transition] (2023), p. 41, 52, indicates that in the context of Union law, mobility not only includes persons, but also goods. In a German legal context, goods are generally not included, cf. Gertz (2021), p. 7.

35 Antonio Fortes Martín, La movilidad urbana sostenible como fenómeno jurídico: el derecho de la movilidad [Sustainable urban mobility as a legal phenomenon: The law of mobility] (2019), p. 35; Elisa Moreu Carbonell, 'Reflexions sobre el papel del Derecho para la movilidad sostenible [Reflections on the role of law in sustainable mobility]', in Andrés Boix Palop/Reyes Marzal Raga (eds.), Ciudad y movilidad [City and mobility] (2014), p. 87, 88.

36 Antonio Fortes Martín, 'La promoción de la movilidad limpia o sin emisiones [The promotion of clean or emission-free mobility]', in Alenza García/Mellado Ruiz (eds.), Estudios sobre cambio climático y transición energética [Studies on climate change and energy transition] (2020), p. 361, 369.

37 Gertz (2021), p. 6 et seq.

38 Gertz (2021), p. 7.

39 Jürgen Gerlach, 'Integrierte Planung – Chancen und Hemmnisse in Deutschland [Integrated planning – opportunities and obstacles in Germany]', in 1. Internationale Wuppertaler Verkehrstage (2005), p. 31, 31.

40 Gerlach (2005), p. 31.

41 Gertz (2021), p. 1, 7.

2. Mobility Planning

Mobility is a very challenging and ambitious task. At a municipal level, the (local) transport situation is determined by numerous factors.[42] To anticipate conflicting issues and coordinate measures not only with themselves, but also with any possible conflicting goals or interests[43], a (mobility) planning instrument is necessary[44]. Without a decent mobility plan, which results out of (the process of) mobility planning[45], it is not possible to overcome (urban) mobility deficiencies.[46] Occasional mobility improvements are insufficient and do not have enough substantial impact to resolve mobility-related issues:[47] an overall, long-lasting mobility concept is required. A mobility plan therefore ensures a certain type of procedure guided by a long-term vision.[48]

3. Urban Mobility Planning

The range or area of a mobility plan can differ.[49] When the mobility plan has a local territorial scope, it usually refers to an urban mobility plan. It can address one single city, but also several, sometimes with or without the surroundings.[50]

---

42 Georg Hermes, 'Gewährleistung umweltverträglicher Mobilität für alle [Ensuring environmentally friendly mobility for all]' (2020), 53(3) Die Verwaltung, p. 311, 327.

43 Wolfgang Kahl/Sophia Effinger, 'Instrumente des Umweltrechts (Teil 1) [Instruments of enviromental law (Part 1)]' (2022), 44(12) JURA, p. 1394, 1395; Wolfgang Kahl/ Klaus Ferdinand Gärditz, Umweltrecht [Environmental law], 13th ed. (2023), § 4 Rn. 50.

44 Hermes (2020), p. 327; Stefan Fimpel, Planerische Neuausrichtung der urbanen Mobilität [Planning reorientation of urban mobility] (2022), p. 60.

45 Cf. Kahl/Effinger (2022), p. 1395: 'Ein Plan – das Ergebnis einer Planung – (...) [A plan – the result of a planning process – (...)]'.

46 Cf. Sachverständigenrat für Umweltfragen (ed.) (2012), Rn. 484.

47 Cf. Fimpel (2022), p. 59; Moritz Reese, 'Nachhaltige urbane Mobilitätsentwicklung – Potenziale eines Gemeindeverkehrsplanungsgesetz [Sustainable urban mobility development – potentials of a municipal transport planning law]' (2020), ZUR, p. 401, 401.

48 Cf. Rupprecht Consult (ed.) (2019), p. 10.

49 See for example Art. 101.2 Ley 2/2011, de 4 de marzo, de Economía Sostenible (BOE-A-2011–4117).

50 The definition of Rupprecht Consult (ed.) (2019), p. 9 states 'cities and their surroundings'. Yet, an urban mobility plan usually addresses one municipality, although it can also have a wider range and cover several municipalities. At the end of the day,

4. Sustainable Urban Mobility Planning

Finally, a SUMP is, as its name suggests, sustainable. Legally speaking, this term lacks a clear and homogeneous definition.[51] Nevertheless, it can be specified by some characteristics. An urban mobility plan is sustainable when it not only tries to minimise or exclude any type of environmental damage but follows an integrated approach by including the development of all transport modes and involving all relevant stakeholders and citizens, using a transparent and participatory approach.[52] At the same time, a SUMP aims to promote economic models with low consumption and less energy dependency, as well as improving the access to transportation for people with reduced mobility.[53] In other words, an urban mobility plan is sustainable when it pursues not only ecological improvements, but also other factors such as social equity, health improvements and economic viability.[54]

II. Germany

Germany has been working with mobility plans for a long time. After the Second World War, it introduced so-called *General-* or *Gesamtverkehrspläne*.[55] These plans were particularly used by larger municipalities to expand their (transport) infrastructure.[56] They primarily focused on flowing and stationary motorised traffic, while other types of transportation methods such as bicycle or pedestrian traffic were nearly irrelevant.[57] As a result,

this term gives an idea but is – in this context- neither legally nor elsewhere accurately defined.

51 Moreu Carbonell (2014), p. 80.

52 Moreu Carbonell (2014), p. 80 et seq.; Rupprecht Consult (ed.) (2019), p. 10.

53 Moreu Carbonell (2014), p. 81; Rupprecht Consult (ed.) (2019), p. 10 et seqq.

54 Cf. Moreu Carbonell (2014), p. 81; Rupprecht Consult (ed.) (2019), p. 10.

55 Bundesinstitut für Bau-, Stadt- und Raumforschung, Konzepte für den Stadtverkehr der Zukunft (2019), p. 14; Carsten Gertz/Gunnar Polzin, 'Stand der Verkehrsentwicklungsplanung – Ergebnisse einer Städteumfrage in Deutschland [Status of transport development planning – results of a survey of cities in Germany]' (2009), 12 StVT, p. 769, 769.

56 Bundesinstitut für Bau-, Stadt- und Raumforschung (2019), p. 14.

57 Markus Hesse/Rainer Lucas, Verkehrswende: ökologische und soziale Orientierungen für die Verkehrswirtschaft [Transport Transition: Ecological and social orientations for the transport industry], (1990), p. 7: 'Fuß- und Radverkehr sind in den Ballungsräumen sprichwörtlich an den Rand gedrängt [Pedestrian and bicycle transport

mobility planning in urban areas focused on motorised private transport and promoted a car-friendly city.[58] Motorised private vehicles 'invaded' public spaces and became the dominant transportation tool.

In the 1980s, doubts arose regarding this car-based dominance.[59] Mobility plans evolved to so-called *Verkehrsentwicklungspläne* (VEPs), which backed off from promoting motorised private vehicles and pursued a cross-vehicular approach that actively included non-motorised transports.[60] Over the years, these plans matured to a 2nd generation of VEPs by using different kinds of eye-catching names to promote a '*Paradigmenwechsel*'[61] (paradigm shift) and renewing their planning methodology and content.[62] These new VEPs have many similarities to SUMPs. Both plans essentially have the same methodological and content-related requirements, which is why both terms are practically used synonymously.[63]

Nowadays, many German municipalities have implemented a VEP.[64] Nevertheless, mobility planning in Germany has always been lacking legal regulations.[65] Apart from one regional exception,[66] there are no legal reg-

---

are literally pushed to the margins in metropolitan areas.]'; Bundesinstitut für Bau-, Stadt- und Raumforschung (2019), p. 14; Carsten Gertz, 'Zukunft der Verkehrsentwicklung – Viele Pläne – (k)eine Strategie [The future of transport development – many plans – no/a strategy]' (2007), Planerin, p. 51, 51.

58 Bundesinstitut für Bau-, Stadt- und Raumforschung (2019), p. 14.

59 Bundesinstitut für Bau-, Stadt- und Raumforschung (2019), p. 15; Gertz (2007), p. 51; Michael Frehn/Ludwig Korte, 'Renaissance der kommunalen Verkehrsentwicklungsplanung [Renaissance of muicipal transport development planning]' (2005), 119 Raumplanung, p. 82, 82; cf. Robert Schnüll, 'Brauchen wir eine neue Art von Verkehrsentwicklungsplänen? [Do we need a new type of transport development plan?]' (2009), StVT, p. 506, 507.

60 Bundesinstitut für Bau-, Stadt- und Raumforschung (2019), p. 15; cf. Schnüll (2009), p. 507.

61 Bundesinstitut für Bau-, Stadt- und Raumforschung (2019), p. 16.

62 Cf. Gertz (2007), p. 53.

63 Bundesinstitut für Bau-, Stadt- und Raumforschung (2019), p. 18; Forschungsgesellschaft für Straßen- und Verkehrswesen e. V., Hinweise zur Verkehrsentwicklungsplanung [Guidelines for transport development planning], (2013), p. 5; Wulf-Holger Arndt/Fabian Drews, Mobilität nachhaltig planen [Planning sustainable mobility], (2019), p. 13 et seqq.

64 See for example Rupprecht Consult, Bestandserhebung und -analyse SUMPs [Inventory and analysis survey of SUMPs], (2023), p. 5 et seqq.

65 Bundesinstitut für Bau-, Stadt- und Raumforschung, Rechtliche Bausteine einer kommunalen Mobilitätswende, (2023), p. 22 et seqq.; Arndt/Drews (2019), p. 6; Gertz/Polzin (2009), p. 769.

66 Cf. Reese (2020), p. 403, according to which Berlin is currently an exception with its Berlin Mobility Act (MobG), introduced in July 2018.

ulations concerning VEPs; the introduction of a mobility plan is neither legally mandatory, nor are there any regulations addressing its content or scope.[67] The methodology and content of these VEPs can basically always differ.[68] VEPs are therefore categorised as 'informal' plans.[69] Informal planning refers to planning instruments or planning procedures that are not legally formalised, standardised and (directly) legally binding.[70] Informal plans stand out due to their lack of or very little legal standardisation[71] as well as their high level of flexibility[72].

While informal planning does have its advantages,[73] its particularly high flexibility leads to serious issues. Just to point out two:

On the one hand, the quality of VEPs varies significantly. In the absence of (nationwide) legally binding requirements, there are unlimited planning options for mobility plans. Mobility planners are not obliged to follow any planning standards. Consequently, the level of detail and scope of VEPs differ – sometimes considerably.[74] A gradual deviation is not surprising, as a mobility plan should be tailored to local conditions and can therefore

---

67 Sibylle Barth/Hubertus Baumeister, 'Elektrifizierung des ÖPNV als kommunale Pflichtaufgabe ohne Finanzausgleich? [Electrification of public transport as a municipal mandatory task without financial compensation?]' (2024), IR, p. 43, 47; Gertz/Polzin (2009), p. 769; Gertz (2007), p. 51; Forschungsgesellschaft für Straßen- und Verkehrswesen e. V., Empfehlungen für Verkehrsplanungsprozesse [Recommendations for transportation planning processes], (2018), p. 17.

68 However, at least in large cities, a similar standard has apparently emerged, Carsten Gertz, 'Weiterentwicklung der Verkehrsentwicklungsplanung [Further development of transport development planning]', in: Tillmann Bracher/Dieter Apel (eds.), Handbuch der kommunalen Verkehrsplanung [Handbook of municipal transport planning] (2016), p. 2.

69 Bundesinstitut für Bau-, Stadt- und Raumforschung (2019), p. 22; Baumeister (2024), p. 47; Moritz Reese, 'Für die Verkehrswende ein Gemeindeverkehrsplanungsgesetz [A municipal transport planning law for the transport revolution]' (2018), ZUR, p. 321, 321.

70 Rainer Danielzyk/Martin Sondermann, 'Informelle Planung [Informal planning]', in Akademie für Raumforschung und Landesplanung (ed.), Handwörterbuch der Stadt- und Raumentwicklung [Handbook of urban and spatial development] (2018), p. 963, 964.

71 Danielzyk/Sondermann (2018), p. 964; Dietrich Henckel/Kestervon Kuczkowski/PetraLau et al. (eds.), Planen – Bauen – Umwelt: Ein Handbuch [Planning – building – environment: A handbook] (2010), p. 227.

72 Danielzyk/Sondermann (2018), p. 964.

73 Cf. Forschungsgesellschaft für Straßen- und Verkehrswesen e. V. (2013), p. 44.

74 Rupprecht Consult (2023) p. 12; cf. Gertz (2007), p. 51; Bundesinstitut für Bau-, Stadt- und Raumforschung (2023), p. 23; Reese (2018), p. 321.

differ depending on the actual city.[75] However, excessive disparities to the commonly applied methodology[76] can have a negative impact on effectively overcoming the challenges of mobility.

On the other hand, it's the lack of formalisation of mobility plans that not only allows the corresponding municipality to choose *how*, but also *whether* a VEP will be developed. If a municipality finally decides to establish a VEP, its actual realisation and following implementation is not necessarily secured. Yet, adequate funding and personnel resources are crucial for its success.[77] If these requirements cannot be assured, a VEP as an informal (sustainable) urban mobility plan will not be taken seriously on a local-political level.[78] Its implementation process may just as well be stopped after a new political shift.[79]

III. Spain

Like Germany, Spain has also been working with SUMPs for quite a while. In Spain, SUMPs are called *planes de movilidad urbana sostenible*, short *PMUS*. These plans first debuted in the 21st century.[80] The first wave of SUMPs began in 2005, when an institute affiliated to the Spanish Ministry of Ecological Transition and Demographic Challenge, the IDAE[81], promoted several mobility plans for the purpose of shaping urban mobility in a

75 Rupprecht Consult (ed.) (2019), p. 24.

76 Cf. Rupprecht Consult (ed.) (2019); Forschungsgesellschaft für Straßen- und Verkehrswesen e. V. (2013); Forschungsgesellschaft für Straßen- und Verkehrswesen e. V., (2018).

77 Sachverständigenrat für Umweltfragen (ed.) (2012), para. 531; Arndt/Drews (2019), p. 26 et seq.

78 Bundesinstitut für Bau-, Stadt- und Raumforschung (2023), p. 23.

79 Cf. Arndt/Drews (2019), p. 4.

80 Vincent-Carlos Barduhn, 'Los Planes de Movilidad Urbana Sostenible (PMUS) [Sustainable urban mobility plans (SUMP)]' (2025), https://www.idluam.org/blog/los-planes-de-movilidad-urbana-sostenible-pmus/ (last accessed: 8 June 2025). Although there were already first experiences with integrated mobility planning during the nineties of the 20th century, see Pilar Vega Pindado, 'Una decade de planes de movilidad urbana sostenible en España 2004 – 2014 [A decade of sustainable urban mobility plans in spain 2004 – 2014]' (2016), 36(2) AGUC, p. 351, 355.

81 Instituto para la Diversificación y Ahorro de la Energía, see https://www.idae.es/.

sustainable manner.[82] The IDAE initiated a pilot project phase in which a couple of SUMPs were launched, offering technical and financial support.[83] These initial SUMPs, mostly elaborated in the Autonomous Community of Madrid, lacked a methodological approach; indeed, their development was mostly improvised.[84] As a result, the IDAE published in the following year a methodological guide called *Guía práctica* on how to elaborate and implement a SUMP.[85] From this moment on, newly developed SUMPs followed the orientations of this guide[86], resulting in SUMPs that were elaborated and implemented in a systematic and structured manner.[87] Simultaneously, the IDAE signed a number of agreements with several Autonomous Communities to award subsidies if SUMPs were developed.[88] Thus, until the economic crisis began in 2008, more than 100 SUMPs were developed and implemented throughout Spain.[89]

Due to the impact of the financial crisis and reduced budgets, the IDAE had to take a step back from its subsidised program.[90] Up until 2013, the number of elaborated SUMPs descended, concluding with the IDAE finally terminating its subsidised program.[91] This did not imply the end of SUMPs in Spain at all. In 2014, Spain introduced a new national law. With the *Ley 2/2011 de 4 de marzo de Economía Sostenible*[92] (LES), for the first time, the SUMPs were addressed in a nationwide manner. Art. 101 LES not only defined the concept of a SUMP (par. 1), but also its territorial scope (par. 2) as well as its minimum content (par. 4) and alignment to other planning

82 Vega Pindado (2016), p. 358; Pilar Vega Pindado, Los PMUS – Balance desde la perspectiva ecológica [The SUMPs – assessment from an ecological perspective] (2017), p. 17.
83 Vega Pindado (2017), p. 17.
84 Cf. Vega Pindado (2017), p. 17.
85 The guide can be found in https://www.idae.es/publicaciones/pmus-guia-practica-para-la-elaboracion-e-implantacion-de-planes-de-movilidad-urbana (last accessed: 8 June 2025).
86 Vega Pindado (2017), p. 17.
87 Barduhn (2025).
88 Vega Pindado (2017), p. 18; Vega Pindado (2016), p. 359.
89 See the image in Vega Pindado (2017), p. 17; Vega Pindado (2016), p. 358.
90 Barduhn (2025).
91 Pilar Vega Pindado, Los PMUS en España [SUMPs in Spain] (2019), p. 66; Vega Pindado (2017), p. 18.
92 Ley 2/2011, de 4 de marzo, de Economía Sostenible (BOE-A-2011–4117).

instruments (par. 3).[93] Furthermore, Art. 102 LES states that as of the 1st June 2014, the granting of any aid or subsidy to regional administrations or local entities included in the General State Budget Law and intended for urban or metropolitan public transport requires the beneficiary entity having the corresponding SUMP that is consistent with the Spanish Sustainable Mobility Strategy.[94] This led to the introduction of 55 SUMPs in 2014 in order to be eligible for public transport subsidies.

Ultimately, the relevance of SUMPs rose again at the beginning of this decade. Spain introduced a new law, the *Ley 7/2021, de 20 de mayo, de cambio climático y transición energética*[95] (LCCTE) which regulates SUMPs in its fourth title named "mobility without emissions and transport". Art. 14.3 LCCTE requires certain municipalities, especially those with a minimum of 50.000 inhabitants, and insular territories to adopt SUMPs before 2023. These mandatory SUMPs will introduce mitigation measures to reduce mobility emissions and must include, at least, a series of measures specified in Art. 14.3 a) – i) LCCTE. Among these measures is the establishment of low emission zones before 2023, Art. 14.3 a) LCCTE. Accordingly, the mandatory introduction of SUMPs was promoted in about 150 municipalities and, in these included as a mitigation measure, the introduction of a low emission zone.[96]

IV. Comparison

Regarding SUMPs, Spain is legally some steps ahead of Germany. The national legislator took an important first step with the LES by narrowing down some basic aspects. While the LES received some criticism due to its

---

93 In detail Antonio Fortes Martín, 'La movilidad urbana sostenible, en la encrucijada de lo urbanístico y lo ambiental [Sustainable urban mobility at the crossroads of urban planning and the environment]' (2015), RDAM, 31 (2015), p. 169, 196 et seqq.

94 The law was postponed and entered into force on 1 June 2014, Vega Pindado (2016), p. 359.

95 Ley 7/2021, de 20 de mayo, de cambio climático y transición energética (BOE-A-2021–8447).

96 El Confidencial, 'Los 149 municipios españoles que tendrán que poner en marcha zonas de bajas emisiones en 2023 [The 149 Spanish municipalities that will have to implement low-emission zones in 2023]' (2023), https://www.elconfidencial.com/motor/2023-01-13/149-ciudades-pondran-en-marcha-zonas-zbe-2023_3557064/ (last accessed: 8 June 2025).

very thin-skinned normative approach regarding sustainable mobility[97], it closed a gap that Germany is still having issues with. In Germany, the term 'SUMP' is still not commonly used everywhere. Mobility plans vary in their terminology, making it hard to identify at first sight whether the respective plan is actually a SUMP and not some other type of (sectoral) plan.[98] Since Art. 101.1 LES was introduced, Spain has ruled out this issue. Furthermore, by establishing a minimum content in Art. 101.4 LES, the expectations of a SUMP are somewhat clearer. Every Spanish mobility plan must list a set of measures to adopt which promote sustainable urban mobility, while in Germany, mobility plans may (only) have a strategic priority.[99] Spain has therefore formalised and standardised SUMPs on a national level with the LES and, based on this, taken a next step for some municipalities with the LCCTE.[100]

D. Outlook

SUMPs significantly impact Germany's and Spain's urban mobility. Both countries have lots of experience with this instrument. While Spain has formalised and standardised SUMPs on a nationwide level, Germany's VEPs remain informal. This informality has been more of a burden than a relief. To become a more powerful instrument for sustainable urban mobility, SUMPs must be legally formalised, standardised and perhaps even (directly) legally binding.

The importance of SUMPs will continue to rise in the near future. In 2024, the EU introduced a new regulation concerning the Trans-European Transportation Network (TEN-T).[101] SUMPs act as a cornerstone of European urban mobility policy. It is expected that until 2027, every Member

97 Cf., for example, Fortes Martín (2020), p. 369: 'déficit normativo [regulatory gap]'.

98 Gertz (2016), p. 6; Rupprecht Consult (2023), p. 5, 41; Arndt/Drews (2019), p. 13 et seqq.

99 Cf. Gertz (2016), p. 10: 'strategieorientiert [strategy-oriented]'.

100 Furthermore, several autonomous communities have decided to implement regional mobility laws, while hereby regulating SUMPs on a regional level, see for an overview Vega Pindado (2019), p. 81.

101 Regulation (EU) 2024/1679 of the European Parliament and of the Council of 13 June 2024 on Union guidelines for the development of the trans-European transport network [2024].

State will implement SUMPs in their major cities.[102] Thus, all Member States will have to deal with SUMPs. Both Germany and Spain have the advantage that, due to their past, they can rely on plenty of experience. Still, both Member States need to intensify their efforts by offering SUMPs a proper legal environment. If SUMPs are not adequately formalised, standardised and – at best – (directly) legally binding, their effectiveness may be limited, and sustainable mobility will be harder to reach.

102 See Art. 41 I b) i) Regulation (EU) 2024/1679 which obliges every Member State to adopt and monitor a SUMP in every urban node by 31st of December 2027.

Law, power and the climate crisis: proposing a critical theory approach for EU sustainability law

Kate O'Reilly

A. Introduction

What, and whom, is sustainability law for?[1] This chapter begins with the premise that to answer this question we must consider how the ways in which we *do* legal scholarship shape the unsustainable social structures of the societies that we live in. By centring law as a social institution that produces and stabilises patterns of social ordering, this chapter reflects on a pathway for a critical approach in sustainability law scholarship in the European Union (EU) that is grounded in the Frankfurt School's critical theory of society.[2]

Critical theory operates in a space outside of the epistemological boundaries of conventional legal approaches, which are predicated on an assumption of law as a neutral force or mere instrument of social engineering that reacts to and acts upon the world while remaining, to a large degree,

1 Drawing on the same question proposed by Isailović concerning EU law, see Ivana Isailović, 'Introduction: Critical Legal Approaches in EU Law – Reflections on New Research Directions' (2024) 15(4) Transnational Legal Theory, p. 493.

2 The critical theory tradition referred to throughout this chapter is the Frankfurt School's critical theory of society.

isolated from the realm of the social.[3] What place ought critical theory have in sustainability law scholarship, and by extension legal scholarship more generally? While EU sustainability law scholarship does engage in substantive critique,[4] critique without reflexivity promotes crises.[5] As Koselleck argues, the abstracted moral critique that characterised the Enlightenment project was detached from the institutional reality of politics and power dynamics in society. This disconnect gave rise to instability when critique crystalised into ideological programmes that fostered the historical crises in Western Europe.[6] Like the Enlightenment philosophical project, sustainable development is grounded in a universalised normative vision of a socially just and ecologically viable social order.[7] This is a social order radically different from the extractive capitalist model of economic growth that lies at the centre of contemporary social ordering.[8] Grand visions of sustainable development also risk hardening into prescriptions on development that are detached from the social and that undermine social and ecological sustainability.[9]

The discussion in this chapter reflects on how a critical approach can provide an alternative frame for answering: what, and whom, is sustainability law for? In Section B, the analysis explores how law, when positioned as a social institution, produces and sustains processes of global warming. The failure of conventional legal approaches in capturing the complex entanglement of law with the climate crisis will be traced, alongside the role that legal scholarship plays in disconnecting the collective imaginary

3 For an exception to this see scholarship from the critical legal studies movement in the US and the revitalized field of law and political economy scholarship engage in critical approaches to law, see for example Anna Grear, 'Deconstructing Anthropos: A Critical Legal Reflection on "Anthropocentric" Law and Anthropocene "Humanity"' (2015) 26(3) Law and Critique, p. 225.

4 For an exposition of the disconnect between law that promotes energy communities, and the material reality of these legal entities see Björn Hoops, 'Two Tales of the Energy Commons Through the Lens of Complexity' (2025) 25 Global Jurist, p. 1.

5 Reinhart Koselleck, Critique and Crisis: Enlightenment and the Pathogenesis of Modern Society, Thomas McCarthy (tr.), MIT Press (2000).

6 Ibid.

7 On sustainable development as a grundnorm, see Klaus Bosselmann, 'International Environmental Law in the Anthropocene: Towards a Purposive System of Multilateral Environmental Agreements' (2013) 2(2) Transnational Environmental Law, p. 285.

8 Kate Aronoff et al., A Planet to Win: Why We Need a Green New Deal (2019).

9 Eduardo Gudynas, 'Debates on Development and Its Alternatives in Latin America: A Brief Heterodox Guide', in Miriam Lang/Dunia Mokrani (eds.), Beyond Development: Alternative Visions from Latin America (2013), p.15, 28 et seq.

of the climate crises from the realities of global warming. In Section C, it will be considered how a critical approach can be integrated into the methodological toolbox of sustainability law scholarship, grounded in the example of Renewable Energy Communities (RECs) in EU law.

B. Diagnosing the role of law in processes of global warming

In the following, law will be positioned as a social institution that drives processes of global warming. Sustainability is first and foremost an issue of social ordering. The social inequalities that prevent sustainable practices, human induced increases in global temperatures, and over-extraction of planetary resources are products of (historically) embedded social structures.[10] Sustainable development policies, such as the EU Green Deal, aim to reconfigure unsustainable patterns of production and consumption using law as a tool for changing market behaviours.[11] By situating law as a social institution, law can be theorised as a part of society that constitutes the social order and stabilises one of several competing normative social logics.[12] This reveals a key epistemological and methodological challenge for sustainability law: how can legal scholarship position law in society when legal analysis treats law as an autonomous system that acts upon society and what does this reframing mean for how we can conceptualise the role of law in processes of global warming.

I. Law as a social institution

Sociological approaches produce knowledge about the nature of society and are concerned with the study of social relations, social institutions and social structures.[13] The social can be defined as 'the general range of recurring forms, or patterned features, of interactions and relationships

10 Sam Adelman/Abdul Paliwala, 'Introduction', in Sam Adelman/Abdul Paliwala (eds.), The Limits of Law and Development: Neoliberalism, Governance and Social Justice (2021).

11 European Commission, The European Green Deal, COM (2019) 640.

12 Roberto Esposito, Instituting Thought: Three Paradigms of Political Ontology (2021).

13 Mitch Duneier, 'Sociology: Overview', in James Wright (ed.), International Encyclopedia of the Social & Behavioral Sciences, 2nd ed. (2015).

between people'[14] while social institutions are more specifically 'a complex of positions, roles, norms and values lodged in particular types of social structures and organising relatively stable patterns of human activity with respect to fundamental problems in producing life-sustaining resources, in reproducing individuals, and in sustaining viable societal structures within a given environment'.[15] This definition does not equate social institutions with (macro) structures or (micro) agency. Instead, social institutions are located at the meso-layer of society and, as Beckers proposes, 'bridge systems and create stable sets of expectations'.[16] The function of law as a social institution is then to stabilise patterns of ordering in society. This is an ontological claim that law is both constitutive of and constituted by the social.[17] This embedding of law in society broadens the scope of what legal scholars can study and calls for alternative methodological approaches.

II. Connecting law with processes of global warming

If law is theorised as a social institution, the frame of analysis expands to include approaches that interrogate how legal institutions shape social structures. Human-induced climate change stems from patterns of production and consumption, where fossil fuels are a leading cause of rising global temperatures. For society, fossil fuels are more than just an energy source. They are a resource through which capitalist processes, facilitated by the coding of law, translate surplus into wealth.[18] They are a medium through which ubiquitous forms of oppression permeate the globe in complex webs of social patterning that span the global north and south.[19] As Malm argues 'The fossil economy has the character of a totality, a distinguishable entity: a socio-ecological structure, in which a certain economic process and a

---

14 Roger Cotterrell, Law, Culture and Society: Legal Ideas in the Mirror of Social Theory (2006), p. 15.

15 Jonathan Turner, The Institutional Order (1997), p. 6.

16 Anna Beckers, Private Law and the Institutional (Re)Turn (2024), p. 1, 5.

17 Roger Cotterrell, 'Law as Constitutive', in James (ed.), Wright International Encyclopedia of the Social & Behavioral Sciences, 2nd ed. (2015), p. 550, 550 et seqq.

18 Katharina Pistor, The Code of Capital: How the Law Creates Wealth and Inequality (2019), pp. 6 et seqq.

19 Marcel Llavero-Pasquina et al., 'The Political Ecology of Oil and Gas Corporations: TotalEnergies and Post-Colonial Exploitation to Concentrate Energy in Industrial Economies' (2024) 109 Energy Research & Social Science, p. 1.

certain form of energy are welded together'.[20] This captures the interconnectedness of fossil fuels and capitalist modes of production where energy systems constitute the social order (of which the economy is part).

The concept of carbon lock-in brings this entanglement into sharp relief as it looks beyond economic theory to analyse why industrialised societies struggle to decarbonise.[21] Path dependency in industrialised countries leads to carbon lock-in through an interplay of social norms that legitimise high-carbon practices, technological infrastructures built around fossil fuel energy systems, and governance structures in energy systems produced by public and private institutions. For Unruh, these forces create a Techno-Institutional Complex (TIC), a self-reinforcing system that is deeply resistant to change.[22] The co-dependency of fossil fuels and capitalist ordering in TICs foregrounds the interwoven and messy complexity of the super-wicked problem that is the climate crisis.[23] Law is a part of this entanglement, and yet conventional doctrinal and theoretical approaches elide social complexity through frames that narrow by selecting what is and what is not relevant for law.[24]

III. Sustainability law and the great derangement

Conventional legal scholarship contributes to what Ghosh calls the 'great derangement'; the collective inability within dominant cultural forms to imagine and narrate the climate crisis.[25] In the following, I sketch out three propositions that highlight why the climate crises is not caused by human technologies alone but is sustained by an epistemological blindness to the realities of the climate crises and how we are conditioned to know and produce knowledge about the world.

---

20 Andreas Malm, Fossil Capital: The Rise of Steam Power and the Roots of Global Warming (2016), p. 12.

21 Gregory Unruh, 'Understanding Carbon Lock-in' (2000) 28 Energy Policy, p. 817.

22 Ibid.

23 Graeme Auld et al., 'Managing Pandemics as Super Wicked Problems: Lessons from, and for, COVID-19 and the Climate Crisis' (2021) 54 Policy Sciences, p. 707, 709 et seqq.

24 On the simplification of wicked problems through legal frames in the context of private property, see Lorna Fox O'Mahony/Marc Roark, Squatting and the State (2022), pp. 209 et seqq.

25 Amitav Ghosh, The Great Derangement: Climate Change and the Unthinkable (2016), pp. 11, 135.

First, law was central for structuring capitalist ordering in Western societies; it did not simply respond to the emergence of capitalism.[26] Historically, law has stabilised capitalist and anthropocentric rationalities, while modern legal categories constitute and stabilise these logics. Capitalist rationalities and modes of ordering have spread across the globe through processes of imperialism, colonialism and the liberalization of markets, made possible by western legal institutions such as private property and freedom of contract.[27]

Second, the global capitalist order depends on structural inequality.[28] Legal categories are not neutral but instead reflect and reproduce the inequalities that animate the global order. The introduction of the Brundtland's conceptualisation of sustainable development in 1987 signalled a recognition that the climate crisis is fuelled by poverty and inequality between the global north and south.[29] The costs of decarbonisation are not born equally.[30] Countries in the global south struggle with decarbonisation during a period of industrial development that depends on fossil fuels. While at the local level, the individuals, communities and industries who already experience structural inequality are disadvantaged by processes of decarbonisation.[31]

Third, law constitutes structures of power. Privilege and disadvantage are scaled, reproduced and stabilized through law.[32] Legal scholars do not deal in neutral legal categories but participate in the reproduction of power dynamics.[33] Liability doctrines offer an example of this dynamic by defin-

26 Pistor (2019).

27 Gareth Austin, 'Capitalism and the Colonies', in Larry Neal/Jeffry Williamson (eds.), The Cambridge History of Capitalism (2014), p. 301; Beckers (2024), p. 9.

28 Jason Hickel et al., 'Imperialist appropriation in the world economy: Drain from the global South through unequal exchange, 1990–2015' (2022), 73 Glob. Environ. Change, p. 1.

29 Iris Borowy, Defining Sustainable Development for Our Common Future: A History of the World Commission on Environment and Development (Brundtland Commission) (2013).

30 Ghosh (2016), pp. 145 et seq.

31 Benjamin Sovacool et al. 'Dispossessed by Decarbonisation: Reducing Vulnerability, Injustice, and Inequality in the Lived Experience of Low-Carbon Pathways' (2021) 137 World Development, p. 1.

32 On the role of law in the distribution of privilege and disadvantage, see Martha Albertson Fineman, 'Vulnerability Theory and the Trinity Lectures: Institutionalizing the Individual' (2025).

33 Pierre Bourdieu, 'The Force of Law: Toward a Sociology of the Juridical Field' (1987) 38 The Hastings Law Journal, p. 814.

ing what counts as harm, who can be held accountable, and the interests legitimised and protected through law. While climate litigation cases in the Netherlands signal a shift in recognising the accountability of both public and private actors, they also expose the doctrinal barriers that arise in the context of liability as a legal institution capable of recognising the harms that arise from climate change.[34] These limitations reflect the active role that tort law plays in stabilising a social order that recognises accountability for certain forms of conduct while excluding others.[35]

C. Critical theory and sustainability law

The discussion in this section introduces critical theory as a methodological approach for the toolbox of sustainability law scholars that aim to study the embeddedness of law in society. While it is not possible to offer a comprehensive account of the premises of critical theory and critical theoretical approaches, the following introduces the core concepts of ideology, reflexivity, and the dialectical using the case of RECs in EU energy law to give substance to these abstracted concepts.[36]

I. From criticism to critique as method

The interdisciplinary critical theory tradition of the Frankfurt School is united by a commitment to a critique of the failures of modernity and to the transformation of the oppressive social structures that reproduce domination, alienation, and inequality. Critical theory in this vein is 'as a branch of social theory that seeks to critique and transform power rela-

34 Hoge Raad, 20 December 2019, C/19/00135 Rechtbank Den Haag, 26 May 2021, C/09/571932.

35 Wendy Bonython, 'Tort Law and Climate Change' (2021), 40(3) UQ Law Journal, p. 422.

36 For a comprehensive discussion of critical theory and EU law, see Päivi Johanna Neuvonen, 'A Way of Critique: What Can EU Law Scholars Learn from Critical Theory?' (2022) 1 European Law Open, p. 60, 60; see also Emilios Christodoulidis/Ruth Dukes/Marco Goldoni (eds.), Research Handbook on Critical Legal Theory (2019); and the special issue 'Critical Legal Approaches in EU Law' (2024) 15(4) Transnational Legal Theory, p. 493.

tions and structures that thwart political and social emancipation'.[37] It is an approach that combines critique (deconstruction) with emancipation (transformation).

Like critical theory approaches, critical theory in law encompasses a diversity of methodological approaches[38] that align on the shared aim to 'describe and critically analyse the inner logics of the law in light of their continuous reproduction and legitimation of intersecting forms of power asymmetries based on gender, class, race and sexuality – among others'.[39] Critical legal approaches interrogate the rationalities and normative commitments embedded within the logic of law's institutions. Neuvonen observes that within EU law scholarship, critique has become a buzzword, where critical interventions are characterised by a 'persistent imbalance between the zest for critical research and the thinness of critical methodology'.[40] What she is pointing to here is a difference between approaches that critique law substantively, such as the failures of EU energy law in promoting renewable energy communities,[41] and a critical approach that engages in an immanent critique of law, such as tracing the contradiction between law's commitment to a just transition and the market-based rationalities embedded in the legal frameworks that regulate RECs.[42] Another concern relates to the emancipatory aims of critical theory, which are inherently political in nature. On the one hand, the critical scholar engages in the negative project of understanding the failures and contradictions in society. On the other hand, the critical scholar also engages in the positive project of developing a better alternative to the object of critique. Legal scholarship tends to view law and legal knowledge as apolitical, which is in no small part due to legal positivism and how legal education is organised.[43] This leads to the belief that a neutral and objective critique of law is possible, reducing the negative dimension of critical theory to pure description.

37 Päivi Johanna Neuvonen, 'The "Crisis of Critique" in EU Law', 7 May 2025, https://verfassungsblog.de/the-crisis-of-critique-in-eu-law/ (last accessed: 16 July 2025).

38 See Christodoulidis/Dukes/Goldoni (2019).

39 Isailović, (2024), p. 493.

40 Neuvonen (2022), p. 60.

41 Hoops (2025).

42 On a critical account of the energy transition, see Mariusz Baranowski, 'Critical Theory of the Energy Transformation: Sociology's Approach' (2023) 7(4) Societies Register, p. 7.

43 Ubaldus de Vries, 'Law in Context – Towards a Reflexive Approach in (Dutch) Legal Education', in Emma Jones/Fiona Cownie (eds.), Key Directions in Legal Education: National and International Perspectives (2020).

It also elides the positive dimension of critical theory and precludes an engagement with what alternatives are possible and how they can be translated into the language of law.[44] Critical approaches to EU (sustainability) law must therefore engage with ideology and integrate both reflexivity and dialectics into critical legal methodologies.

II. Ideology

The concept of ideology is central to critical theory.[45] The emancipatory commitment of critical theory demands of a critical scholar that they engage in a critique of the ideologies in society that lead to oppression. Ideology tends to be defined in two ways. First, as an analytical concept that describes 'an intellectual framework, a way of talking, or a set of beliefs that helps constitute the way people experience the world'.[46] Second, is the value-laden understandings of ideology as 'a kind of mystification that serves class interests, promotes a false view of social relations, or produces injustice' or 'a way of thinking and talking that helps constitute and sustain illegitimate and unacknowledged relationships of power'.[47] Haslanger offers a third view of ideology as a cultural technē gone wrong.[48] A cultural technē is the framework of meaning we use to understand and interact with the world.[49] It includes the 'social meanings (...) that provides tools for interpreting and responding to each other and the world around us, and does so in ways that facilitate (better or worse) forms of coordination'.[50] We unconsciously use cultural technēs to navigate daily life, such as when we buy Disney princess dolls for girls and male superhero figures for boys. Ideologies permeate these interpretive horizons that colour how we view and

44 For alternative methodological approaches see Anna Beckers/Gunther Teubner, 'Sociological Jurisprudence and Digital Technology: The Need for Cross-Disciplinary Analysis' (2024) 18 Court of Conscience, p. 137.

45 Raymond Geuss, The Idea of a Critical Theory (1981), pp. 2 et seq.

46 Jack Balkin, Cultural Software: A Theory of Ideology (1998), p. 3.

47 Ibid.

48 Sally Haslanger, 'Going On, Not in the Same Way', in Alexis Burgess/Herman Cappelen/David Plunkett (eds.), Conceptual Engineering and Conceptual Ethics (2020), p. 230, 232.

49 This view aligns with the concept of practical consciousness of Giddens, see Anthony Giddens, The Constitution of Society: Outline of the Theory of Structuration (1984), p. xxiii.

50 Haslanger (2020), p. 232.

understand the social. A critique of ideology therefore requires reflexivity and a method of dialectical reasoning to confront how relations of power shape the production of knowledge for 'There is no power relation without the correlative constitution of a field of knowledge, nor any knowledge that does not presuppose and constitute at the same time power relations'.[51]

The example of RECs in EU law allows us to trace how ideology operates through cultural technēs (that emerge from law and policy narratives) and how it shapes the normative direction of the just energy transition. EU law recognises, promotes and supports RECs.[52] Definitions in the recast Renewable Energy Directive (RED III) invoke an image of RECs as local, grassroots collectives consisting of environmentally conscious, empowered individuals who willingly participate in the clean energy transition with projects that produce renewable energy.[53] The normative vision embedded in the RED III positions RECs as localised, not-for-profit and democratised legal entities that pursue environmental and social goals within the broader context of liberalised energy markets.[54] RECs are portrayed as socially conscious legal entities that pursue social and environmental aims, forming communities characterised by active participation and democratic governance, where proximity to the REC project ensures equal opportunity for local individuals to participate.[55] In EU policy discourse, energy communities are a mechanism for transitioning to a just decarbonised economy and must be 'strengthened to allow local communities, citizens and companies to join forces and invest in clean energy projects at local level; thereby allowing them to produce, sell and consume their renewable energy'.[56] This framing positions RECs as a material site where the abstract aims of social justice and environmental protection intersect, obscuring that RECs function within the overarching rationality of liberalised energy markets.[57] A critical approach to the study of RECs then begins with an exposition

51 Michel Foucault, Discipline and Punish: The Birth of the Prison, Alan Sheridan (tr.), Vintage Books (1995 [1975]), p. 27.

52 Council Directive (EU) 2023/2413 of 18 October 2023 amending Directive (EU) 2018/2001, Regulation (EU) 2018/1999 and Directive 98/70/EC as regards the promotion of energy from renewable sources, and repealing Council Directive (EU) 2015/652 [2023] OJ L, 2023/2413 (RED III).

53 Art. 2(16)(a) RED III.

54 Art. 2(16)(c) RED III.

55 Art. 2(16)(a), (b) & (c) RED III.

56 European Commission, 'An Affordable Energy Action Plan', 26 February 2025, COM (2025) 79 final, p. 8.

57 Art. 22 RED III.

of the ideologies in energy law and policy that obscure underlying power relations as well as the structural inequalities that permeate processes of decarbonisation that are collectively (re)produced through law.

III. Reflexivity and dialectics

Alongside the centrality of ideology in critical theory, the combination of reflexivity with dialectics gives critical theory its critical form and is what distinguishes critical theory from traditional theory.[58] Reflexivity without the dialectic reduces the scholarly analysis to the subjective position of the scholar, while dialectics without reflexivity risks a reproduction of the oppressive structures of power the scholar aims to deconstruct and transform.

As socialised beings, the presumptions (practical consciousness) of an individual are a pre-condition for knowledge production.[59] As Fish states, an open mind is an empty mind.[60] This means that all knowledge is partial because no one can reason from a 'view from nowhere'.[61] Reflexivity requires that we make explicit the position from which we engage in critique by clarifying our underlying epistemological and ideational position (positionality);[62] no one exists outside of society or the power relations within society.[63] While engaging in critique, the scholar assumes a normative vision that serves as the foundational interpretive horizon against which to distinguish between the emancipatory and oppressive structures in society that are the object of study. Whether we make our interpretive horizons explicit or not does not negate the existence of this normativity. Reflexivity requires that as scholars we reflect on our positionality, that we make explicit the frameworks that guide our critique *and* that we reflect on how the methods that we use to produce knowledge are themselves shaped by ideologies and relations of power.

---

58 Max Horkheimer, Critical Theory: Selected Essays, Matthew J. O'Connell et al. (trs.) (1972).

59 Balkin (1998), p. 273.

60 Stanley Fish, There's No Such Thing as Free Speech, and It's a Good Thing Too (1994), p. 117.

61 Donna Haraway, 'Situated Knowledges: The Science Question in Feminism and the Privilege of Partial Perspective' (1988) 14(3) Feminist Studies, p. 575.

62 Neuvonen (2022), p. 72.

63 Judith Butler, Gender Trouble: Feminism and the Subversion of Identity (1990), p. 2.

Moving on to the centrality of dialectics for critical theory, a dialectical process '(...) moves from an initial positive (thesis) through its rejection (antithesis) to a transcendent synthesis or 'sublation' (...) that maintains both moments, and preserves the transcended in the act of overcoming it'.[64] Combined with reflexivity, dialectical reasoning is a process through which we can draw out the contradictions in society (immanent critique). For EU sustainability law, dialectics are a means to move beyond a critique of the substantive content of law to tracing the contradictions that are embedded in the normative structure and rationality of law itself.[65] This immanent critique exposes the contradictions between the ideals and values of EU sustainability law and the material reality of the social that is (re)produced. The nature of the contradictions that emerge depend on the interpretive frame adopted by the scholar. These frames should prioritise marginalised perspectives, with critical feminist theories offering just one of several potential approaches.[66]

RECs allow us to consider how reflexivity and a dialectical approach can expose the contradictions in EU energy law. The forms that RECs take are diverse and yet the same cannot be said of their members. REC members tend to be financially secure and highly educated home-owning individuals, small and medium enterprises, or local municipalities.[67] Decarbonisation disproportionately burdens low-income households, renters, immigrants, precarious workers, and other marginalized groups.[68] These disadvantaged persons experience financial and social barriers that prevent participation in energy communities. Legal frameworks such as the RED III, designed to promote participatory energy governance and a just energy transition in the EU, stabilize existing economic structures and patterns of inequality by distributing privilege and disadvantage.[69] The legal frameworks that govern

64 Emilios Christodoulidis, 'Critical Theory and the Law: Reflections on Origins, Trajectories and Conjunctures', in Emilios Christodoulidis/Ruth Dukes/Marco Goldoni (eds.), Research Handbook on Critical Legal Theory (2019), p. 10.

65 Neuvonen (2022), p. 87.

66 Julia Wood, 'Critical Feminist Theories', in Dawn O. Braithwaite/Paul Schrodt (eds.), Engaging Theories in Interpersonal Communication: Multiple Perspectives (2008).

67 Jasmine Arnould/Diana Quiroz, 'Energy Communities in the EU: Fulfilling Consumer Rights and Protections' (2022), https://www.beuc.eu/sites/default/files/publications/BEUC-X-2023-010_Energy_communities_in_the_EU-report.pdf (last accessed 13 August 2025), pp. 24 et seq.

68 Ibid.

69 To trace this distribution, vulnerability theory can provide and interpretive frame, see Fineman (2025).

RECs are not neutral; they reproduce and stabilize a capitalist rationality of sustainable development as one of several competing normative visions of sustainability. A contradiction then emerges (anthesis) between the normative vision of RECs portrayed in EU law and policy and the material reality of RECs that exclude disadvantaged and marginalised groups from participating and benefiting from renewable projects. This brief example illustrates how a critical legal approach can both embed and critique sustainability law within society. The critical legal analysis that could follow from this example would engage in the challenging doctrinal task of translating emancipatory alternatives into the language and logic of law and legal doctrine.

D. Conclusion

Sustainable development calls for social transformation, where law is viewed as a tool for driving change. The pressures of the climate crisis demand a turn from this view of law as a neutral instrument that acts upon society to an understanding of law as a social institution that constitutes and stabilizes patterns of social ordering. Conventional legal approaches are insulated from the role that legal institutions play in producing and sustaining extractive, capitalist modes of ordering. In doing so, legal scholarship contributes to the 'great derangement' of our time by thinking through frames that obscure the entanglement of law in processes of climate change. Drawing on the Frankfurt School's commitment to emancipation and critique as method, a critical theory approach was explored as a methodology for EU sustainability law scholarship. The concepts of ideology, reflexivity, and the dialectic in critical theory illustrate how legal frameworks, such as the RED III, that are designed to promote sustainability, democratic participation and equality, work to embed existing inequalities in society under the guise of the normative vision of a just and inclusive energy transition. The emancipatory aim of critical theory highlights that legal scholarship, while epistemologically insulated from the social, is not apolitical. The key insight that can be drawn from this chapter is that by understanding how law reproduces (rather than merely responds to) the climate crisis, EU sustainability law scholarship can identify, critique and transform the legal institutions that structure processes of global warming.